Integration Models: Templates for Business Transformation

MW01254331

SAMS

Integration Models: Templates for Business Transformation

Copyright © 2000 by Laura Brown

International Standard Book Number: 067232055x

Library of Congress Catalog Card Number: 00-106886

Printed in the United States of America

First Printing: September 2000

02 01 00   4   3   2   1

Trademarks

Warning and Disclaimer

Associate Publisher
Tracy Dunkelberger

Acquisitions Editor
Loretta Yates

Development Editor
Sean Dixon

Managing Editor
Thomas F. Hayes

Project Editor
Leah Kirkpatrick

Copy Editor
Cindy Fields

Indexer
Aamir Burki

Proofreader
Harvey Stanbrough

Technical Editor
Elena Oliker

Team Coordinator
Cindy Teeters

Interior Designer
Anne Jones

Cover Designer
Jay Corpus

Production
Ayanna Lacey
Heather Hiatt Miller
Stacey Richwine-DeRome

Contents

About the Author

Since 1984, Laura Brown has helped business and technical managers deliver systems solutions, and has worked as senior technical advisor and management consultant to Fortune 500 companies. Laura is president of System Innovations, founded in 1994 as a consulting firm specializing in enterprise application integration, data warehousing and Internet design.

She was a vice president of Marketing Information Systems at NationsBank where she managed the development of product statistics databases for NationsBank Marketing.

Laura's client list includes, among many others, the following companies:

- Nationwide Insurance, where she designed and developed a Marketing prototype, introducing integration modeling techniques
- Synergistic Solutions, Inc., where she developed the UML architecture models for Web-based systems providing enterprise application integration to SSI's clients
- Norrell Services, where she delivered enterprise-level Business Models, defining how Norrell's future processes will be integrated and automated

Laura has also represented systems integration consulting firms such as Digital Equipment Corporation, Computer Professionals, Inc. (CPi), and Naviant to their clients. She presented Integration Modeling techniques at the first OMG-sponsored EAI Workshop in February 2000, and speaks regularly at conferences and in educational forums.

Acknowledgements

Elena Oliker, of MATIS, Inc., for being the technical editor of the book.

I especially thank David Treadway at Synergistic Solutions, Inc. for granting permission to use models developed for SSI and their case histories in the book. It was through SSI that I met Eric Ericson, of Logical Solutions, who introduced me to the use case tree structure in UML modeling.

Melanie Smallie, for believing in me as an author and her husband Larry Smallie for his enthusiastic support. Jeri Kagel, for readings of the early chapters and feedback.

Alexa Selph, for her editing on early drafts, which hopefully made the book more accessible to non-technical readers.

Mabel Brown, my Mother to whom I am grateful for always thinking of me as a writer.

And finally Carl Rainey, for his ongoing love and emotional support as my significant other, life-partner and partner in creative endeavors.

Dedication

This book is dedicated to Dennie Doucher, a friend and inspiration.

Introduction

The techniques and tools that this book introduces provide a proven approach to delivering Enterprise Application Integration (EAI), offering examples from actual practice, and exploring the steps to follow for its day-to-day implementation. Originally designed for companies undergoing significant merger and acquisition activity, Integration Models have evolved into a working toolkit for bridging the gap between business and technical models. They provide a core of flexible models that have been employed successfully across several different industries, including

- Telecommunications
- Transportation
- Financial Services
- Software Development (Vendor)
- Employment Services
- Insurance
- Internet Services
- Marketing and Sales
- Wireless Services

Origins of Integration Models

After deregulation in banking began in the mid-1980s, the Atlanta, Georgia-based bank I worked for started acquiring community banks, expanding the region of its operating reach. Soon the marketing applications that I managed for the bank began to need information extracts from the computerized systems of not only the many Georgia branches, but those of new branches in Florida and South Carolina as well. Before the feeding frenzy of acquisition was over, we were integrating extracts from over 100 different legacy systems to produce a warehouse of product performance and customer information for marketing purposes.

Because many other areas in the bank also needed to merge the systems of acquired branches, a task force sponsored by the bank's advanced technology group was developed, providing in-house consulting on integration to other areas of the bank. The efforts of this team, which I joined, focused on how new techniques and tools could address the integration needs that many areas of the bank were experiencing. We began to develop a set of principles for integration that later evolved to serve in similar situations for other companies operating in different industries.

In the 1990s, through industry consolidation and other factors, many other companies were beginning to see an increasing need for integration services. One such company, in the employment services sector, saw consolidation give rise to integration needs at the enterprise level. Working with that company, we applied integration modeling to support the merging of multiple acquired companies with divergent operating models. We found that the techniques and tools of integration that worked in banking carried over quite nicely to the staffing business. Later, of the many industries that saw deregulation in the 1990s, telecommunications is perhaps the most significant for today's economy. There again, the integration of multiple divergent platforms became a driving business requirement, and integration models helped my client's companies meet that requirement. In today's marketplace the need for rapid delivery of integrated technology solutions has only increased.

It was out of this milieu of increasing integration needs and decreasing timeframes that the techniques and models introduced in this book originated. Begun as a mechanism for helping one company survive multiple mergers of its systems, the models proved useful on the next contract, where I was able to reuse the same models for the same kinds of issues. The same held true for subsequent engagements, and the models began to evolve into a kind of toolkit that went with me from one client to the next, providing a starting advantage on some of the toughest issues my client companies faced.

The Toolkit

Through a process of trial and error, and some fortuitous discoveries, the toolkit grew and became a working set of templates. These templates, applied with integrative methods developed initially at the bank and subsequently refined, always seemed to provide a missing piece of what client companies needed and they never failed to deliver improved integration.

It was when I discovered Erich Gamma's book *Design Patterns* [0.1] that I found a wonderful affirmation of what these templates were—a way of encoding knowledge, a sort of collection of best practices, and a catalog. And through Gamma's book, I discovered the earlier work in architecture design, *A Pattern Language* by Christopher Alexander [0.1], which put forth a rich catalog of design patterns for the discipline of building houses, towns, and roadways. These earlier works helped me see how the patterns I had been collecting and refining could be formalized and shaped into a catalog of templates that would support the integration of any company's systems.

Influences That Shaped the Approach

Long before finding these two books that helped me put integration models into perspective, there were a couple of influences that helped form the basis from which the models grew. They provided a foundation in terms of the approach that was adopted in these integration projects and the methods that evolved to support that approach.

One was in the form of a partner I found in the days of integrating systems at the bank. Elena Oliker was a colleague who became a true partner and supporter, with whom many projects were undertaken and completed. Working together, we formulated many of the principles that underlie the approach of integration modeling. And many of the first models that later became the toolkit were formulated in partnership with Elena. You'll see the appropriate entries in the acknowledgements section of the book, but I mention her here as well because her ideas were so important to the direction integration models continued to follow, even after we had both moved on to working on other projects separately. Though working separately, we always retained our friendship and working relationship behind the scenes, so her influence was always a part of how integration modeling took shape.

It was through our partnership that the ideas in this book were first formulated, field tested—sometimes on ourselves and the success or failures of our partnership, sometimes on our clients who had pressing needs for integrative techniques—and then reevaluated based on the results. And it was out of that early laboratory we built together that the central themes of the book were germinated. The focus on context, the interplay between foreground and background, short term and long term, form and function, linear and nonlinear thinking, all were part of the ideas we incubated together.

The other influence that shaped the ideas behind the current work was a book called *Composing A Life*, a collection of the life stories of five women, examined from an anthropologist's perspective [0.3]. The author, Mary Catherine Bateson (daughter of physicist Gregory Bateson and Margaret Mead, the author of *Coming of Age in Somoa*) traces the uniquely feminine style of weaving a life. It is a style that is made up of advances mixed with many setbacks. In creative endeavors, particularly in the lives of women, she asserts, we learn that sometimes the best progress does not occur in linear fashion. In the male-oriented world of singular focus, creating with a capital "C," projects are conceived, they are capitalized, and they proceed from start to finish without interruption. The resources assigned to the project are protected from intrusions, and the simplest, most direct path is followed to bring the project to a conclusion. In a way, this single-focus style is seductive—in a way it's intuitively obvious—how else can we get anything done?

But in the realities of day-to-day experience, we often go without this luxury of singular focus, and often it serves us better than we know. In *Composing a Life*, Mary Catherine Bateson articulates the understanding that sometimes the way is unclear, that sometimes we must fall back and regroup and rethink. Sometimes the way is blocked and we haven't the wherewithal to unblock it ourselves, but must wait. It is foreign to the impatient mind of corporate America, this concept of biding our time. Yet it is an idea that can be useful in the larger scheme of things, even in the corporate world where project timeframes are dictated by the bottom line.

Even in the corporate world, there are times when a project is blocked, whether because of company politics, lack of funding, or outside business influences. When this happens, the project can stop, formally disbanding with its resources reallocated to other projects, or it can simply go underground for awhile, popping up somewhere else with new sponsorship.

In the latter case, where an initiative perhaps loses focus or resources, but continues in the background, integration models have also proven valuable. They are a tool set that is useful when my clients' projects have the spotlight and I need to move quickly, but also when my clients' projects suffer setbacks, and they have to go underground. Integration models can move into the foreground, providing structure and organizing principles for the enterprisewide architecture, but they can also move into the background and serve in the same role with no supporting resources.

Just Do It

When I recently presented the models at an Object Management Group technical workshop, someone in the audience asked about how to get management support for using integration models. My answer was, as Nike says, "Just do it!" Don't sell it to your manager or client, just start using integration models and let the value speak for itself. You don't really need special funding to learn and apply the techniques and approach of integration models. You're doing the work anyway. Management doesn't have to understand how you do your job—they just have to benefit from it.

When we depart from the management of command and control, as many companies in the new economy are doing, we also depart from the notion of an all-knowing, all-seeing manager who controls the work of those who report to him. We allow the emergence of expertise as a source of authority, as it was in the guild system, with master craftsmen and mentoring through apprenticeship. It is a system where power is determined not by position in a hierarchy of control, but rather is conferred by knowledge. And it is one of the models that is being revived in support of the changing mode of system development today.

Increased Autonomy

In today's e-development landscape, the fact that teams are Internet-enabled means those team members operate with greater autonomy than ever before. Examples range from the telecommuting that is made possible by advanced telecommunications to the new mindset of self-direction and independence that Tom Peters extols in his recent book, *The Brand You 50*, of the Reinventing Work series [0.4]. These forces for increased autonomy at work lead to greater separation and a greater need for approaches that reunite all the pieces, whether human or other resources, without imposing the outmoded controls that no longer apply. The approach of integration modeling is designed to operate in this new freedom, providing ways of connecting without hierarchical control.

Intuitive Approach

One change wrought by the Internet and other technological advances is the increasing pace of information delivery in our society. Business information comes in from many diverse feeds 24 hours by 7 days a week, comprised of business news wires, competitor intelligence, and industry analysis.

The average consumer is bombarded with smaller bytes of information delivered at more rapid rates than ever before. The result of this information overload is that people begin to bypass the old ways of taking in information, through the rational mind, and move more and more toward a higher organization of perception. As the quantity of information becomes too much to comprehend straightforwardly, the intuitive side of the brain takes over and evaluates the information on the basis of "impressions" delivered through the senses. These intuitive readings, which bypass the rational mind, are becoming the currency of the future for advertising, in both traditional and Internet delivery media.

Integration models employ a similar device, by speaking to the intuitive side of the brain and embedding meaning and information visually in the form of the model. The approaches that integration modeling recommends are designed to work with the intuition, building iterative processes that incorporate logical steps for the rational mind, while allowing room for the intuitive side to operate too.

Intuitive Design

Another front on which intuitive design is prominent is the design of the user interface, whether as Web site on the net or as a GUI screen providing a unified interface to disparate business applications. The goal of intuitive design is to create for the user the experience of *flow*. Flow is a term coined by Mihaly Csikszentmihalyi, author of *Finding Flow* (*The Psychology of Engagement with Everyday Life*) and *Creativity*. It means what athletes and musicians think of as "being in the zone."

According to Csikszentmihalyi, "flow tends to occur when a person faces a clear set of goals that require appropriate responses. Another characteristic of flow activities is that they provide immediate feedback. They make it clear how well you are doing.... Flow tends to occur when a person's skills are fully involved in overcoming a challenge that is just about manageable."[0.6]

The techniques and tools presented in this book are designed with flow in mind. They include mechanisms of immediate feedback, providing a sense of perspective and a way to focus on context and the dynamics of interactions. Also they provide ways of understanding the viewpoint of the user of a system, such that any designed interaction that user has with the system will be based on a knowledge of the user's priorities and preferences. Indeed, it will be based on how the user sees the world.

Aim of the Book

This book is aimed first at technical managers who are often on the front lines of *EAI* projects, experiencing up close and first hand the need for proven strategies and methods of enterprise application integration. Whether that manager is the chief technology officer, technical lead, or systems architect, the book offers a knowledge base in integration methods and a catalog of templates to provide a starting point.

Other people who can benefit from reading this book include

- System integrators, for whom it offers modeling techniques that have been used successfully for carving out the project specifications and establishing business goals for consulting contracts.
- IT strategists and architects, who need to ensure a coherent strategy for their organization's application systems integration, and who need workable, proven techniques to help achieve consistency and cost-savings.
- Members of the project teams that support and deliver enterprise application integration projects.
- Business application vendors of DBMS, ERP, business application, and front office systems, who must ensure that their products integrate with *EAI* software.

Organization of the Book

Part I, "Techniques for Enterprise Application Integration," defines enterprise application integration, exploring the increased need for integration techniques in today's complex business environment. It introduces the context for *EAI* and the ways to determine whether your company or the industry in which it operates has an increased need for integration. It further discusses the approaches and techniques of integration modeling, and gives an overview of the catalog of Integration Models.

Chapter 1, "The Context for Enterprise Application Integration (EAI)"—This chapter defines *EAI* and introduces the factors producing an increased need for enterprisewide integration.

Chapter 2, "Introduction to Integration Models"—Chapter 2 introduces the concept of Integration Models and places them in context between the mental models of the business view and the computer-aided software engineering (CASE) or object-oriented models of the technical view.

Chapter 3, "The Environment for Integration Modeling"—This chapter addresses the way Integration Modeling fits in with the organizational components of the IT department. The chapter discusses the place of integration models with regard to other project deliverables and how they place other models, specifications, and designs in a larger context. An operating model for setting up teams on a project basis is provided.

Part II, "Catalog of Integration Models," provides a set of modeling templates that readers can use to improve integration on any business or technology project. Models with formatted descriptions are presented, giving details on the following attributes:

- Template Description
- Template Discussion
- When the Template Applies
- Examples
- Benefits and Consequences
- Template Realization
- EAI Applications
- Templates That Work Well with This Template

Chapter 4, "The Cycle Template"—The Cycle depicts a life cycle or cyclical process, which is characterized by repetition, evolution, and the features of self-reinforcement and self-correction.

Chapter 5, "The Seed Template"—The Seed is a generator or transformer structure depicting a situation where a core component produces, collects, or contains an array of results.

Chapter 6, "The Web Template"—The Web template depicts a network of nodes (or endpoints) and connectors (or arcs). It is useful in modeling network routing and for performing complex path analysis and optimization.

Chapter 7, "The Flow Template"—The Flow template is utilized by process and flow analysis to trace the course of information, goods, services, and communications.

Chapter 8, "The Wave Template"—The Wave template is used to describe the layers of a system, environment, or network. Layers help manage complexity.

Chapter 9, "The Ring Template"—The Ring is useful in depicting the chaining of events, people, devices, or network addresses. Whereas the Cycle models directional processes, the Ring models peer-to-peer relationships.

Chapter 10, "The Cell Template"—The Cell template supports modeling of categorization and compartmentalization. The Cell is useful for analysis of distribution systems, geographic division, and behaviors at the local versus global levels.

Chapter 11, "The Tree Template"—The Tree is a structure utilized to model systems whose characteristics include complex branching, diversification, and the implementation of distribution alternatives.

Part III: "Applying Integration Models," gives real-life examples showing how the techniques can be applied to specific kinds of projects. This part includes sample models, case studies, and lessons learned in the field.

Chapter 12, "Case Study: Enterprise Resource Planning (ERP)"—This chapter provides a composite example for using Integration Models in the Employment Services sector to provide the basis for an ERP implementation.

Chapter 13, "Using Integration Models to Synthesize Industry Models"—This chapter describes how to use the frameworks in extracting the models of a given industry and applying them to your company.

Chapter 14, "Data Strategy, Warehousing, and Architecture with Integration Models"—This chapter explores the application of Integration Models for defining data architectures, warehouses, and overall data strategy.

Chapter 15, "Case Study: Integration in Telecommunications"—This chapter discusses how to apply IM to define the integrated platform in environments fragmented by growth without architecture or by merged operations.

Chapter 16, "Conclusion"—Discusses how Integraton Models help us to understand the current problem set and suggests some future directions for the catalog.

Techniques for Enterprise Application Integration

I

1

The Context for Enterprise Application Integration (EAI)

Business systems are living systems, naturally integrated in the manner of social organizations. Complex and multitextured, they are reflected in the computer systems that evolve to automate business processes. However, when computer systems are designed, the complexity and multitextured nature of the integrated business system is often reduced. When the complexity goes, so does much of the integration that it provides. What's left is the portion of the system that is simple enough for standardization. What's lost is the complexity and the connections that comprise integrated systems.

Without that complexity, systems become rigid, lack integration, and can be difficult to use. When computer systems are built without integrative techniques, the resulting fragmentation of both information and process can greatly reduce their capability to do what they're meant to do: speed up and enable business processes through computer automation. Speeding up a business process is possible because computers can perform tasks much faster than their human counterparts can perform them. Enabling a business process means using computers to not only speed up and make a process more efficient, but also to support the redesign of processes in ways that can only be conceived through technological innovation.

For example, the process of designing a product can involve many steps and the passing of design specifications between those steps. To speed up that process, one could automate the production and distribution of specifications by electronic means. To enable the process, one could introduce a newly feasible technology, designing a new process that only twenty years ago would not have been possible. A shared database, with check-in and check-out features allowing version control and source integrity, would revolutionize the process of product design. It would allow steps that were formerly sequential to be performed concurrently, drastically reducing the overall development time frame.

Both the goals of speed and enabling are put at risk by systems approaches that result in the fragmentation of information and process. For instance, a national bank's sales systems can't be used to manage relationship selling—the strategy of selling new products to current customers based on the existing relationship—because the systems don't depict the whole customer relationship. In many cases, determining all the accounts involved in a given customer relationship requires looking at multiple customer databases and manually compiling the information.

Another example is the telecommunications provider who can't quickly respond to a request for high bandwidth services from a business customer because the engineer who handles provisioning requests must access seven different computer systems to find available facilities or physical circuits that can be assigned to the account.

These two simple examples are not isolated instances. Most large companies today have successfully integrated their communications network so that services such as companywide electronic mail and employee listing databases are considered routine. However, many higher-level business processes, such as service delivery, remain untouched by integration efforts. In fact, stories like these of systems that fail to speed up or enable business processes are more the norm in today's computing world than not. In these instances, the advent of new business models, such as relationship selling and the introduction of new product lines, has out-paced the application of enabling computer technology. Integrating new business models and new product lines increases the complexity of the processes that must be enabled, and indicates a need for techniques that help manage complexity in the design of automated solutions.

Business Reasons for EAI

Many companies are faced with systems and processes that are so fragmented that they slow down such business functions as service delivery and customer support. These are critical business functions, yet often slower than the companies would like. One example is a telecommunications provider that required 90 days to provide services for high-capacity business customers because of convoluted process steps involving numerous non-integrated computer systems.

First, the order manager handles the service order, assigning resources, logging and tracking the service order's progress, and rerouting the request when necessary. When problems are encountered while performing a task associated with a work step, the order manager must invoke contingencies, sometimes with the help of the order-management system, and sometimes going outside the capabilities of the system.

Next, before the assignment process begins, a circuit route determination is completed. The routing identifies the criteria to be used for the selection and/or ordering of the piece parts making up the end-to-end service. After an engineer has identified the requirements, the assignor begins the search for inventory to fulfill them. When a spare unit is found in inventory, the assignor reserves it for use with the service. However, if a spare unit is not found by the system, it doesn't necessarily mean there is no spare unit. Usually it means that manual procedures must be used to search a number of systems that might turn up spare inventory. Meanwhile, portions of the inventory that fall outside the provider's domain must be supplied by trading partners, and requests are initiated to acquire services from them.

After the assignment has been completed, circuit design and service installation are performed, again through the use of computer systems that often are separate or only partially integrated. The process of shepherding a service order through multiple steps involving multiple supporting systems can be interrupted at any point along the way, extending its eventual completion even farther into the future.

Instances like this have engendered the development of a new type of integration that applies not just to one computer system and its internals, but to multiple computer systems as they interact. By automating the process steps and integrating the multiple systems used for provisioning, tying legacy systems together with a single graphical interface for engineers, this provider eliminated lag times and shortened the overall process dramatically. With the application of *Enterprise Application Integration* or *EAI* systems, this provider reduced the 90 days provisioning time to a matter of a few hours. The need for this new type of integration is becoming increasingly apparent as more companies get more of their processes automated. Sooner or later, companies find that they have a need for solutions they can apply to applications operating across the entire enterprise. Hence the term, *Enterprise Application Integration*.

Fragmented Systems

The previous examples show what happens when application systems are fragmented, operating in isolated departmental "islands," and unable to share information across application boundaries. Whereas the lack of techniques for handling complexity is part of the problem, the result of past practices in business management is the other part. Frederick W. Taylor, in his book *Principles of Scientific Management*, published in 1911, taught managers to break the work down into simple jobs and hire unskilled workers to perform those simple jobs [1.1]. The role of managers was to control the work and do the thinking for the workers. According to Taylor, workers do and managers think, plan, and control. This view resulted in the breakdown of businesses into functional units acting as hierarchies of command and control management.

In actual practice, the business community tends to overcome the problems introduced by Taylor's methods by connecting their business functions using the rules of a social network. But the legacy that Taylorism has left embedded in our computer systems is that applications tend to function as stove-pipes, where self-contained units perform one function for a business and avoid all contact with systems performing other functions. Such isolationism leads to the fragmentation seen in systems today. Looking across the enterprise means looking across one stove-piped system after another. Although business people can still function day-to-day, the new business models they want to employ require more than these fragmented legacy systems can offer.

The drive to embrace e-commerce and conduct business on the Internet requires new levels of integration between the online front end and the supporting back office systems. Delivering new ways of collaborating with customers and suppliers, also Internet-enabled, creates more new demands for integration of legacy systems containing the information those customers and suppliers need. Web portals attempt to provide a single point of access to all enterprise applications and spawn new needs for specialized portals for special audiences, all dependent on the integration of legacy applications.

Part of the role of enterprise application integration is to deal with the fragmentation of application systems caused by the divide and conquer strategy of Taylorism. The need for EAI is becoming increasingly urgent, for three key reasons.

Three Key Reasons for Urgency

Three trends in today's business environment provide reasons for the urgent need for integration:

1. Mergers, acquisitions, and regulatory changes

   When companies merge and grow by acquisition, the integration of diverse systems becomes important for back-office merging of operations. Regulatory changes create new opportunities for mergers and concurrently generate the requirement for more integration to support compliance with those regulations.

2. Supply chain movement

   The increasingly important supply chain movement strives to link all parties along a particular supply chain in order to move supply closer to demand. The necessary sharing of information with customers, suppliers, and supply chain partners requires the flexible integration of key Enterprise Resource Planning (ERP) and business systems.

3. e-Commerce and Internet applications

   New e-commerce and Internet applications, such as online marketing, sales, and customer service, must be integrated with back-office applications and databases providing functions such as order-fulfillment, sales tracking, and inventory control.

New Demands on Aging Systems Infrastructures

These business and technology trends are characterized by new demands and pressures on aging systems infrastructures that were never designed to support this kind of load. These infrastructures evolved over time, often without formal design, to meet the needs of yesterday's information climate. In many companies, they developed on an ad hoc basis to address the isolated concerns of different departments at different times.

As priorities shifted from one arena to another through the changing agendas of corporate politics, systems were sometimes completed, sometimes abandoned. Like a Dali painting of great staircases ascending into the clouds where they terminate in thin air, computer systems were partially built and installed, then forgotten, but left in operation, producing useless reports that nobody understood. The resulting base of legacy systems can be confusing and chaotic to maintain or change when new requirements surface. And systems maintenance tasks to support new requirements can take a surprisingly long time to complete.

In this climate of ad hoc development and unstructured growth, a cottage industry sprang up. Systems work was taken outside of corporate Information Technology departments through outsourcing to vendors whose service alleviated some of the problems in-house teams encountered. These vendors specialized in maintaining a stable environment where projects could be completed without political interference, the relationship to legacy systems could be minimized, and then the finished system could be plugged into the customer's environment. The main problem then was that these outsourcing vendors put controls on the scope of a project. They could get the project finished, but couldn't keep up with changing requirements of the real world. Often, by the time the system was "plugged in," the company's needs had changed.

Neither the outsourcing vendors nor the hiring company in this scenario was addressing the deeper issues of integrating application systems across the entire company. By attempting to reduce the complexity (by outsourcing the project and then freezing all changes) the vendors and the hiring company were actually magnifying the underlying problems, while getting even farther away from the root of the problem.

A True Story

Consider the following true story of Mac, (not his real name), a sales representative from a large provider of employment services before it achieved integrated systems:

> *Mac, from Sales, has finally gotten his client, Bill Smith, to agree to a face-to-face meeting to discuss follow-on business. He's excited because Bill's company is a big client and a lot is riding on this sale, so he's not leaving anything to chance this morning. He's wearing a $500 suit, he's got all the collateral sales materials the client could possibly want to see, and he's even got his laptop with a fancy new calculator program that enables him to generate a price quote on the spot.*

> *But as soon as he sits down across the desk from Bill, he suspects something is wrong. Bill's not smiling as big as usual and he seems to be keeping his distance this morning. Mac's antennae are shouting, "Something's wrong!" but he doesn't have a clue what it might be.*
>
> *"So, Mac, your company services a lot of accounts for us all over the country, right?"*
>
> *"That's right, Bill; in fact, that's one of the reasons we're a good fit for you locally. We know your company, how you like to do things; it won't take much to ramp up operations here based on what we're already doing for your company."*
>
> *"So what can you tell me about the problems in Denver last night? I understand Tom's still waiting on his morning reports…."*
>
> *At this point, Mac knows he's dead in the water. It's happened before, and even though he went through the roof last time, it's happening again. Nobody called to brief him, and now instead of making the sale, he's got to pacify an angry client even though he had nothing to do with the problem.*

If Mac had known ahead of time that the Denver account had encountered processing problems the night before, he could have come prepared to give Bill a status update immediately, putting to rest any lingering fears Bill might have had about facing the same problem. Instead, caught off guard and ill informed, Mac unwittingly let the client know that in his company, the left hand didn't know what the right hand was doing.

Mac was not the only one to suffer from that company's lack of application integration. Important new business that could have been written that day was lost, and Mac's co-workers would tell you that it happens all the time. Small, single-location accounts are not a problem in this respect because the sales rep usually knows about any activity on an in-town account. But keeping up with the big accounts, where the big contracts originate, is often a convoluted nightmare. Customers merge and move, they divest holdings and enter new lines of business, and without integrated systems to track these developments across the country and internationally, the sales force is in the dark when having information matters most.

After this company integrated its applications enterprise-wide, setting them up so that problems in Denver can easily be reported in Atlanta, an early warning system generated and delivered a trouble report to Mac before he went out on any customer call. Now, if a large multilocation client experiences problems anywhere in the country, Mac knows to expect questions and develop strategies beforehand for handling concerns.

What Is Enterprise Application Integration?

By focusing on the context for computer systems, EAI pulls together the more traditional types of integration that occur in the systems environment. It uses techniques from all types of integration, but with an added emphasis on integrating applications across the enterprise.

Traditional Kinds of Integration

The need to integrate computer systems is nothing new and there exist traditional ways of integrating systems at the levels of information, function, network, and equipment. Wherever systems development is going on, you'll find the need to integrate new systems into the existing base of systems, data sources, and infrastructure.

This section reviews the existing types of integration and introduces a definition for enterprise application integration:

- **Information Integration**—This addresses the spectrum of knowledge from data collection to information analysis, intelligence, and adding business value.
- **Functional Integration**—This deals with the process support delivered by applications and how they work together.
- **Network Integration**—This focuses on the physical network of computer devices and their interconnections.
- **Systems Integration**—This refers to the integration of diverse technical components and the functionality they support.

Information Integration

New levels of sophistication in data gathering and interpretation have evolved in recent years as companies have progressed from merely gathering data to understanding and using that data more wisely. As raw data becomes increasingly available, its sheer volume discounts the benefit of merely collecting facts. The sorting, filtering, and interpretation of that data turns it into information that can be applied for business benefit. When information is used for activities such as customer profiling to predict buying behavior or to create market performance forecasts, it becomes business intelligence on which actions can be based.

The next tier of business information results when, for example, customer profiles are used by 1:1 marketing strategies, such as those popularized by Don Peppers and Martha Rogers in *Enterprise_One to One*. They advise that "instead of selling as many products as possible over the next sales period to whoever will buy them, the goal of the 1:1 marketer is to sell one customer at a time as many products as possible, over the lifetime of that customer's patronage." [1.2]. Such marketing strategies use customer-specific data from profiles to inform "push" technologies that provide custom-tailored purchase opportunities to clients. The results can add business value to data already configured for forecasting.

Not so long ago, information alone was assumed to confer power, as the saying goes, but in today's information-rich computing world, less is becoming more. Information that is narrowed down by filtering, analysis, and profiling has become the new currency. The model in Figure 1.1 depicts the continually narrowing focus of information that has occurred in recent years.

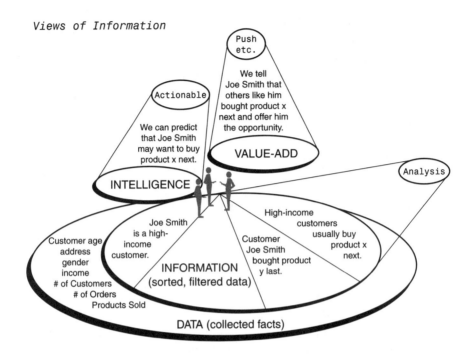

Figure 1.1   The Views of Information model depicts the
continually narrowing focus that information assumes.

Data is the broadest and most plentiful category. The largest pool on the model represents data. Data is defined as collected facts that are without any high-level structure or direction. Customer data includes pieces of information such as customer name, address, and income range. Other data that companies collect include facts such as number of products sold, type of products sold, number of customers, and number of orders.

Sorted, filtered data is the next tier, called *information*. Information is organized by its use in business analysis. Information allows us to categorize customers and make certain assumptions about them based on that categorization. The fact that Joe Smith has an income between $50,000 and $100,000 is data. Characterizing this income range as a high-income range and combining it with the fact that high-income customers have certain behaviors turns the data into information.

An even smaller pool of information is *intelligence*: information that can be acted on because it combines our knowledge about customers into predictive profiles. It is organized by the actions that are based on it. Given that Joe Smith is a high-income customer who bought product x last year, a company can predict that he will want to buy product y this year, because most high-income customers do. Intelligence is information that has been combined in such a way that a company can take action based on it.

The smallest pool of information is that which adds value directly to a transaction by offering opportunities to which the customer is most likely to respond. A company determines these opportunities and presents or "pushes" them using new technology, such as a Web site that recognizes the returning customer and makes product recommendations. Amazon.com is an example of such a company. As Amazon adds new product categories, existing customers automatically receive recommendations in those categories based on the customer profile Amazon maintains for them.

The infrastructure needed to accomplish this vision of highly sophisticated business intelligence requires layers of information integration. Not only must data collection be planned, but also its sources must be understood and communicated. Their semantics, the meaning of data fields belonging to business entities, must be reconciled from one system to another.

The difference in information semantics between systems is the usual stumbling block to information integration because meaning gets lost in the translations. Thus, when a loan system at a bank stores a piece of information that is called "thirty days past due," it is critical to know how the system arrives at the value of that data. Does it equate "thirty days" with a month, and if so, how does it make adjustments for thirty-one day months? What adjustments are made for twenty-eight day months or those with twenty-nine days? Does the system pro-rate for fewer or more days or make some other allowance for them?

When performing financial calculations, differences in the definition of any of these terms can render numbers from different systems incompatible, and you can end up comparing apples and oranges unintentionally. When we say the semantics must be reconciled, we mean systems must know about differing definitions of data elements, as in the previous example, must be able to translate from one system's definition to that of another, and must make the translation available to the other system. In other words, if system A defines "thirty days past due" as thirty days, and system B defines it as a month, which is sometimes thirty and sometimes thirty-one days, any calculations shared by these two systems must compensate for the possible one day difference somehow. Otherwise, system A will consistently charge less for past-due balances.

Functional Integration

Functional integration, or application integration, addresses the combination of disparate computer systems into one system that uses a common set of data structures and rules to deliver the required functionality for a business area. Applications are generally grouped by the business area that owns or uses them, with integration efforts focusing on the applications within that business area, as shown in Figure 1.2.

Functional integration is limited to the applications within the boundaries of a given business area.

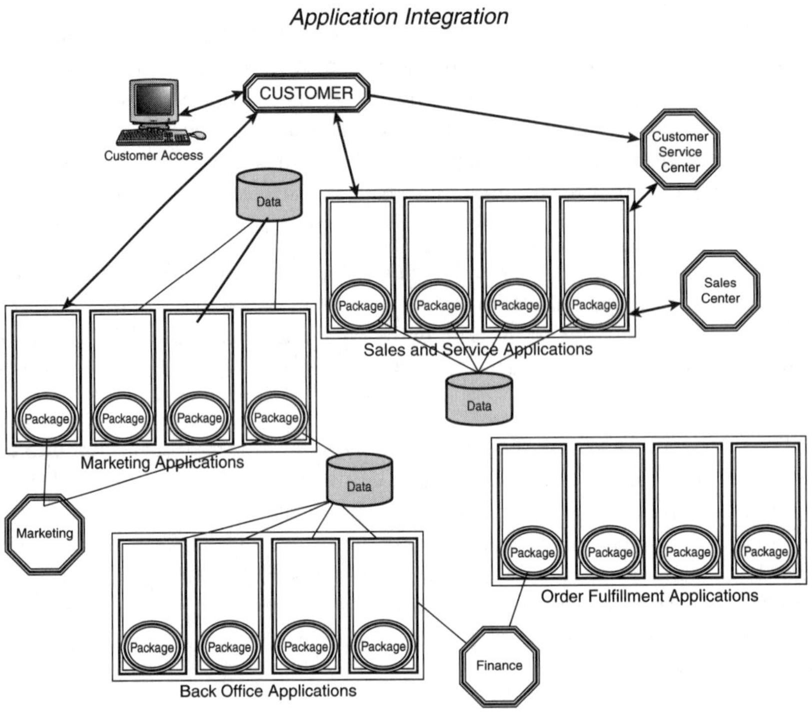

Application Integration

Figure 1.2   Application integration focuses on the integration
of the applications for a given business area.

Many ways of achieving functional integration exist. The outsourcing discussed earlier in this chapter is one method that companies have pursued for addressing the need to make applications function together.

Purchasing integrated packages of application systems is another common approach to functional integration. Vendors in vertical markets define the applications common to an industry, integrate the component applications within the package, and market complete solutions.

Packaged applications can successfully address the needs of one business area. Sometimes they can address the needs of two or three combined business areas. But they fall short in providing solutions that can span the enterprise in today's business reality for the following reasons:

- **Closed and proprietary systems**—Part of the issue is that the technology employed by such packages is often closed and proprietary, so plugging them in to the existing infrastructure is difficult.
- **Lack of advantages of newest technology**—Packaged applications can tend to fall behind the curve of technical innovation, so that all capabilities needed for a competitive advantage are not present.

Outsourcing, packaged applications, and company internal integration schemes are ways that companies pursue the functional integration of application systems. When the integration requirements are truly local and not enterprise-wide, functional integration can be an important building block in a company's systems architecture.

Network Integration

Network integration focuses on combining the elements of the hardware platform that is selected to support a company's computer automation. Standard protocols such as TCP/IP (Transmission Control Protocol/Internet Protocol) are used to provide network connections. Routers, hubs, and front-end devices running communications processors, storage, and computing devices and facilities with their modes of connection are all included in network integration (see Figure 1.3 below).

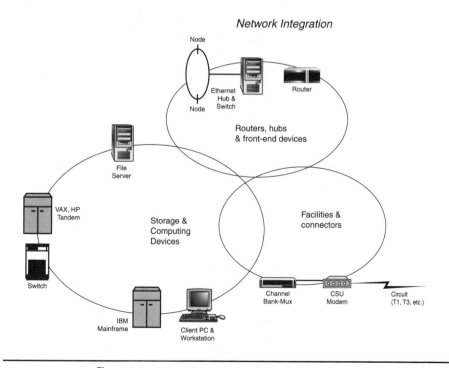

Figure 1.3 Network integration focuses on combining the elements of a company's hardware platform.

Network integration is routinely accomplished in most companies today, with equipment vendors supplying integrated network solutions with predictable results. Quantifying such deliveries has become fairly straightforward in today's environment.

Systems Integration

The focus of systems integration is combining software, hardware, and the necessary network components to deliver a complete solution. Systems integrators specialize in providing and combining pre-fabricated technical components (computers, application packages, and so forth) to resell to customers. Solutions generally include one application or a suite of applications needed for a business area, as seen in Figure 1.4.

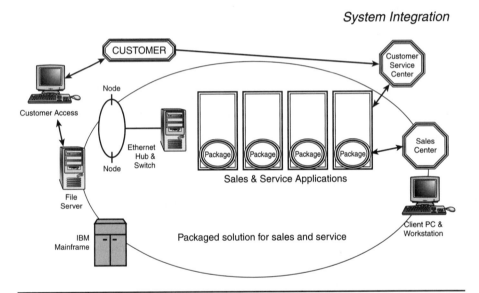

Figure 1.4   Systems integration focuses on complete solutions for a given business area.

Vendors and companies have traditionally combined these four types of integration (functional, information, network, and system) as needed to deliver solutions.

Limitations of Traditional Kinds of Integration

Although all the traditional kinds of integration are necessary and valuable in their place, they fall short of meeting the needs of many business requirements. Each of them covers an arena, such as *information* or *function*, but that arena is too specific, too local, and too detailed for some types of requirements. Applications cover vertical divisions of functions. For instance, sales and service applications support the functions of customer acquisition, customer retention, order taking, and customer service. They store information about those functions and they are designed to help make those processes faster, easier, and more efficient. They organize the information and processes accordingly. When the requirements call for data that slices horizontally across the organization (like market strategy, e-commerce and Internet portals) or process support that occurs horizontally across business functions (like reengineered processes and supplier and customer integration) traditional forms of integration fall short. Network and systems integration occurs at the hardware level. Higher levels of integration call for conceptual, not just physical compatibility.

Enterprise Application Integration

The market often defines enterprise application integration as the use of middleware that enables the rapid integration of legacy, packaged, and new applications into new business solutions. This definition can be broadened by removing the reference to any specific implementation, and by including concerns that reach beyond specific application solutions to pre-defined business needs. A meaningful definition must include the significant fact that EAI addresses the context for application systems as well as the systems themselves. In fact, the techniques introduced in this book will rely on an Escher-like reversal of foreground and background to place a new emphasis on context, as depicted in Figure 1.5.

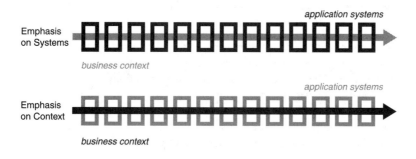

Figure 1.5   EAI requires shifting the emphasis from
computer systems to their business context.

Traditional forms of integration typically place the emphasis on the computer systems and their internals and how to combine the technical components for efficiency. EAI includes the collaboration of technical components, but shifts the emphasis to the context in which those computer systems must perform, including the business goals and models. Thus, a more comprehensive definition of EAI reads as follows:

> Enterprise Application Integration is the process of placing hardware, software, and the business process in context so that when they are combined the interfaces between components become seamless, information can be easily shared, and systems working together can achieve synergy.

To better understand this definition, I will break it down and discuss each idea in turn.

Seamless Interfaces Between Components

From the enterprise perspective, computer systems are the components that make up the overall architecture of a company's systems. Ideally the computer systems will merge into the background and the business use of these tools of automation will come to the fore. This shift in focus requires that the computer systems act as components in a larger operation where the differences between the components have been resolved.

For instance, the application used by a company's sales force to track customer leads, contacts, and sales might be one component. That one component can have several different versions in a large company, when different sales offices have implemented the same system differently, or have even installed different software. It's not uncommon for sales offices in separate geographical locations to operate independently from each other, installing and maintaining their own computer systems separately. When that is the case, those systems probably will not be able to inter-operate and share data because their definitions for that data, and for the operations applied against it, won't match. So a company's sales systems in Omaha won't be compatible with the same company's sales systems in Akron.

Another component might be the software used by the marketing department to forecast customer demand for services or products and to track promotions, market trends, and customer behaviors. This type of software often uses an entirely different scheme to represent customer information, with definitions that are meaningful to marketing but not necessarily meaningful to sales. Marketing tends to look at trends among demographically defined groups of customers, for example, whereas the sales department is more likely to track information on contacts with a specific customer.

Both the sales and marketing software components store information about customers, but from two or more different perspectives, often with different definitions of what information is needed about customers. To say that the interfaces between these components are seamless means that in spite of their different relationships to the customer, the computer systems have been configured to use compatible definitions of important pieces of customer information. The operations or business rules applied against that data (such as calculations, transformations, and categorization,) are also compatible. In other words, they have seamless interfaces that basically become irrelevant to the business owner's ability to use them to conduct business.

Data Sharing

In 1996, in *Data Management Review,* David Newman wrote "Data, data everywhere, but not a drop that's uniform, consistent, or integrated" [1.3]. He was referring to the many issues that can make sharing data between systems a challenge. For example, each of the following presents its own issues:

- Determining the best source for a particular type of business information, and whether different sources will be required for different times in the life cycle of that information

- Knowing whether more than one source will be required to get the whole picture

- Knowing when the same piece of information is captured more than once and how each capturing system defines and formats that piece

- Understanding the timing of updates and changes to data, and how they affect its capture

All these issues must be addressed for data to be successfully shared and integrated.

Systems Working Together in Synergy

When interfaces are seamless and data is shared, the resulting synergy tends to enable entirely new ways of doing business, furthering the evolution of the industries in which they occur. Synergy, in this context, can be defined as the combination of components working together to produce something more than the individual components could achieve on their own.

For example, 1:1 marketing is one new business model that's received much attention in the industry press. Amazon.com has built much of its success upon the Internet implementation of this new model. The synergies Amazon.com has achieved include integrating sales and service customization with the collection of customer information and the interactivity of the Internet. That interactivity has enabled Amazon.com to track customers' buying behavior and to juxtapose that information with customer profiling data. The resulting "something more" is the capability to predict customer behavior and intelligently recommend next purchases.

Delta Airlines provides another example of integrating revenue and market performance tracking with reservation systems and forecasting software to create synergies. Enabled by the deep integration of diverse computer systems, these synergies enable the airlines to practice revenue management, which increases revenues by adjusting price and product availability based on customer demand. To see how synergy affects industries in convergence you only need to look at a company like Microsoft, where the components being synergized are actually the industry components of software development, financial services, publishing, and entertainment. Finding new ways of integrating these components has continually renewed Microsoft's competitive advantage.

Table 1.1 depicts these and other examples, giving the new business model, the company employing the new model, and the components that are working together in synergy.

Table 1.1   **Company synergies table shows new business models enabled by systems working together in synergy**

New Business Model	Example Company	Synergizes Components
1:1 Marketing	Amazon.com	Sales & marketing Order fulfillment Mass product customization Collection of customer information Internet interactivity
	Dell Computer Corporation	Sales & marketing Order fulfillment Mass product customization
Revenue Management	Delta Airlines	Revenue tracking Market performance tracking Reservations/bookings Demand forecasting
	Bureau of Alcohol, Tobacco and Firearms (ATF)	Taxpayer accounting Collection actions Audits of claims Review & approval of applications for permits
	Hilton Hotels Corporation Reservations	Sales force automation
Convergence	Microsoft	Internet interactivity Software development Financial services Publishing Entertainment
	AT&T (through merger with Tele-Communications, Inc. and joint venture with Time Warner)	Voice services Media and entertainment Broadband communications services Cable TV

As this shows, enterprise application integration is the complex process of fitting hardware, software, and business processes together to enable new business solutions. Its characteristics include

- Emphasis shift from systems to context
- Seamless interfaces between components
- Data sharing
- Systems working together in synergy

Architectural Infrastructure for Integration

Traditional forms of integration focus on the following levels of technical architecture:

- Logical application architecture
- Physical technology architecture

Enterprise application integration requires an architectural infrastructure that addresses both the business and technology sides of the equation.

Logical application architecture and physical technology architecture are driven by the demands of the business processes and the information they employ. At the same time, the capabilities of the application and physical architecture determine what is feasible in the process and information landscape.

Business Process

Business process describes the functionality that must be delivered and supported by the application systems. At the highest level, business process describes the core processes that a business carries out to conduct business. A core process can be defined as one that starts with contacting the customer or the market and extends to the collection of payment for services or products delivered, or to the generation of new market dollars.

Core processes are differentiated from subordinate processes, sub-processes, and procedures. The latter delineate some of the steps required to deliver on one or more phases of the overall process but do not extend all the way from customer to payment.

For example, a core process in an employment services company might be to provide temporary staffing to a client. The core process would start with customer contact, include taking the order and delivering the service, and end with invoicing and collecting payment. End to end, the core process extends from customer to payment. A subset of the core process might be service delivery, which covers only one step in the entire core process.

Core processes are understood, designed, and optimized using business process engineering. To automate defined subsets of the business process, they are generally captured at the use-case level, where the use of a system is documented as a series of interactions between the end user and the system interface. Use cases help define the requirements for process automation, providing the first layer of rigorous definition from which technical design models can follow.

Three interrelated architectures support the delivery of the business process requirements:

- Information architecture
- Application architecture
- Technology architecture

Along with the business process component, one of the architectures, the information architecture, is business-oriented, whereas the other two are technology-oriented, as shown in Figure 1.6.

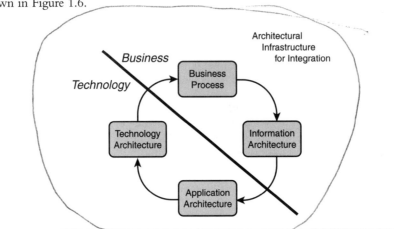

Figure 1.6   Business process is delivered by three interrelated architectures.

Information Architecture

To be accessible, information must be structured, mapped, and organized so that the significant pieces of business information can be retrieved. To create that organization and mapping, the subject areas that are of interest to the business across the organization must be defined. The types of data and its sources that are either in current use or required for assembling the desired information in each subject area must also be determined.

Information architecture defines the way that company data is structured for accessibility, navigability, and comprehension. Too often companies don't understand the need for information architecture, and they attempt to catalog and store data at one level of detail only. When designing a single system, the logical design of entities and their relationships leading to the design of physical databases can be sufficient. But when you attempt to integrate and combine multiple systems with multiple data sources, logical and physical design is not enough.

Combining long lists of data elements derived from existing systems without a sense of context, structure, or relationship makes the data incomprehensible. This approach creates an ocean of data that is difficult if not impossible to navigate. Subject area analysis at the enterprise level is required to organize the overall data picture. Figure 1.7 shows the desired relationship of logical and physical data design to information architecture.

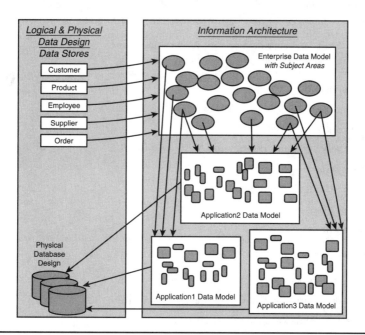

Figure 1.7   Relationship of logical and physical data design to information architecture.

After data is organized through information architecture, to be maintainable it must be stored once rather than in multiple redundant databases. Mechanisms are needed for recognizing when a piece of data has been changed, added, or deleted, and for tracking and distributing those events across the subscriber base for the information.

For data to be understood, it must be quantifiable. The source of the data, its unique perspective on the data, any timing considerations in the completeness of the data, and the credibility of the source are all factors that must be known. The semantics applied to the data must also be known. All this information is referred to as *metadata*, or data about the data, and must be delivered with information to make it useful and understandable.

Application Architecture

Application systems work together to deliver the required automation of business processes. Sometimes one system will automate an entire core process, as in the case of an Internet storefront that interacts with the customer, accepts orders, and engages order-fulfillment automatically, whether it takes place online as does a product download or offline as does a UPS-delivered product. More often a suite or portfolio of application systems is needed to automate all the requirements of a core process. For example, a typical business operation would have one application for customer service, one for order acceptance, and one for order fulfillment. The application architecture describes how these components are structured to work together.

For applications to manage data or support business functions, they must access a variety of systems services and perform many tasks:

- Data collection
- Data storage
- Data security
- Data movement and transformation
- Information presentation
- Data retrieval and updating
- Data analysis
- Data summary

The following are also important targets for automation:

- Diagnostic processes (for example, troubleshooting)
- Monitoring processes (for example, fraud detection)
- Process control (for example, workflow)
- Critical decision support (for example, loan authorization)

By using the application architecture, application systems are categorized according to their different processing characteristics. Standard reusable components are defined for application use, whereas unique applications are customized. Thus, a company can maximize the synergy of like applications.

Applications are analyzed and broken down into components, which are assigned functional responsibilities and technology choices. Where the component will reside is determined, and the layer within the architecture is determined. Some standard types of application architecture include

- Two-tier architectures
- Three-tier architectures
- N-tier architectures

These tiered approaches can include a user desktop client, a Web server, an application server, a database server, a mainframe, or combinations thereof.

Technology Architecture

All the specific computers, operating systems, database management systems, computer languages, and peripheral devices required to execute software programs and manage their input and output are referred to as the *technology platform*. These components must be configured to meet the requirements of the computer software and integrated to provide the basis for operations.

The technology architecture describes the platforms on which the application components operate. It specifies client machines versus server machines, types of systems that are interconnected using networking, and their topology, location, and modes of connectivity.

Company Risk Factors for Integration

In many companies, as increased automation turns up the heat, certain factors emerge as trends in the development of information technology. These trends can be designated as risk factors that indicate when a company has an increased need for integration. These risk factors include

- System development without architectural planning
- Previous data integration failures that have created negative perceptions to be overcome
- Dramatic changes in the role of marketing
- Dramatic changes in the role of IT

System Development Without Architectural Planning

When systems are developed without architectural planning, the resulting systems environment can end up looking like a "crazy quilt," a patchwork of home-grown systems and databases developed without architecture, much like a city that grows without a city plan until no one knows exactly where the streets go anymore.

Computer systems are usually built by the dictates of a corporate initiative. They happen in large companies when one business user gets funding approved and buys, builds, or assembles the desired system. In small- to medium-sized service companies like software development firms, they happen in response to customer demand. The developer rarely stops to question where the latest customer-requested application fits into the bigger picture. Normally, she just nails down enough requirements to proceed, without worrying about potential ties to other systems.

In other companies, the lack of architectural planning is a symptom of focusing on short-term deliverables. Like politicians, executives are driven by the bottom-line results they can deliver in the near-term. In the absence of a balanced long-term perspective, the short-term wins out and whatever can be delivered in three months will be—again without reference to the bigger picture.

After several years of this opportunistic type of development, the "crazy quilt" presents a growing burden of overlap, shortfall, and disconnected databases. A company in this situation will experience an increasing need for integration as requirements come up that can only be addressed by information gleaned from more than one of these disjointed data sources.

Previous Data Integration Failures Have Created Negative Perceptions to Be Overcome

When a desire to build a warehouse of data for management reporting, marketing, and service statistics exists, previous data integration failures can reduce the effectiveness of any new initiative. Largely a question of perception, the presence of previous failures denotes an environment where the necessary trust will be hard to build.

Data integration through warehousing initiatives requires cooperation between several project sponsors or stakeholders, unlike typical technology projects that have one clear owner. The costs and benefits become difficult to quantify and must be parceled out over several user communities. By definition, data integration crosses the usual boundaries of application ownership because it requires information from multiple computer applications. Not only do the sponsors have to share the assets of a data warehouse, but they must be able to work together to define how those assets will be configured and represented in the warehouse.

If they haven't failed at it before, and if a trust can be built between departments accustomed to competing for resources, the results of a cooperative integration project can be stellar. But if previous failures have set organizational units against one another with polarized positions already formed, mending that damage can add significant overhead to the work required of the project team.

Beyond the psychological factor, actually requiring the team to incorporate artifacts from previous failures can severely impair their ability to succeed. But it often happens because no one wants to admit the earlier projects actually failed, and managers sometimes see the re-use of the artifacts as redeeming the earlier effort.

Dramatic Changes in the Role of Marketing

In many companies, the role of marketing has changed in recent years, from providing market research and sales support to developing strategies that can change the course of a company's future. This new role produces a growing demand for information that supports strategic decision-making.

When marketing was about mass-marketing consumer goods to the waiting public, research and customer behavior studies determined what the customer wanted, at what price, and within what parameters of time and place. Marketing provided this research and sales support through largely manual processes, and their share of the IT dollar was relatively small. Marketing requests that computer jobs be run to extract a list of customers for direct mail approaches were generally delivered last at the end of the month. And for direct mail purposes, the delivery of such information was considered timely and sufficient.

As the mass market has given way to the niche market, the role of marketing has shifted from developing products for mass markets to mass customization of products based on customer demand. Marketing requirements for more customer information, for information that would enable relationship selling and customer profiling, have begun to surface. The old methods of collecting customer information through survey, observation, and sampling have become insufficient. Suddenly, the information requirements have changed dramatically.

The new role of marketing has introduced the following requirements at polar opposites:

- Summarized homogenized data from diverse application sources that supports strategic decision-making
- Detailed customer behavior, demographic, and buying history that supports relationship selling and one-to-one marketing

Together, these widely divergent requirements can place enormous pressure on the existing systems, which usually are not configured to respond to either one.

Dramatic Changes in the Role of IT

As information technology has matured, the expectations for technology have changed from carrying out tactical plans defined by the business strategist to enabling strategic advantage. The pursuit of new technologies for the promise of strategic advantage has resulted in companies incorporating IT strategies into the overall corporate strategy, rather than permitting the corporate strategy to dictate IT strategy. This change represents a fundamental shift in the relationship between IT and business from IT as subordinate to business, to IT as enabling partner to business.

The paradigm shift is evident in business today, where dot-com companies rule the NASDAQ. Technology is no longer just a supporter, but has become the central (sometimes the only) priority, as is the case with new Internet startups. The emerging role of IT is that of influencing, whereas the business generates demand, as illustrated in Figure 1.8.

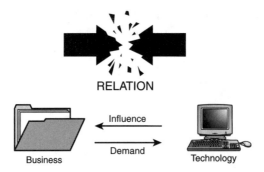

Figure 1.8   The emerging role of IT is to influence
the business application of new technologies.

The more a company has adopted the new paradigm, the greater the demand will be for systems that are

- Faster, in terms of both the development cycle and the performance delivered, because speed to market is as crucial in Internet time as high-performance
- Stronger, for handling multiple concurrent transactions
- More strategic in their objectives

All this adds up to greater integration.

Industry Risk Factors for Integration

Just as companies can experience certain conditions that raise a red flag indicating greater need for integration, entire industries can become more susceptible to the issues of integration. When certain factors come into play, these industries can be said to have an increasing need for integration. Industry risk factors include

- Rapid industry consolidation
- Convergence blurring the lines between industries
- Decreasing technology life cycles
- Reduced product-development cycles

Rapid Industry Consolidation

Deregulation and competitive pressures are producing rapid consolidation in one industry after another. The dynamics of this consolidation increase the pressure on infrastructures of all kinds, but especially on technical systems. As companies merge, systems that were developed in diverse environments suddenly must function together as one. But often these systems are so different in their design that it's difficult to combine them without major restructuring.

Convergence Blurring the Lines Between Industries

In addition, the lines between industries are blurring, as the convergence of television cable, telecommunications, and Internet technologies attests to. Not only do companies merge, but also industries themselves can merge and mutate into new forms, with entirely new ways of doing business. Enterprise application integration is in the forefront at companies deploying the technology required by these new business models today.

Decreasing Technology Life Cycles

Technology life cycles are decreasing. As Jeff Erlich, the CIO of National Data Corporation, a leading provider of information services and systems for the health care and payment systems markets, points out, "The time it takes to learn a new technology is greater than the half-life of what you're trying to learn. They're becoming shorter lived, so to learn it in the classical sense is not physically possible. By the time you've barely understood it the technology is gone."

When the enabling technology constantly changes and evolves, keeping up with that technology becomes an issue in itself. As market demands force the adoption of ever-evolving products, integration depends on the compatibility of new releases with old platforms, languages, and operating systems.

Reduced Product Development Cycles

Competitive pressures to reduce product development cycles are mounting. Global competition combined with technical innovation has created an environment in which the window of opportunity for new products is shrinking rapidly. Products that formerly required years to develop are now being produced in months or even weeks and rushed to market by streamlined teams.

To determine whether your company is encountering a higher need for integration because of the internal operating environment or industry forces, review the following checklist of company risk factors:

- System development without architectural planning
- Previous data integration failures creating negative perceptions to be overcome
- Dramatic changes in the role of marketing
- Dramatic changes in the role of IT

Also, the following industry risk factors can indicate an increased need for integration:

- Rapid industry consolidation
- Convergence blurring the lines between industries
- Decreasing technology life cycles
- Reduced product development cycles

Conclusion

Many companies find that today's business environment presents challenges that require new tools and new methods of solving problems stemming from integration issues. For computer systems to actually deliver on the promises of automation—faster, better ways of doing business than ever before—these integration issues must be addressed.

EAI represents the next logical step in the evolution of technology that started with the automation of isolated business processes and has grown to affect how business across an entire company is done. It has far-reaching consequences for the extended life of systems belonging to a company's legacy. At the same time, EAI and the technologies it produces help define future possibilities for the growth of new systems.

2

Introduction to Integration Models

Integration models originated on integration projects carried out in companies doing business in diverse industries. They have been collected and formalized to provide a pattern language for integration. The templates embody common solutions to integration issues, providing a visual syntax for depicting and combining the elements of those solutions. Similar to the pattern language represented in Erich Gamma's *Design Patterns: Elements of Reusable Object-Oriented Software* [2.1] or its precursor, *A Pattern Language* [2.2], Christopher Alexander's treatise on patterns in architecture design, integration models formulate some common approaches to integration issues and present them as patterns in a catalog.

Integration models differ from the design patterns cited previously because the models are more background formulations, designed to provide an organizing principle for the modeling of integration issues and their solutions, whereas design patterns focus more on the design of physical implementation. Sometimes integration models are useful in the early and high-level modeling work of a project. Sometimes they filter down into detailed and physical design models, but generally their application is broad, focused more on the dynamic context for systems building and less on the physical design of implementation solutions.

Integration modeling provides a core of flexible models that were both developed and discovered on integration-related projects. Each of these models acts as a template or pattern, representing a particular dynamic that can be harnessed to deliver improved integration.

Integration Models Bridge the Gap Between Business and Technical Views

A common problem in technical projects is a gap between how technical people see the world and how business people see the world. If you've ever tried to present an entity relationship diagram to a business audience, or to senior executives, you know about this problem. Only a business user with a decidedly technical bent will sit still for the lengthy explanations required for understanding most technical models. For those designing a system solution who need the guidance, buy-in, and concurrence of business representatives, this difference in viewpoints can become the Great Divide. Too often, technical people resolve this dilemma by trying to build system solutions without the guidance, buy-in, and concurrence of business representatives. The solutions they devise under such circumstances will always fail to deliver business value.

Another typical approach is to build the technical models and then attempt to educate the business representatives on how to read, relate to, and update those models. This approach usually fails because the disciplines of technical modeling are complex and abstract. There is too much to learn, especially for an audience that has no other use for the knowledge except to verify the contents of one set of models.

The integration modeling approach is to start not with technical models, but with the business viewpoint. First, viewpoint analysis models that capture the essence of one or more points of reference for the business are built. These models are not technical and do not require that the user learn an intricate modeling notation to understand them. They are designed so that the details of the model become irrelevant and the visual pattern of the model conveys the information. You work with the business area representative at that level, using the view models to reflect the business concerns and problems, and applying integration models to resolve those concerns. Then you take the resulting new models and translate them to the technical team. The team then carries the selected integration models forward into the technical implementation models.

This approach enables the business area representative to focus on business concerns, using the view models as tools, without having to learn the intricacies of arcane modeling notations. The technical team is then briefed on the business viewpoint, and uses the integration modeling results as a basis for technical models. This means that if the business representative ever has to be exposed to those models, he will recognize the patterns and have some visual clues to relate to. He will also be more likely to relate to a technical model that provides some clear visual organization taken from the integration models.

A key role of integration models is to bridge the gap between the business view and the technical view. Figure 2.1 shows the relationship between business models, technical models, and integration models.

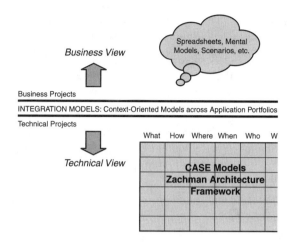

Figure 2.1   Integration models bridge the gap between business and technical models.

Business Models Are Task Oriented

Business projects are often illustrated and supported by various models developed formally or informally by the business lead for the project. Formal business models include such practices as

- Mental models
- Future scenarios
- The revenue "S-curve" for market penetration
- Spreadsheets
- Bar charts

Additionally, various strategy gurus introduce the following techniques:

- The business diamond of re-engineering
- Value chain and core competencies
- Various implementations of quadrant or association matrix modeling

Informally, many project leaders develop a sort of "story," often complete with a favorite illustration that is drawn and erased every time the pitch is made.

Technical Models Are Analytical and Formalized

On the technical side, Computer-Aided Software Engineering (CASE) and object-oriented modeling provide various types of analysis and design models supported by software tools, aiming to make the "push-button" generation of computer programs (or code) a reality. These models are characterized by their analytical objectives: decomposition, enumeration, separation, delineation, and classification.

Unlike the business models described previously, technical models require rigorous notation in order to make their automation possible. They also generally appear rather cryptic and hard to decipher for the uninitiated, making them inappropriate as vehicles for illustrating technical solutions for most business people.

Formalized by John Zachman in his *Architecture Framework* [2.3], technical models attempt to answer the following questions:

- What? (Data)
- How? (Process)
- Where? (Network node)
- When? (Events)
- Who? (Owner, business area)
- Why? (Strategy)

These questions are applied to designing the technical components of a system. The models progress through increasing levels of detail and across changing perspectives of complexity. Many different models are utilized for technical analysis and design, including

- Entity relationship diagrams
- Decomposition diagrams
- Activity diagrams
- State charts
- Flow charts
- Data-flow diagrams
- Use-cases models
- Collaboration diagrams
- Class diagrams

Integration Models Are Context Oriented

Integration modeling occurs at the intersection where business and technical modeling overlap, and runs throughout all levels and viewpoints, providing the glue that ties the pieces together that have been separated through analysis. Whereas technical models are analytical (separating out the components), and business models tend to be task-oriented (getting the job done), integration models are oriented toward clarifying the context. They capture multiple perspectives and can function on more than one level at a time.

CASE and object-oriented models observe rules that are used to define and master "the box," but integration models are about getting "outside the box" without losing sight of it. They are about seeing the big picture without losing touch with the details.

What Do Integration Models Do?

Integration models help you deal with integration issues. The focus of this section is on what they do for the project, such as enabling you to concentrate on the background in which systems operate, and capturing multiple perspectives. They also function on more than one level and depict issues that occur across application portfolios. Ways that they can provide placeholders for infrastructure requirements analysis are also discussed.

Clarify Contexts

Integration models help place the technology in the background and bring the business use to the foreground. They accomplish this by treating systems as context and focusing on the dynamics of systems interactions. Overall, does a specific business activity follow a cycle? Does it require a web of connections? Or does it contain layers of complexity? How does it function? Questions like these will help define which integration models are selected.

The design of a revenue data warehouse in the airline industry provides an example. The business intelligence team was collecting use cases representing use of strategic revenue data by marketing and forecasting analysts. The team kept getting tripped up by the special timing requirements of flown revenue accounting. Data collected at the point of sale differed widely from statistics captured after the passenger had actually completed the flight. The team needed to understand the timing considerations of the revenue information update cycle and place the use cases in a context that made sense of their position within that cycle.

A model similar to the one shown in Figure 2.2 utilized the Cycle template to focus on the iterative nature of the revenue information update cycle and was used to place the numerous use cases in context.

Before the revenue information update cycle model was developed, the use cases lacked organization and were hard to comprehend. Marketing and forecast analysts knew that data was incomplete at earlier points in the update cycle, but had a hard time conveying the related timing requirement to the business intelligence team. After the revenue information update cycle model was introduced, the use cases made sense and the warehouse requirements fell into place as a schedule was developed showing which use cases could occur at what points in the update cycle.

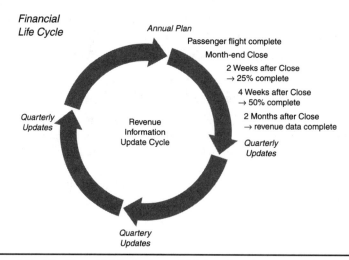

Figure 2.2   The Financial Life Cycle model helps place the use cases in context.

Table 2.1 shows a sample of a similar schedule.

Table 2.1   Use Case Schedule Versus Revenue Information Update Cycle

Update Cycle Milestone	Use Case Allowed
Passenger flight complete	Monitor flight leg performance
	Forecast QSP share and compute share gap
	Monitor and analyze origin and destination revenue
Month-end close	Identify and counter competitive threats
	Monitor and analyze load factor
	Monitor and analyze traffic growth
Two weeks after close	Forecast demand and fares
	Update and analyze origin and destination revenue
	Update and analyze traffic growth
Four weeks after close	Update and analyze origin and destination revenue
	Update and analyze traffic growth
Two months after close	Update and analyze origin and destination revenue
	Update and analyze traffic growth

The introduction of a cyclical integration model in this example clarified the business context, providing a guiding organizing principle for the use cases. It cleared up the confusion about how the use cases related to the timing of business events, and enabled the team to focus on business analysis rather than tracking down timing issues. The use cases themselves became part of the background, and the work of the team focused on gathering information at all significant points in the cycle.

Capture Multiple Perspectives

Part of the role of integration models is to help capture multiple perspectives. Because they are a flexible set of modeling templates, integration models can apply in a variety of different settings. They can model the dynamics of a customer scenario, showing what's important about how a customer might interact with a Web site, for instance. Or they can be applied to the computer operations environment, depicting a series of computer systems and devices that support customer interaction.

Integration models can also define how organizational components will interact. For example, you can reinforce the relational nature of modern project teams by choosing to use the Ring model to depict the teams in an organization, rather than using the standard org-chart with its hierarchical structure. The idea is that integration models are flexible enough, and focused not only on technical, systems concerns, but also on dynamic patterns of interaction and collaboration.

Function on More Than One Level

Integration models can be utilized to focus in on significant details of a process or system or to bridge across systems at a very high level. Again, this is because they concentrate on the dynamics of a situation, not on the implementation technology. Thus integration models are useful in modeling business processes and process flow, while also offering the benefits of organizing and clarifying the dynamics of more detailed models.

The level that is captured depends on the perspective being described. For example, when developing a data warehouse of customer information in a financial institution, you need to understand the structure of customer relationship information. The tree structure can be selected to support the branching diversification of the components of information. The template highlights the dynamic of branching and focuses the model on the composition of the required data. The Tree template appears in Figure 2.3.

TREE
The Tree is a structure utilized to model systems whose characteristics include complex branching, diversification and the implementation of distribution alternatives.

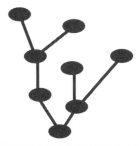

Figure 2.3   The Tree template is a structure utilized to model systems with characteristics that include complex branching, diversification, and the implementation of distribution alternatives.

The resulting model shows the possible levels of customer relationship, from household to individual customer to account relationships with the customer (see Figure 2.4).

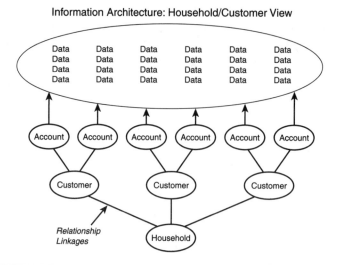

Figure 2.4   The Information Architecture model shows the hierarchy of data as it pertains to customer households.

Suppose the team that was using the information architecture for the customer households model to build a decision-support system for marketing needed to design the actual use with desired entities and attributes. A more detailed data model could be developed, depicting the decision-support use of the required information. The Seed integration model (see Figure 2.5) helps focus in on the technical details.

SEED
The seed is a generator/transformer structure depicting a situation where a core component produces, collects or contains an array of results.

Figure 2.5   The Seed model is a generator/transformer structure depicting a situation where a core component produces, collects, or contains an array of results.

The Seed model provides the element of a shared repository, in this case represented by the fact table in a star schema multidimensional model (see Figure 2.6). Levels of customer relationships from the information architecture model become the dimensions on the star schema. This model in turn becomes the basis for detailed entity relationship diagrams that drive the design of the physical database.

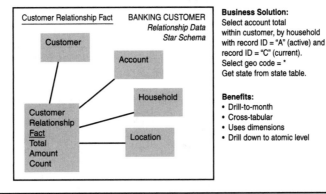

Figure 2.6   The Marketing Data Mart—decision support usage model provides the basis for more detailed physical entity relationship diagrams.

Cross Application Portfolios

Some companies place all the application systems that are used by a business area (for example Marketing, Finance, Operations, Sales, and so forth) in a *portfolio*, or suite of application systems, for that business area. Applications within a portfolio are more likely to be well-integrated. Those in separate portfolios are rarely so.

One role of integration models is to provide a way to focus on aspects of doing business that takes place across application portfolios. For example, in one project, the Cell template (see Figure 2.7) helps define subject areas for a publish-and-subscribe implementation that serves shared data across the entire corporation.

The Cell template helps the team to compartmentalize the information requirements while keeping its global nature in perspective. The model in Figure 2.8 was presented to business executives as the first in a series of Cell-based models that pulled together the data requirements at the subject-area level. Subsequent models in the series defined the topics in each subject area and drilled down into the more detailed business use of the information. The end result was a set of context-oriented models that were devised for the business owners and that received their unqualified endorsement.

CELL
Cell models support modeling of encapsulation, inheritance & messaging.
Analysis of distribution systems, geographic division -
behaviors at the local versus global levels.

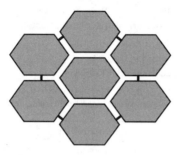

Figure 2.7   Cell models support modeling of encapsulation, inheritance, and messaging. They are useful for analysis of distribution systems, geographic division, and behaviors at the local versus global levels.

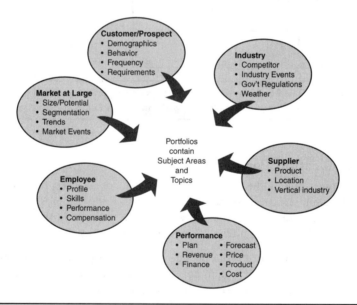

Figure 2.8   Portfolios contain subject areas for a publish-and-subscribe system.

The subject area models then became the roadmap for the data architecture devised to support the distribution of data. Technical design models (entity relationship diagrams and physical design models) were then developed to build the actual technical components for publish-and-subscribe implementation.

Provide Placeholders for Infrastructure

When they cross the lines between application portfolios, integration models can highlight opportunities for economies of scale or reuse of a variety of technical assets.

They can also provide placeholders for pulling together an infrastructure. For example, during a Y2K analysis at a wireless services company, integration models helped one client get their arms around their equipment inventory so that their Y2K liabilities could be better understood.

In the wireless services industry, application systems are in some cases less a concern than the equipment that houses them. The application systems are easy enough to identify, inventory, and analyze using standard Y2K techniques. But the equipment inventory is much less understood because it is an area that has grown without design to accommodate needs as they surface in various locations. It isn't managed centrally, though some of the equipment is managed out of a network operations center (NOC). A widely distributed cellular network with local variations in installation details, such as equipment type, operating software version, and so forth, exists. It is tied to a data network, with some products delivering voice services, some delivering data services, and various combinations thereof.

To quantify what equipment is in the field, you first must model the equipment scenarios. Then you are in a position to start assigning management responsibility for the Y2K analysis of liability. For instance, you need a model that will help you manage the complexity of the data network, which could be thought of as layers of hardware connections that cooperated together. The Wave template (see Figure 2.9) depicts the layers of the data network.

WAVE
The wave template is used to describe the layers of a system, environment or network. Layers help manage complexity.

Figure 2.9   The Wave template describes the layers of a system, environment, or network. Layers help manage complexity.

The layers are defined by working with the network engineers, and then equipment is categorized by layer and filled in. The resulting model appears in Figure 2.10.

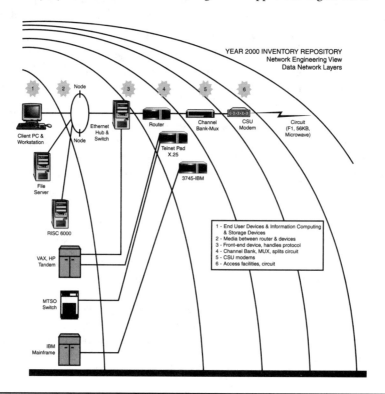

Figure 2.10   The Wave template is the basis of this model that defines the layers of the data network for a Y2K analysis.

To read this model, you start at the left side and move to the right across the waves of network layers. Those layers are described as follows:

- The first layer contains all the PCs and workstations, file servers, RISC 6000 computers, VAX, HP, and Tandem machines, MTSO switches, and IBM mainframes in the company.
- The second layer contains the media between routers and devices, including the Ethernet hub and switch and network nodes.
- The third layer contains the front-end devices for handling protocol, and includes routers and telex pads.
- The fourth layer contains the channel bank, MUX (circuit splitter), and covers channel bank MUX devices.

- The fifth layer contains CSU modems.
- The sixth layer references access facilities and circuits.

After the layers are understood and populated with all the devices in use, meetings are held with technical managers to determine and assign management responsibility for each layer.

This illustrates how integration models help define the infrastructure for cellular systems.

What Integration Models Are Not

Although it is important to understand what integration models are and can offer, it is just as valuable to know what they are not and what they do not attempt to do. Integration models do not replace any of the existing mechanisms of systems design, modeling, and implementation that are in use today. They are not intended to do away with existing paradigms or to make them obsolete. However, they do offer an enhancement to what current mechanisms provide. In providing pattern examples, integration models show how current models can be organized to improve their usefulness.

Integration models are

- Not modeling notations
- Not CASE or OO analysis and design models
- Not business models
- Not rigorously defined for automation
- Not one more level of detail or abstraction

Not Modeling Notations

Many modeling notations are in use today, and most are supported by one or several modeling tools. Recent efforts in the object-oriented programming community have made great strides in standardizing on the modeling notation delivered by the *Unified Modeling Language, (UML)*. The UML is limited to object-oriented methods and is somewhat narrowly focused on implementation solutions, making it less than optimal for business process modeling. Other notations like Peter Chen's well-known data modeling, "Chen Diagrams," and James Martin's notation, have been in use for decades. The vendors of various tools have adopted their use.

Integration modeling does not attempt to replace any existing modeling notations, although it can be implemented in virtually any of them. It offers patterns for organizing models developed in any notation, which can help clarify the dynamics of any model.

The patterns themselves are simple. They give you the archetype.

Then you can adjust and customize them as you apply them to a specific model. The model will retain the essentials of the pattern, but is not confined by the pattern. As such, the patterns provide a core of flexible models that have been used successfully across several different industries.

Not CASE or OO Analysis and Design Models

Integration models do not replace CASE models, such as those specified in John Zachman's architecture framework, nor do they replace object-oriented models for analysis and design of systems. They can be used to provide an organizing principle for these types of models, and the resulting models will appear more coherent and meaningful in their visualization of technical design. The best modeling experts tend to organize their models according to some such structuring principle, which usually goes unacknowledged although it is an important background element. Integration models are a collection of these types of structures, found successful in many systems and other models and abstracted to create a set of templates.

Not Business Models

Integration models can be used to organize a business model, but they are not the same as business models. Business models are task-oriented and often very informal. One type of business model is the mental model, defined by Peter Senge in *The Fifth Discipline* as "deeply held internal images of how the world works"[2.4]. Mental models are akin to beliefs, as closely held assumptions that are not typically examined consciously. Senge and others have proposed methodologies for surfacing these mental models and for testing and improving them to enhance organizational performance.

Mental models shape a company's way of doing business, its priorities, cultural biases, and expectations about the marketplace. For instance, recent successes in the Internet marketplace have revolutionized the business models that are accepted and expected today. As a result, having a Web presence is now simply part of the cost of doing business, whereas it once was a competitive advantage. This change in expectations represents a change in the current mental model in the marketplace.

Integration models provide a visual language that can be used to depict the integration aspects of mental models, showing where a particular dynamic comes into play in the mental model. They can be useful in organizing mental models, but are not a type of mental model.

Another type of business model is the business process model, popularized by Mike Hammer in *Reengineering the Corporation [2.5]*, which is used to analyze and redesign the methods of getting work done in light of the new capabilities that can be introduced by technology. Integration models can extend the existing visual language utilized for the modeling of these redesign strategies. They also provide new images and new ways of organizing business models.

Not Rigorously Defined for Automation

The introduction of rigor is required to automate the process of developing technical models. Modeling tools require that the modeling notation be precise, strictly conforming to a set of standards, or conventions, which is built into the tool design as rules for model construction. The tools then offer varying levels of validation and enforcement of the imbedded modeling rules.

Integration models are not intended as a modeling notation or language, and intentionally avoid assuming the rigor that is required by tools for automation. Their goal is to provide a flexible background pattern that can be adapted to many different settings and consistently applied. If they were to appear in a modeling tool, it would be as a format similar to the "snap-to-grid" format currently employed by many drawing tools.

Not One More Level of Detail or Abstraction

Finally, integration models are not intended to insert another level of detail or abstraction into the deliverables of a project. One issue that must be addressed when deploying modeling tools is that the level of abstraction they introduce presents a significant learning curve for the users of the tool. Integration models do not add to this problem by adding layers. They are applied to the existing levels of detail and abstraction to help tie them together.

Benefits of the IM Approach

Jeff Erlich, CIO of National Data Corporation, says of new technology, "those who are successful treat it like an organic thing and try to figure out its behavior. Anything sufficiently technically advanced begins to look like magic. Treat it like magic, and you can succeed"[2.6].

Typical automation approaches attempt to "divide and conquer" a process by breaking it down into its constituent parts and getting a grasp of them individually. These approaches manage complexity by separating systems out into simple parts, which are then dealt with en masse through the "magic" of automation. Thus, the usual standardization approach removes the rough edges to make business processes fit the mold selected by technologists, but often loses important distinctions along the way.

Treating technology like magic means you treat it like it has a life of its own, like a living system. Rather than analyze and redesign, you leave the system in place and work around it through context-based approaches.

To successfully build for synergy in new technology, integration modeling adopts an approach that will do the following:

- Integrate key indicators
- Customize easily
- Scale up or down, as needed
- Handle multiple views
- Provide feedback mechanisms

Integrating Key Indicators

Living systems have behaviors. They have indicators that can be observed to get clues to what's going on. As one example, to diagnose illness, health practitioners look for symptoms and run tests to pick up statistics that might be out of range. Another example is conservationists determining the health and vitality of ecosystems by monitoring key indicators. In the Pacific Northwest of the United States, the reason conservationists are concerned over the possible extinction of the spotted owl is that the bird has been identified as a key indicator for the entire ecosystem of the rainforest there. If the spotted owl disappears, it has far-reaching implications for the whole system.

With other, non-biological systems, one can observe similar profiles. In economics, the gross national product, employment statistics, and the Dow Jones Industrial Average are well-known leading indicators used to predict system behaviors. In each, the system under observation is not totally predictable, but rather amorphous, with many variables. It operates best within certain definable boundaries, and the expert who wants to manage the system concentrates on drawing those boundaries and establishing the criteria of operation.

To translate the management of a living system using key indicators into the terms of a technology project, you would specify a new system in broad strokes, defining high-level requirements and describing what project success would look like. The resulting *critical success factors* act as key indicators, and are used to measure progress over the life of the project. Having established parameters against which to assess any success helps resolve the requirements at the higher level before moving into more detailed and rigorous descriptions for implementation.

Customizing Easily

The approach must be customizable according to the individual project or situation. It must be structured enough to provide a backbone on which to build, yet flexible enough not to interfere with the dynamic nature of the business automation process. Many methodologies start out with good intentions, but get bogged down in so much added work that no project manager in his right mind would stick it out. Instead, he gets into the thick of the project and starts dumping steps of the methodology when time runs short. Better to have an approach that anticipates it: In the world of technical projects, time is always short. You're better off learning to live with it and being prepared accordingly.

A customizable approach eliminates unnecessary steps up front, selecting only the critical activities. It also provides some criteria for determining which steps are critical and which can be eliminated, delivered through a process that supports making conscious decisions with well-understood and documented rationales behind them.

Scaling Up or Down, as Needed

Scalability is another key feature of the desired approach. It must apply to many situations, small and large projects, local, or enterprisewide. Especially as more applications move onto the desktop, into n-tier architectures, and see Internet or intranet deployment, the importance of scalability is increasing for all aspects of technology. Integration occurs at all levels and at all times. It is an ongoing process that is sometimes fitted in on-the-fly, sometimes planned in a more structured manner. The chosen approach should work for both extremes—the large, complex, high-end project, and the small, contained, local project—while meeting the needs of those that belong to the continuum in between.

Handling Multiple Views

In contrast to "divide and conquer," the integrative approach draws the big picture from one viewpoint, and then moves to the next viewpoint and describes it again. It's what an old Warren Beatty film referred to as *The Parallax View*—the tendency for people, places, and objects to appear differently depending on where the observer stands. Multiple views lend perspective and provide another way of handling complexity. As each view is drawn, differences between it and earlier views are resolved.

A feedback mechanism is a way to help those involved with a project become clear about the goals, requirements, and design decisions made in the project. In technology projects it is important to have a clear vision of where you want to go, and to maintain and update that vision along the way. It is equally valuable to be able to make implementation compromises along the way, mechanisms of getting the job done in practical terms.

The important thing is to know when you've compromised the vision for the sake of speed or technical feasibility, and to make the choice to compromise a conscious choice. This principle becomes significant in technology projects, where minor deviations at the design level tend to be amplified at the implementation level. It is a well-known rule of software engineering that problems caught in the design stage take far less resource to correct than do those that are allowed to persist into the programming stage. Feedback mechanisms can help make the design choices more conscious.

The Catalog of Integration Models

Based on the experiences of many software projects, the catalog of integration models offers a distillation of best practices in the integration arena. Not intended as an exhaustive list, the models represent the patterns found useful on projects in many different industries. The reader is invited to test the models included in the catalog and share experiences in working with them, and also to add to the catalog as new patterns that cannot be accommodated by the existing set of models are discovered.

Overview of the Catalog

Chapters 4–11 provide a catalog of integration models with formatted descriptions giving details on the following attributes:

- **Template Description**—Describes the template and its characteristics.
- **Template Discussion**—Discusses the dynamics of the template.
- **When This Template Applies**—Suggests the kinds of integration issues and project settings in which the template can be applied.
- **Examples**—Details examples of the application of the template to specific instances.
- **Benefits and Consequences**—Lists the benefits and/or consequences to be considered when selecting this template as a solution.
- **Template Realization**—Discusses how the template is realized into subsequent business or technical models. Because the implementation model for integration projects is middle-out, the translation from the template into other types of models will occur in both business and technical directions.
- **EAI Applications**—Gives EAI-oriented examples for applying the template.
- **Templates That Work Well with This Template**—Discusses how to combine the template with one or more other templates and suggests some typical combinations.

The names and descriptions of the integration models are listed here to give you an overview:

Cycle (Chapter 4)—The Cycle template depicts a life cycle or cyclical process, which is characterized by repetition, evolution, and the features of self-reinforcement and self-correction.

Seed (Chapter 5)—The Seed template is a generator/transformer structure depicting a situation where a core component produces, collects, or contains an array of results.

Web (Chapter 6)—The Web template depicts a network of nodes (or endpoints) and connectors (or arcs). It is useful in modeling network routing and for performing complex path analysis and optimization.

Flow (Chapter 7)—The Flow template is utilized by process and flow analysis to trace the course of information, goods, services, communications, etc.

Wave (Chapter 8)—The Wave model is used to describe the layers of a system, environment or network. Layers help manage complexity.

Ring (Chapter 9)—The Ring template is useful in depicting chaining of events, people, devices or network addresses. While the cycle models directional processes, the ring models peer-to-peer relationships.

Cell (Chapter 10)—The Cell template supports modeling of categorization and compartmentalization. It is useful for analysis of distribution systems, geographic division, and behaviors at the local versus global levels.

Tree (Chapter 11)—The Tree template is a structure utilized to model systems with characteristics that include complex branching, diversification, and the implementation of distribution alternatives.

Preparing to Apply Integration Models

The IM approach introduces two feedback mechanisms, user scenarios and viewpoint analysis models, which are used in preparation for selecting and applying integration models.

User Scenarios

Narrative descriptions that illustrate a user, business area representative, or a stakeholder's perspective on system usage, scenarios provide a neutral reflection of project concerns. In developing scenarios you are not drawing conclusions, but feeding back the information you are collecting, primarily through interviews and sometimes through surveys and focus groups. The story of Mac from sales presented in Chapter 1, "The Context for Enterprise Application Integration (EAI)," is a scenario to describe the view of the sales organization in a particular situation.

In Web development, scenarios are used to support user interface design, demonstrating the expected flow of events for visitors interacting with the features of a Web site.

Scenarios are crucial to enterprise application integration because they identify potential problems and possible solutions and highlight the most important requirements of a particular system's use. Embracing the multiple use scenarios on a project ensures that you don't end up with narrow design solutions that will only work for one type of user or one type of Web site visitor. Even if you have correctly chosen the dominant user type, belonging to the group that wields the most clout politically, any of the others can and will sabotage a solution that works against their interests.

The rules for developing scenarios are as follows:

> **Capture one viewpoint at a time**—Make it a point to align yourself with the owner of the view, seeing how the world looks from her perspective. Don't try to correct her assumptions, just surface them and describe them.

> **Keep the scenario loose and informal**—Modify its presentation to suit your audience. Some people like verbal feedback with no time committed to writing and reviewing formal scenarios. Others like visuals, and still others want to read a short capsule that captures the essence of what they said to you. Sometimes you need to combine all three. Play it by ear.

> **Keep it focused**—The initial interview should not be longer than one hour. Less is even better. People get to the point more quickly when the time is limited. (Don't get carried away with this though. Ten minutes is not enough. The point is to listen and help your interviewee get to the point.)

> **Keep it short**—One scenario per page. You might have to start with several pages to capture all the information. The process of condensing information into one page will help you become clear about what is essential.

> **Feed it back**—This is your chance to get buy-in and promote ownership from your project constituents. Ask for, listen to, and apply corrections. Then feed it back again.

Viewpoint Analysis Models

Whereas scenarios provide a narrative method of describing the system requirements from more than one point of view, capturing those multiple viewpoints for the design of an integrated solution requires a modeling repository. It must be one that is flexible, easily modified, taken in at a glance by the owner of the viewpoint, and questioned or corrected on the spot.

Viewpoint analysis models are about perspective. They offer a quick way to develop sophisticated knowledge of a problem set by capturing several perspectives against it prior to synthesizing them into one solution.

The rules for developing viewpoint analysis models are as follows:

> **Adopt conventions**—The examples provided in this book suggest conventions that have been used successfully. You can modify these or adopt your own. You need to adopt conventions to have enough structure so people don't get lost, and you need to present them as a preface to reviewing your models.

Go sit with the user—Capture what they see. Use size and position on the model to indicate importance and priority. Let the relative positioning of components tell the story.

Visualize it for them—Start with a best guess and let them correct that. Modeling is easier for the interview subject if you provide the starting point.

Show them other viewpoints—People begin to catch on when they see the variations in views. If a view is too foreign for them, don't show it.

Use their terminology—If marketing calls a system by one name and operations calls it by another, let the two views use two different names. This can provide an important indicator when it's time to reconcile the meanings of the business entities.

User scenarios and viewpoint analysis models set the stage for the solutions-design work that is yet to come. They clarify the issues for integration and let project contributors know you've understood their concerns and prioritized them correctly. Presenting both a visual and narrative description, the two techniques work together to deliver a balanced picture of the business context in which the integration project must proceed.

With scenarios and viewpoint analysis models, you can work your way through a group of contributors, interviewing as needed to understand individual differences in requirements. You will produce one or more models for each viewpoint, gathering an understanding of each perspective.

Depending on the project, it can be possible to combine this step with the application of integration models, shortening the timeline. It depends on the level of understanding in the project group. If the issues are well understood, feel free to skip the preliminary feedback step and move into solution-oriented modeling. If they're not, time spent up front clarifying the issues can be time well spent.

How Integration Models Solve Integration Problems

Integration models help modelers solve integration problems in several ways. The following sections describe a few problems that integration models solve and how they accomplish that.

Integration Requires a Broad Repertoire of Types of Models

Many modelers develop their craft in the focused discipline of either technical modeling or operations research with its quantitative techniques. When the limited techniques from any one field are brought into the integration arena, they fall short because they were designed for a different type of problem set. Integration models provide and extend the modeler's repertoire by offering patterns that have been worked out over time during experiences with many projects. As any modeler knows, there is no substitute for time and experience, but if you can distill the essence of that experience, you can give yourself a distinct advantage. Most modelers have one or two favorite forms that they use to organize every model. One relies on the Tree structure and component breakdowns, while another always follows the Cycle and Flow modeling structures. But modelers seldom use forms and structures beyond their proven repertoire. Integration models are a way of extending your repertoire by choosing to incorporate new patterns.

Integration Projects Have Greater Levels of Chaos and Confusion

Integration projects introduce chaos and confusion because they often span greater area than development projects, and cover less-understood subjects of inquiry. While the typical technical modeler relies on one business expert who knows his subject inside and out, the typical integration modeler must often deal with dozens of subject-matter experts, synthesizing information from many sources. Integration models comprise a sort of toolkit that you can take from one project to another. Tested on multiple projects, they formalize the organizing patterns that have worked in specific instances before. When you have a toolkit, you have resources to call on that help you save time and avoid the confusion of casting about for the right form. They also help bring stability into the chaos of enterprise-wide projects by offering a set of principles that can be applied through the patterns. Having a toolkit makes it possible to take on more, in terms of going into a field you know little about, because you have a known quantity in the toolkit.

Many Unknowns in Integration Projects

Software development projects more often depend on mature technologies in known arenas of practice. Integration pushes the envelope in requiring new technologies, applied to areas where there's less history of formal practice. In formalizing the possible dynamics for a problem set, integration models support your thinking process and give you a set of options to consider when deciding how to model it. It helps to be able to think through a series of patterns for selection, rather than always generating a new pattern. And it gives you a sort of visual language for expressing ideas. If a situation really doesn't fit any of the existing patterns, it can signal you to invest more time and attention in creating a new pattern, which will then be added to your toolkit and carried forward. This was the case with the Wave template, which was added on a project in telecommunications, which called for modeling of the layers of the network. None of the existing patterns quite worked, and adding the Wave opened up a new paradigm for subsequent projects.

Limited Thinking Kills Integration Projects

Good systems builders make lousy systems integrators. The very skills that characterize a good systems builder, such as singular focus, implementation orientation, and linear thinking, will, if applied too rigidly, make integration more difficult. Systems integrators must cultivate the skills of coordination, multitasking and tolerance for ambiguity, which contradict the usual dictates of system development. Integration models take you outside the current boundaries by focusing on the background and context for application systems. Placing too much emphasis on the systems and details sets up a "can't see the forest for the trees" situation, where technologists cannot even imagine a solution. Integration modeling allows you to eschew poring over detailed listings in linear mode, and move into a more intuitive mode of thinking, where you step outside the box and look for solutions from a more holistic perspective.

Lack of an Organizing Principle

Modelers working at the enterprise level struggle with finding the organizing principle for a model, and often end up taking it from the archaic structures already embedded in a business, such as the departmental divisions represented by the organization chart. This defeats the purpose of integration and redesign efforts, which need a way to move beyond the organization's current forms and norms. Integration models provide an organizing principle that depends on the dynamics of a company's processes and business models, not on the internal structures set up for other purposes.

Lack of a Unifying Principle

Integration projects span wide areas organizationally and technically. When many different viewpoints come into play, the integrator can end up moderating between views so different they operate as if they were different languages. Integration models give you a unifying principle, which can carry certain themes from one level to another, from the project's articulation of business issues, through the design and documentation of solutions. When you apply the patterns of integration models to integration issues and then carry those patterns into subsequent models and diagrams, you can infuse a higher level of organization across the levels without boxing yourself in or re-creating existing limitations.

Greater Involvement of Non-Technical People in Developing Technical Solutions

The high priority, high visibility, and far-reaching consequences of many integration projects demand more involvement of senior levels of business management than the usual software development project. Integration models help the integrator present technical concepts to these non-technical people in ways that convey meaning visually.

Many business people are not accustomed to taking in information in the forms that technical people tend to produce. Digging through huge reference manuals or detailed, cryptic technical models to find answers is time-consuming and frustrating to one whose career is not technical. You really have to understand the inner workings of a discipline to make knowing the material well enough to navigate it feasible. When you don't know the details of a discipline, it helps to have navigational cues so that you can find what you need quickly and easily. Models offer those cues by way of visual organization that helps reduce complexity and at the same time reveal insights that otherwise might not be intuitively obvious.

Rules for Selecting and Applying Integration Models

This section combines the selection and application of integration models because this is an integrated and iterative process. The goal is to work back and forth from reviewing and selecting a model to applying it. The examples in Part III, "Applying Integration Models," provide some sample process steps for applying integration models in specific types of projects. The rules for selecting and applying integration models are as follows:

- Model significant characteristics.
- Select models intuitively.
- Combine modeling with research.
- Make the models a living library.
- Create your own templates.

Model Significant Characteristics

Choose the integration model that reflects the most significant characteristics of the subject under study. For instance, when modeling the relationships between organizational components at a theatre company, the Ring model can be chosen to emphasize the peer-to-peer relational qualities of the groups. The Ring model helps portray the qualities more as spheres of influence than as a hierarchy of control.

Select Models Intuitively

Allow the review of scenarios, interviews, and viewpoint-analysis models to provide clues to the kind of process you are modeling. As you peruse the accumulating information, let your intuition inform you on what models to consider.

Combine Modeling with Research

Integration models support the synthesis of diverse sources of information. They provide an organized repository (the model) for the collection of information. As you conduct research through interviews, online searching, and review of project materials, let the intrinsic structure of the information emerge. Capture it with the most similar model and begin to coalesce the information into that structure. As the structure becomes clearer, go back to the research and allow the evolving structure to influence the direction of research.

Make the Models a Living Library

As you work with the models, you'll develop a library of your own of applications to specific projects. This library becomes a toolkit that will shorten the time it takes to do the modeling on the next project. The more you work with the models, the more flexible and accessible they will become.

Create Your Own Templates

You can build examples of your own from the provided integration models, in a language of your choice. If the project you're working on uses UML to design and document, you can build a library of templates in UML to provide starting points for technical models (likewise, with any modeling notation currently in use by your organization). You might not be able to translate all the patterns into a particular notation, but it can be valuable to translate those you can and find other ways of utilizing the rest. It's often possible to build the core of a project's technical models in the language of a specific modeling tool and then use the more flexible PowerPoint or Visio diagramming tools to create models selectively that will position them for a given project.

Conclusion

Integration models can be used to help clarify the dynamics of any model, whether in UML, CASE, OO, or any other notation or language. They are not a notation in themselves, but are more like a background formulation of principles for integration. As such, they can help you allow the technical details to fade into the background and concentrate on business process, context, and integration.

Integration models make the models that are based on them tend to match each other, bringing an organizing principle to all levels in the project repository. They cover a broad spectrum of structures and are applicable at any level. They tell you how the current problem set might work, where it will likely go next, and what its characteristics are. Integration models can also suggest technological options. Some templates translate directly into OO design patterns (see *Design Patterns*, by Gamma et al). For instance, the Seed template translates into Gamma's strategy pattern. Others merely suggest a particular implementation due to their intrinsic pattern, such as the network implications of Rings and Webs.

3

The Environment for Integration Modeling

WHAT KIND OF ENVIRONMENTAL OR INFRASTRUCTURE supports does integration modeling need? That depends on how much you want to do, how fast you want to do it, and where you are today in terms of integration. Because integration modeling is essentially a scalable approach, you can do a lot or a little, working within limited resources, or extending your reach by adding resources.

Many of us learn from working in large corporations that the first step to setting up a project is appropriations: Figure out what you need, get a P.O. authorized, and purchase it. Integration modeling can reverse the order of events so appropriations are the last step we take. When setting up an environment for integration modeling, you can work with what's on hand, gradually building infrastructure by developing a pocket at a time. For a more aggressive schedule, you can rebuild your environment to reflect integration priorities.

What It Takes to Build an Environment

The environment in which integration projects operate is influenced by several factors. Building a workable environment involves adopting integrative approaches in each of these areas. Project approach determines the degree of structure and other supports that will be required to carry out a particular project. The selection of project approach will depend on both organizational and technology factors. How a project is conducted is also interrelated with the structure of the organization in which it's carried out.

Project deliverables, such as documents, models, specifications, and other products of the development process, must be managed with a coordinated strategy. Teams undertaking integration projects will often take on new team structures and operate within different guidelines from ordinary software development teams. The implementation of an integration project will also have different strategies and different pitfalls. New strategies must be devised if these enterprise-wide projects are to succeed.

It is beneficial to recognize up front that integration projects and the teams that carry them out have a different set of requirements and will need different marching orders based on those requirements. They will need unprecedented latitude in scope of responsibility, while concurrently divesting themselves of the usual duties of software development and maintenance teams. The duties of new development include designing, coding, testing and installing software programs within a departmental, targeted domain. New development is primarily focused on completing a system implementation within tight budget and timing constraints, leaving little time for contributing to integration and infrastructure requirements. Software maintenance involves diagnosing problems and designing, coding and installing corrections and new enhancements. Maintenance focuses on ongoing support and troubleshooting, but rarely moves beyond the immediate domain of a system. The duties of an integrator go beyond those of software development and maintenance and will be addressed in more detail in the section titled "Role of the Integrator."

Integrators will require vertical mobility, with permission to disregard chain of command within the limitations of their charter. They will enjoy the privilege of being privy to information that software development and maintenance teams usually don't receive, such as confidential information about the company's strategic plans and product's market positioning because EAI projects usually have such plans at their center.

Differences Between Integration Projects and Software Development Projects

Integration projects differ significantly from traditional software development projects. The business requirements for software development projects are usually well understood and finite in nature. They are specific to the needs of a departmental tactical solution, and are managed with a clearly structured approach. Requirements for integration projects, on the other hand, typically evolve as the project unfolds, and are accomplished with a pragmatic approach, which expects mid-course corrections throughout the duration of the project. Software development delivers tactical solutions to defined problems, specified to solve departmental concerns. Integration delivers the dynamic reuse of enterprise applications, with a focus on the strategically transparent support of new business models.

Software development projects usually occur in a controlled environment where the technical manager has the freedom to select among predefined and standardized platform options. The development of software solutions is generally treated as a black box, with input and outputs defined, where everything inside the box falls under the project manager's control. He will develop local applications, which are built on either a single platform or a distributed platform using local and internal networks. Integration projects generally take place in an uncontrolled environment. The integrator must deal with a variety of technologies, old and new, which are already embedded in existing systems. The integrator works within the confines of the existing architecture.

On software development projects, team members are specialists who apply the discipline of systems engineering to well-defined specifications. The goals of integration involve the re-purposing of legacy systems (usually with little or no documentation available) and their merging with newer technologies in the global Internet arena. Therefore the integrator is usually more of a generalist, with expertise in multiple systems arenas. The integrator must also be skilled at utilizing specialized resources at the right time.

Integration projects extend across the enterprise and its relationships with customers and the supply chain, whereas software development projects usually concentrate on local objectives. The data in these local projects tends to be discrete and contained, easily understood and modeled. Integration, on the other hand, must reconcile data from disparate sources in disparate formats. It is not unusual for an integration effort to require the merging of data from five to ten, or even fifty different application systems (built on different platforms at different times by different vendors). It can also require that the integrated platform account for less structured data from sources such as various Internet sites, or telecommunications software packages where data is scraped from online screens in a "blob" which must be parsed and managed.

The implementation model for software development is usually either top-down, in structured projects that proceed from conceptual design to logical analysis and detailed design and development, or bottom-up, in typical object-oriented approaches. The model for integration projects, on the other hand, is middle-out. It focuses first on the system's use, in the context of business goals. Then it builds simultaneously upward to business modeling and downward to detailed technical design to deliver the system. The project can drive process improvements upward to the business model, as well as incorporate technical efficiencies at the system level.

The model shown in Figure 3.1 summarizes how software development projects differ from integration projects.

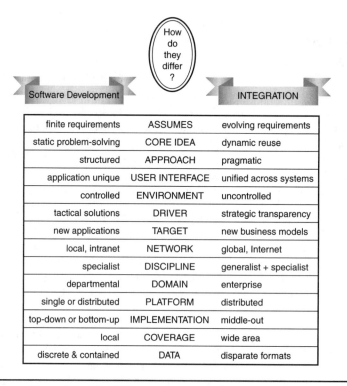

Figure 3.1   The differences between software development and integration projects are significant.

Requirements for the Environment

As we get a clearer understanding of how integration projects are different from software development projects, we can establish a set of requirements for a supportive environment. Based on the differences outlined in assumptions, approach, environment, and so forth, the optimal environment for integration modeling must enable us to

- Capitalize on opportunities in an entrepreneurial way in order to accommodate evolving requirements and new business models.
- Organize skilled specialists using the integration generalist to function on projects that are driven by strategic business needs.
- Recognize the de facto reality of
    - A great variety of immediate business needs.
    - Already existing solutions.
    - Rapidly evolving technologies.

- Utilize existing industry experience and benefit from available components.

- Update project requirements as changes occur and new needs become apparent.

- Manage project deliverables in a framework that allows for iterative development and spontaneous repositioning (mid-course corrections).

Selecting a Project Approach

Every project must define how it will approach the particular objectives that it must satisfy. Integration projects often occur across the functional business lines of a company. They can involve modifying or re-purposing multiple application systems for business goals defined and shared by several organizational units. Therefore the selection of a project approach is based on organizational factors as well as on technology factors.

Three Approaches and Their Requirements

Three basic project approaches can be used successfully on integration projects. They include

- Unstructured

- Structured

- Pragmatic

Unstructured

The unstructured approach sets up an environment of constant learning. Mistakes by team members are welcome and are considered a necessary part of the learning process. They are part of how we learn, and are almost as valuable as no mistakes. Project advances in the unstructured approach will occur in an opportunistic fashion, with the integrator prepared to move quickly when opportunities arise.

This approach requires a high degree of political flexibility and organizational willingness. Integration teams must be allowed to operate outside the usual protocols, depending on the requirements of the individual project.

Structured

The structured approach makes the process explicit. It's for situations in which the process is predefined and planned in detail in advance. It's a better approach for technology projects in which the terrain is well-known, and implementation solutions are built in mature technologies. In structured approaches, the required skill is in laying out the schedule and managing for success. Structured approaches add overhead to a project. You'll need a full-time project manager, and the time to negotiate and lay out the schedule. Taking a structured approach usually inflates an average project's timeline by 30%–50%. You'll be spending time in steering committee meetings, selling and defending project goals and progress. Time will be spent preparing presentations, responding to queries, and explaining project progress.

The structured approach requires adequate time and top-down support. It emphasizes appearance, perception, and communication of project goals. Mistakes are not allowed in the structured environment because the learning is expected to take place ahead of time. Project steps are predefined based on the knowledge acquired, and project goals are about execution, not discovery.

Pragmatic

The pragmatic approach combines aspects of both the structured and unstructured approaches, and defines the required supports to be successful. It utilizes predefined time boxes with flexibility within each time box, and the agility to reconfigure time boxes if needed. The pragmatic approach expects some learning and discovery to take place, but not so much as to derail the project. It acknowledges the value of learning through mistakes, as does the unstructured approach, but it mandates that mistakes are acceptable within defined and limited boundaries. This approach builds in mechanisms for making mid-course corrections. It requires the ongoing involvement of project sponsors because their direction helps keep the project on course and out of difficulties. The pragmatic approach requires the combination of the sponsorship of a "champion" who can help sell the project within the organization, and the reliance upon interested parties. Thus it finds and invites the collaboration of natural allies in building organizational support for project goals.

Choosing the Best Approach

To choose the best approach, you need to think about what your organization can support, what its preferred styles are, and how flexible your particular project sponsor can be. Sometimes the personality of the project sponsor and/or stakeholders will dictate the tone of the project approach. Sometimes another factor or set of factors will determine the choice of approach. In either case, the approach will set the tone for the entire project and as such, it should be selected with care. It is often an organization's first encounter with alternative methods, and can be a valuable introduction to them if handled with precision. Table 3.1 summarizes the three approaches for integration projects.

Table 3.1   **Project approach is selected based on organizational factors and technology factors.**

Approach	Description	Requires
Unstructured	Constant learning	Consistently strong sponsor at mid-level Political flexibility and organizational willingness Mistakes welcome

Approach	Description	Requires
Structured	Predefined	Time and top-down support
		Emphasis on appearance, perception, and communication of project goals
		No mistakes
Pragmatic	Predefined time-boxes with flexibility within them, a "champion"	Combination of sponsorship of and reliance on interested parties
		Willingness to make mid-course corrections
		Ongoing involvement of sponsors
		Careful mistakes

The recommendation for integration projects is usually the pragmatic approach. But if you're in a corporation with a lot of structure and a political environment, and you want to undertake a project that involves cultural change that cuts across boundaries (in other words, an integration project), you'll need a different kind of support. If your project is operating in such an environment, and you are required to follow a structured approach, you will need to secure the necessary time allowance and top-down support from management. You'll need to focus on careful communications and be aware that public mistakes won't likely be tolerated.

But it's also good to know that if you can't meet all the requirements for the structured approach, you can still succeed at integration projects. You'll just have to do it in a different manner. You'll have to lobby more, you'll need a group of supporters, and you'll have to be opportunistic. You must recognize you can't do it under your company's usual structure unless you have all the supports that make that approach work. You can still do it, but it's a different kind of thing to do.

Without the required support, don't try to do it in a structured way. Recognize you need a different approach. One support that can sometimes be provided when time or public support is not possible, is permission to break the rules, permission to go outside the usual structures. Management can make a decision to set up a team with an exceptional charter requiring exceptional rules. Often, this rule-breaking approach is unstructured, requiring the strong sponsorship of a mid-level manager with control over his or her domain.

If you're in a large company, or one with a structured environment, you'll be trained in the expected, structured approach, and that might be the best choice for your project. If you're in a smaller company, a start-up or a vendor, you might find the unstructured approach is perfect for you.

Organizational Factors

The project approach selected for an integration project will depend on the characteristics of your company and the ability to meet the requirements of the approach. Some of the organizational factors that should be considered include

- Structured versus unstructured
- Political versus plain
- Corporate versus entrepreneurial
- Trust versus control
- Autonomy versus security
- High-risk versus low-risk
- Start-up versus behemoth

Structured Versus Unstructured

Larger companies tend to employ more structure, although this varies according to the industry. Banking is traditionally a very structured industry, for instance, whereas telecommunications companies, though quite large in some cases, tend to operate with less formal hierarchy. Recent years have seen the trend toward de-layering and creating flat organizations. Smaller companies, such as Internet start-ups, tend to run much leaner and with less structure. However, as they grow they will often put more structure in place.

Political Versus Plain

Corporate politics places a great amount of emphasis on appearance and perception, with layers of committees that must approve of project activities. Communications is very important in the political setting, and focuses on style, form, and approved mechanisms of distribution. Governmental agencies tend to incorporate many political factors, as do many large multinational corporations. Projects for non-profit organizations, a growing market for the services sector, also frequently originate in a political setting.

Less formal companies, from small to mid-sized usually, will be inclined to speak much more plainly within their own territory. They will likely tolerate less structured approaches, displaying more political flexibility and willingness to pursue new approaches.

It would seem that the politics in larger companies would preclude any but the structured approach, but there are times when the pragmatic approach is more advantageous. In large companies it is rare that the wisdom required for enterprise-wide integration and reengineering efforts is supplied handily and neatly from the CEO on down, in the form of top-down support. More likely, you will get a department head who is more of a maverick and risk-taker (a strong sponsor at mid-level) who is willing to stick his neck out. He can only go so far, and that's why you need the combination of sponsorship and interested parties or allies. You get that person to back the project and as long as he has control of his domain, which often happens, the pragmatic approach can work fine. Your appeal to allies works in synergy with his ability to push the envelope to create a win/win situation for all concerned.

The provenance of executives such as this is usually found in circumstance. Sometimes they are owners of companies that have been acquired, and the acquiring company has adopted a position of non-interference based on performance. Other times, they will be the ones who can get the job done, and other executives will run interference for them. Other times, the company has a reason for leaving them alone. From "We just haven't gotten around to that" to "We know we don't have the infrastructure in place yet, so we put a maverick in there who's good at improvising." This type of executive can be good with integration projects, because he is less bound by corporate politics and is willing to step on toes a little (often he has an uncanny ability to detect just how far is too far).

Corporate Versus Entrepreneurial

Structured approaches, formality, and layers of responsibility that allow managers to delegate and that provide for clear career and succession planning characterize the corporate model. At its best, the corporate model provides authority with the freedom to delegate and the ability to orchestrate the leveraging of significant resources. At the low end of its expression, it can degenerate into a model of anonymous authority, with sanctioned avoidance habits, rather than clearly assigned authority.

At the other extreme, the entrepreneurial model is characterized by autonomy of action, widespread access to information for decision-making, and empowerment at the lowest possible organizational level. Entrepreneurial organizations can be flexible and quick to market with their execution savvy. But they can also experience growing pains, display difficulties in delegation, and lack paths for employees to grow. The entrepreneurial manager can have trouble giving up the control of the business on a day-to-day basis. Determining where your company operates on the scale from corporate to entrepreneurial can help decide the best project approach.

Trust Versus Control

Management style determines whether a company operates with a culture of trust and openness or one of tight controls. In cultures of trust, managers tend to delegate more and give broader powers to subordinates. Trusting cultures are more likely to accept and tolerate mistakes than are more controlling ones.

Autonomy Versus Security

Greater levels of autonomy are more the norm in start-up companies, although many large companies are moving toward greater freedom of decision-making at lower levels in the hierarchy. Companies oriented toward security would be more risk-averse cultures with greater caution around new technology choices.

High-Risk Versus Low-Risk

A high-risk environment encourages open mistakes in the pursuit of business benefits. Risk-taking cultures allow greater flexibility in work style, team organization and team interactions. Low-risk cultures require more careful approaches and less radical changes in accepted team structures and norms.

Start-Up Versus Behemoth

New technology and Internet companies tend to run smaller, leaner and faster, embracing the latest technological innovations. The behemoth company moves slower, though usually with a wider front and broader potential impact. And sometimes today's largest companies are organized locally for start-up nimbleness within pockets of the company. For the integrator, finding or building such pockets can provide a flexible environment for pragmatic approaches.

Technology Factors

The project approach can also be affected by the technology selected. Some factors to consider include

- **Relational technology**—As the name implies, relational technology focuses on relationships between business entities, and requires an increased focus on relationships. It is a non-hierarchical implementation model, and should not be managed using a strictly hierarchical process.
- **Object-oriented**—Object-oriented approaches are iterative and bottom-up in nature. Small teams are organized to provide flexibility, with the intention to build reusable components, which are propagated over the life of a project or projects. Such teams can bring execution savvy to an integration project and are practiced in customizing approaches.
- **Classic**—Classic technology includes mainframe systems, client/server and generally well understood, mature technologies. These are managed using time-boxed approaches. Y2K is an example of a classic project that served integration goals. Its classic management style included the program management structure, with teams delivering updated code according to time-boxed schedules.
- **Highly distributed applications**—When the platform is highly distributed, such as in the Internet project, team norms include resources that are not co-located. Virtual team meetings, telecommuting options, and unique arrangements to bring team members together are often employed.

All these factors should be evaluated in selecting the approach for an integration project. Sometimes they dictate that the completely structured approach will be chosen, and sometimes the opposite. Most often, in my experience, the pragmatic approach has the broadest applicability. For example, a company that is highly structured and practices significant corporate politics would probably choose a structured approach if all the required factors are present. However, if one or more factors are not present, such as time or top-down support, the project could be successful with the modifications of the pragmatic approach. Similarly, a high-risk start-up company would probably select the unstructured approach. However, if circumstances are such that mistakes are not acceptable on a particular project, a safer course would be to adopt the pragmatic approach.

Some projects will opt for the obvious choice for their company profile, but most will find that the pragmatic approach offers the best results for integration. Therefore, we'll cover it in more depth and see it in more examples throughout this book.

Providing the Glue Between Organizational Components

Integration models specialize in providing the glue between the business view and the technical view. They also can take on the role of providing needed integration between the various business units that actually drive the integration project. Integration models may identify business units that were not included in the project originally due to obscurity of relationships caused by tradition, politics, or current technology use. They also help define the scope, context, and extended applications of an integration project. Integration models encompass both the business units driving the requirements and the technical units managing the project.

Specialization and Matrix-Management

Traditional software development approaches have introduced specialization and matrix management (see Figure 3.2) for organizing project resources. In the matrix-managed organization, the human resources are organized according to specialties such as programming, database administration, middleware services, data services, architecture, object-oriented design and development, and Internet services. Grouped by skill set into pools, these resources are then assigned to projects in flexible configurations as the projects come up.

After resources are assigned to a project, the project or line manager, in addition to the manager of their specialty, manages them. Under this arrangement, the employee reports to two managers at once, the one who knows her specialty well enough to provide support and evaluate performance and the one who knows and is responsible for delivering the objectives of the project. The reporting relationship is described as *matrixed* or sometimes as a *primary and dotted-line* reporting structure.

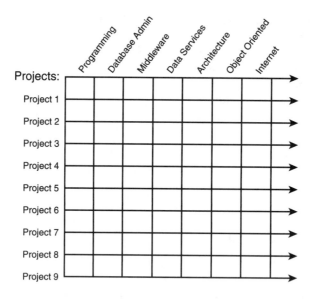

Figure 3.2 Matrix management organizes resources by specialty
and assigns them to projects on an ad hoc basis.

The Advantages of a Matrixed Relationship Include

- A manager who is versed in the skills in which the employee specializes handles the employee review.
- The team in a given specialty can share ideas and support each other's efforts.
- The employee aligned with a specialty can represent the infrastructure goals for that specialty.

The Disadvantages of a Matrixed Relationship Include

- The employee can get caught between differing agendas of the two different managers.
- The line or project manager must share resources with other projects based on the needs of her specialization team.
- Cost justification and cost allocation for specialized groups is difficult.

Introducing the role of the integrator can help us to retain the advantages of this model while addressing the disadvantages. The integrator's sphere of influence is necessarily broad, putting her in a position to help resolve conflicts in project agendas. She can also help identify resource shortfalls and justify and elevate the true resource requirements so they can be addressed.

Role of the Integrator

In its role of building the context for systems components and business initiatives, integration modeling is more flexible and more fluid than both technical and business modeling. It introduces the process for knitting together the fragmented components. As shown in Figure 3.3, the integrator's job is to help pull together the goals of the projects and the disciplines of the specialists.

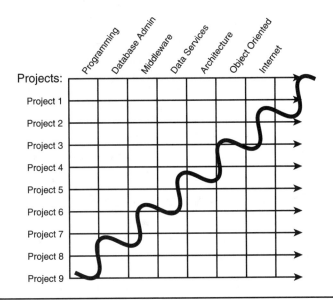

Figure 3.3 The integrator weaves together the project teams and the specialized disciplines they require.

The role of the integrator is similar to the role of the humorist in society at large. The integrator provides commentary, informal correction, and continually reviews the context in which a project is taking place. The role itself requires that the integrator have the freedom to go wherever needed in the organization, and the permission to question whatever needs questioning.

The integration generalist represents the matrix of resources into the larger organization for the technical staffing of projects as they are initiated, planned, and implemented. The integrator must have the willingness to work on multiple projects and the ability to change styles as needed, depending on the particular project. She must also maintain an integrative approach, which looks across, and not vertically, as does the typical project. It's a service role, but one that imposes a broader view on the project when necessary.

Organizational Integration

The first two dimensions of the matrix in Figure 3.3 are project teams and their individual member's specialized skills. The third dimension of the matrix is the business project that organizes all those resources into corporate objectives. The organizational components are the business departments—and project resources get assigned according to initiatives. The business executive sponsors an integration initiative, keeping it focused on business goals and pulling that matrixed pool of resources into a business context.

This is especially true in a technology-driven organization such as an Internet startup. There the business and technology strategy are combined for a singular focus, and all the company's resources are funneled into the business/technology venture. Integration in the Internet company means all primary business processes are executed using technology, realizing the promise of what a classic *Harvard Business Review* article called "Managing by Wire"—the extension of the judgement and skill of a pilot that is achieved by instrument-based flying [3.1]. Only in the case of the Internet start up, it is the judgement and skill of the dot.com's executive team that is extended by technology.

Placing Project Deliverables in Context

Providing context means determining how a system is going to be used. This is the first question asked by system usability design. What will it be used for and by whom? In the traditional systems project, these questions are asked at the front end, the initial broad level of definition that occurs in the strategic planning phase. The next time the usage question is visited is at the detail design level, where the team is specifying the user interface in terms of reports, access to data, online screens, and online activities that must be supported. In object-oriented approaches, we see systems design starting with the user interface and GUI design and moving in bottom-up fashion to determine the architecture and infrastructure requirements.

Integration modeling supports a middle-out approach, starting at the level of context diagrams and moving both up and down in level of detail from there. It asks the usage question early and often.

Integration Models Don't Eliminate Other Types of Models

Depending on the type of organization you're working in, you can have a lot of models that you're required to produce for a new development project or for an enhancement to an existing system. Or the modeling requirements may be fairly limited. One of the advantages of integration modeling is that it is applied to the existing structure. Projects will keep on producing their current deliverables. Integration modeling selectively adds the models that are needed. These additions are made with discretion, not comprehensively.

Integration models don't replace other types of models. They add another dimension to the existing models. So if you think of the Zachman architecture framework [3.2] with its two dimensions, integration models provide the third dimension, which organizes the other two. They also go beyond the current models to extend their reach into the business process view and the organizational view.

Systems Development Life Cycle

Integration modeling extends the usual systems development life cycles (SDLC) because integration projects have different goals. They start in the middle, and organize and influence both the technical (systems development life cycle) and the business process sides of the equation. Integration techniques place business and technology in context, and add another dimension. As such, they can add steps on the beginning of a project, in the middle, or at the end.

Integration modeling permeates the life cycle and provides context by wrapping around some of the deliverables found in the standard life cycles. It can broaden or add depth to certain phases of the life cycle, but basically, it doesn't alter the life cycle for software development.

Some of the standard life cycle templates in common use in today's technology projects include

- **Classic (waterfall)**—Standard mainframe technology, characterized by the stepwise procedure through predefined phases. Minimal overlap is allowed between phases. Requirements must be specified in detail early in the life cycle, with minimal changes or departures once the project is underway.
- **Time-boxed**—Similar to the waterfall, except the lock step between phases is more pronounced. No overlap is allowed between phases, and a phase does not commence until its predecessor is complete. Requirements completed in advance of each time-box.
- **Object-oriented**—Designed to accommodate the bottom-up methods of system specification. Iterative and focused on reusable components. Requirements evolve based on dynamic models.
- **Rapid application development (RAD)**—Employs prototyping to drive out requirements. Requirements for the final product do not have to be cast in stone early in the life cycle. Proof of concept delivered early in the life cycle.

Integration modeling treats these different templates as options to be applied depending on the requirements of a given project. Part of the role of the integrator is to select the SDLC to be employed to carry out the objectives defined by the integration project.

Repositories

Integration models do not require any particular repository or tools. They can be utilized successfully in PowerPoint or Visio models, without tool integration. But they can also be applied to your existing tool set. It is advisable to build a set of integration model templates in whatever tools and modeling notations your project is using to provide a basis for modelers to draw on. These templates are the concrete expression of the integration models. They can be built in most modeling tools with a minimum of effort, to become a template library for projects.

Model Management

Model management is the process of defining how your organization will use and apply various modeling techniques and how it will store and integrate the deliverables they produce. The model management framework tells the project manager how to position the models within the project life cycle, offers options to select from, and shows how models are used. It provides mechanisms for managing project models at the enterprise, logical, and physical levels. Model management will determine the requirements and design for a modeling repository and the version control (check-in/check-out facilities) that it will need.

The model in Figure 3.4 shows a generic strategy for model management in context.

The model shown in Figure 3.4 supports a model management strategy that allows widespread use of technical models using several options. The models are stored in a purchased repository tool, which is installed and supported by administrative personnel. Modeling specialists such as data analysts and database administrators have full permission to read and write to models stored in the repository based on their security profiles. Business analysts, project managers, and developers have the ability to read models from the repository, but not update them. Project managers and business users who need a more convenient access to the models can read them using their publication to the company's intranet.

In setting up a managed modeling platform, an inventory and assignment of existing models can be necessary to populate the initial implementation. Plans are then developed to standardize management of the company's existing model inventory and ensure that newly developed models follow those standards.

Building Proactive Communications

Part of the role of the integrator is to provide mentoring for project teams and consulting to project managers. The goals of such mentoring and consulting are to deliver technology transfer and project planning mechanisms that are consistent with integration strategies. By stepping in to work with project teams, teaching a few team members at a time, the integrator can train those team members to become the local experts on integration. This promotes the seeding of project teams with local experts to produce an increased understanding and awareness of the integration strategy and its applications.

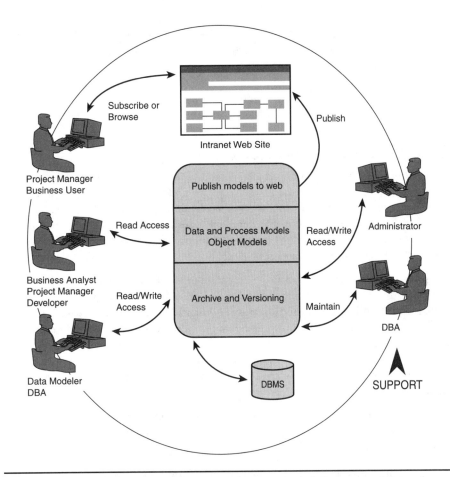

Figure 3.4   Model management in context shows a generic infrastructure, defining the roles and functions required for managing the modeling process.

Mentoring and consulting to project teams and managers allows them to support and carry out the integration objectives and action plan as proposed in early project stages. Other mechanisms that can be employed, depending on project needs, include

- **Targeted training**—Training that is tailored to the needs of an integration audience, which helps teams set expectations and helps managers understand the role of the integrator and the integration team.
- **Handbooks**—Depending on the goals of the integration project, the team might want to develop handbooks of project information for dissemination among the groups that are affected.

- **Overviews**—Overviews presented to management, employees, customers and suppliers can introduce the goals of the project and head off confusion and *scope creep*.
- **Intranet delivery**—Defining a home page for the duration of the project to store project contacts, goals, handbooks of project information, schedules, and deliverables is a useful way to facilitate the communications on a large project.

The Operating Model for Integration

In the course of one integration project, we found ourselves dissatisfied with the available operating models within the IT arena. So we undertook a benchmarking study to identify another industry with similar parameters and requirements. This benchmarking effort led us to examine the entertainment industry, and especially theatre companies, as a new model. With today's merging of Internet and entertainment industries, this finding might not seem surprising at all.

We spoke with an operations manager at a large urban theatre company, who described the prevailing operating model in that industry. Jane Bishop (then operating manager at the Alliance Theatre Company, in Atlanta, Georgia) told us that "Theatre is the only collaborative art form. To get a play out, you set the opening night and then fit everything in. To put on a play, creative designers come and go from all over the country. Many of the specialists required are hired on a seasonal basis." Jane helped us to review the workings of a modern theatre company and understand its operating models so that we could apply them to our IT objectives.

We saw many similarities between this theatre's operational requirements and those we had identified for our integration environment. Some of the principles that emerged from our application of the theatre-company operating model include

- **Collaborate**—Integration projects are based on collaboration. They organize skilled resources that come together for the duration of a project, and then separate for reassignment to another project.
- **Set up a positive environment**—Unified field theory tells us that resonance is everywhere. You should be able to feel the customer service at the door. You should be able to feel a positive environment when you walk in. This requires creating an environment where people can be themselves. Our theatre source told us, "If you can create an environment in which everyone feels like an artist, that's the whole thing."
- **Leaders stand for people**—Grace Hopper, mathematician and rear admiral of the U.S. Navy, referred to the expression "managing people" as a misconception: One can manage projects, machines, materials, and so forth; however, people can only be led, (or misled), but not managed. She said, "You manage things, you lead people. We went overboard on management and forgot about leadership. It might help if we ran the MBAs out of Washington" [3.3].

Leaders stand for people: They believe that people can do just about anything; that doesn't mean they always will, but the stand is that people are the ones who make it all happen.

- **Make room for fun**—Our theatre contact reminded us that some scientists claim that you can tell when a shift in perception or a project breakthrough is about to occur because there's a lot of laughter going on.

- **Conduct seasonal reviews**—Instead of annual performance evaluations, our theatre model recommends giving reviews at the end of a project, to critique performance on a project basis.

Portable, Virtual Workspace

The workspace for integration is defined by visits to project meetings, telephone contacts, electronic connections, face-to-face meetings, and networking. Integrators will often work on multiple projects, so it makes sense that they come to project engagements equipped with portable laptop PCs, loaded with the modeling tools in standard use. They will require Internet connections for research and administrative support and may require programming tools for prototyping of requirements.

Integration team members operate through scheduled interviews with key business area representatives to gather information, in the field or at headquarters as the situation dictates. They also meet with technical managers for guidance and to provide consultation. On occasion, an integrator needs to visit various software development team's meetings, but the bulk of actual work of integration is completed outside the implementation project team. There the gathered materials are transformed into the models that upon validation and dissemination will facilitate the integration of applications across the enterprise.

Teams Assembled on a Project Basis

The integrator cultivates and maintains relationships with the various organizational units within a company, and with the external providers of products and services to that company. Thus he can offer internal clients access to extensive resources brought together on a project-by-project basis to deliver custom business solutions.

People working on an integration project can be drawn from teams that are organized according to the matrix management model discussed previously, or they can function in more classic arrangements. When they are assigned to the integration project, they can very well need new organizational forms that provide greater flexibility and political agility and that encourage improvisation. The requirements will shift depending on the nature of the project goals. We can consult with futurist Alvin Toffler, author of *POWERSHIFT*, for some new organizational forms to consider.

Toffler writes, "A company could conceivably have within it a monastery-style unit that writes software…a research team organized like an improvisational jazz combo…a compartmentalized spy network, with need-to-know rules, operating within the law, to scout for merger or acquisition possibilities...."

He describes the rebirth of the modern company, along non-bureaucratic lines, as not implying structurelessness. However, Toffler notes "It does suggest that a company, in being reborn, may cease being a mule and turn into a team consisting of a tiger, a school of piranhas, a mini-mule or two, and who knows, maybe even a swarm of information-sucking bees.... The business of tomorrow may embody many different formats within a single frame" [3.4].

The structure of teams for integration projects will vary. They can adopt very different structures than those we are accustomed to in software development arenas. Just what kind of structures depends on the needs of the individual project. If you're integrating platforms to provide a unified interface, a team of integration weavers that can pull together the strands of many GUI apps may be needed. If your project requires technology for crawling the World Wide Web to seek and compile information, the information-sucking bees may provide a useful image.

Partnership Model

Integrators enter into projects as partners with the client. The partnership model is based on open communications, trust, and the ability to benefit from the unique contributions of each individual. As Figure 3.5 shows, the partnership model provides a map for the integration of two or more parties, whether companies, provider and client, or partners in strategic alliance.

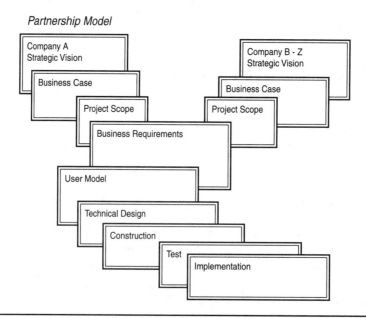

Figure 3.5 The partnership model supports the integration of two parties or more.

The partnership model is also effective in providing the reengineering and process improvement that is often a central component of the EAI initiative. It defines the required steps that partners will follow, indicating where those steps are separate and where they overlap.

Strategic Vision

The model starts at the level of defining strategic vision for both parties, whether of company strategy, product strategy, or market strategy. This step is performed separately, though certainly results can be shared and can inspire the parties to find synergies between similar visions. It includes

- Understanding your goals and parameters for the project in question.
- Defining the target customer or audience demographics.
- Initiating the marketing strategy.
- Delineating the expected budget range.

Business Case

The next step is the business case, which elaborates the economic models to explore the anticipated costs and benefits of the project or collaboration. This step also includes the review of statistical information on the use of current products and services and of competitor's products and services. The goal of this review is validating the direction of the product or service strategy.

Project Scope

Project scope is evaluated next, with boundaries drawn in terms of what is in-scope and what is out of scope. Defining the scope helps clarify the goals, parameters and focus of a project so that subsequent changes and additions can be recognized and evaluated before being added.

Business Requirements

The definition of business requirements is the first overlapping step in the partnership model. We develop a more specific vision, indicating data needs, data definitions, process specifications, object and event models, and target customers. The parties will build a joint list of project requirements and establish the initial project approach plan at this stage. Customer value assessments also begin at this stage. Partners can employ surveys or interviews with potential customers to learn about how they assess the value of an offering.

The remaining steps in the process have a joint focus, whether one or both parties actually perform the steps. This shared focus clarifies the singular outcome expected from the process of working together.

User Model

The user model defines the user interface, which can consist of an Internet site design, online graphical user interface screens, queries, reports, and other outputs such as checks or statements. Use cases help capture all the scenarios depicting how the project will be used when implemented.

Component Design

Next the partners define the logical components needed to develop the project deliverables and support the business processes required. They define the technical architecture requirements, logical data model, and sources of required information. Working together, they decide on the features the project will implement and the options for doing so. They also define the human resources that will be required by the project and work together to locate and select appropriately skilled service providers for every stage of the project.

Required technology will be defined, including platform selection (development language and application, database and Web servers) and tools and techniques for development. Partners will also identify any needed vendors for the project, from data providers to other services.

Development estimates of time and cost are finalized at this stage, and a release strategy is put in place. The release strategy should be characterized by short development cycles (average 3 months), prioritization of needs and the use of reusable components which allow the parties to benefit from prior experiences on similar projects.

Construction

The construction phase includes the development of any components, program code, and executables that are needed to implement the design. Unit testing occurs on each component at this stage. Whether one or both partners are involved in actual construction, the planning and management should be done cooperatively.

Test

The test program must also be managed jointly, covering seven different dimensions of system performance, including

- **Functional requirements**—Getting the job done
- **User interface**—Desired "look and feel"
- **Integration**—Seamless interplay between components
- **Stress**—Traffic volume, database, and application server performance
- **Regression**—Changing the changes (configuration management)
- **Acceptance**—Applying customer scenarios
- **Production performance**—Ongoing tuning and performance monitoring

Implementation

Ongoing monitoring and support provide follow-up on the project's performance and help in defining subsequent releases to update and accomplish both parties' vision over time.

Implementation Strategies for Integration Projects

Integration projects often span the enterprise, requiring widespread acceptance for their success. To develop that acceptance, we can utilize the 80/20 rule to help us understand how to promote the goals of the project. We can assume that 20% of the audience is already on our side, as the early adopters of the enterprise. These early adopters are quick to embrace change, will readily see the value of the initiative, and will likely provide their support.

Another 20% will be opposed, or indifferent. As slow adopters, they will not be easy to convince, and will remain cautious for the duration of any new initiative. These skeptics can raise valuable questions that help us run a tight ship, but their contribution usually comes later in the project. Initial efforts require more support than criticism.

The remaining 60% is our target audience, because they have yet to decide. We can expect they will have a reasonably open stance, coming around if we provide sound reasons. The following strategies will help build that support in the implementation of your integration project.

Utilizing "Early Returns" to Promote Your Project

If we work with the 20% already on our side to create early successes, and then see that they are well publicized, we have a means of influencing the remaining 60%. For example, on one data warehousing project, the project's steering committee identified the "low-hanging fruit"—data subject areas that could be sourced (pertinent systems identified and data extracted) with a minimum of effort and brought into the data warehouse quickly. These early returns were used to help build credibility for the project and secure ongoing funding from stakeholders.

As the project defines the areas of highest need for integration, the recommendations will specify an action plan for near-term and long-term objectives. Early returns will be defined as a part of the near-term deliverables.

Selecting and Developing Component Sponsors

The action plan will be broken up into component projects that deliver key objectives. For each component, we identify a sponsor who provides support and resources for those objectives. These sponsors act as co-sponsors to the project "champion" who drives the overall integration effort. Their areas of control become the place the integration team sets up a laboratory for testing and proof of concept on the plan. As the laboratory setting produces results, they are propagated across the remaining business areas.

Launching Prototypes and Pilot Projects

Prototypes are built to demonstrate the "look and feel" of the application, allowing for rapid validation of information requirements. Checkpoints are established every 60–90 days to provide for ongoing corrections and prioritization of expenditures. Allowing the greatest flexibility, this approach also provides ongoing validation of requirements, easy incorporation of new requirements, which are surfaced through prototyping, and early delivery of predefined components of data and application functionality.

Defining Success Criteria

Because they are evolving in nature, it is important for integration projects to acknowledge milestones achieved and project successes along the way. The integrator must help define clear criteria of project success, with measurable milestones and indicators of project achievements that can be used to

- Promote the goals of the project.
- Predict the course of similar future projects.
- Identify where the project falls short and plan ways to recover.

Some examples of success criteria for integration projects include

- Ability to reference one source of information for all needs of a given business initiative, regardless of interdepartmental boundaries. (Define the business initiative, such as marketing's capability to track and predict performance of specific products.)
- All aspects of a given business transaction can be conducted electronically. (Define the business transaction, such as a customer places an order online at the company's Web site and receives order confirmation through email within a specified time frame, while product shipment is initiated automatically.)
- One unified interface to all information and process intelligence needed to complete a particular business transaction. (For example, a telephone service company can complete the provisioning of DS1 services without leaving the primary terminal interface for a specified percentage of cases.)

Organizing the Chaos of an Integration Project

Integration projects have a higher level of chaos because of higher levels of autonomy, less controlled environment, and their global intent. It is important to harness the chaos without demanding that it be controlled in standard ways. This implies iterative approaches and facilitating the project as a process of discovery.

Iterative approaches enable the team to test out assumptions through prototyping, and to apply the knowledge gained to the next phase of the project. Continually testing and proceeding allows for a constant balance of theory and proof.

Although integration projects often deal with existing systems, they are usually venturing into uncharted territory. Whether it's undocumented and little understood legacy systems or harnessing new technology for business advantage, they involve making discoveries along the way. The integrator must expect to incorporate discoveries into the project plan, and must prepare project sponsors accordingly.

Recognizing and Avoiding Common Pitfalls

The course of an integration project differs from that of a software development project, and the things that can go wrong will be different too. The chances of success are improved by recognizing and avoiding the pitfalls that are common to integration efforts:

- **Lack of tolerance for ambiguity**—The fast pace of technical innovation means that technology selections made today might not be relevant even six months from now. The best project managers understand that a "best guess" must be taken today and revisited at implementation. One advantage of all types of modeling is that models support the ambiguous nature of the real world. Graphics are more equivocal than narratives. Models can be developed without slant, framed by the required structure, and built into the required deliverables. That way more than one group can utilize the models. A business group can plug them into their approach one way, while the technical team can use them in design documents without having to make changes.

  When project managers have a hard time with ambiguity, they can inadvertently sabotage an integration project. This problem usually manifests as demands that project participants spell everything out in advance: deliverables, schedules, decision-points, and outcomes. Integration projects are evolving, and the project goals can shift as new technology appears or other circumstances dictate. They require iterative approaches and do not lend themselves to standard project planning techniques.

- **Demanding resources be 100% allocated**—The integrator must be able and willing to perform independently. He must be able to multitask between several different projects. Similarly, management needs to allow people to have more than one project—more than one focus. In that way, the integrator can be the glue that holds together several different projects, just by being there. Part of the integrator's job is to be somewhat outside the set, to hold an infrastructure viewpoint. Integrators work with implementation projects that require a leadership with blinders on. We need that singular focus to get things done. But we also need an integrator who sits in and is aware of what the independent projects are doing.

The point of the integrator's presence is not to control or to enforce standards. That defeats the purpose. We want her on the team as an enabler, reminding the team of outside influences when appropriate—working out the solutions, not trying to enforce standards. The integrator is there as someone who can help a project team leverage their resources, and can get that team's buy-in by demonstrating her own value.

- **Scope creep**—*Scope creep* is the tendency to keep adding more and more requirements to a project, particularly when in the early stages, before any requirements are actually implemented. Integration projects are particularly prone to scope creep, because they cross application boundaries. Taking an iterative approach helps solve this tendency. Iterations should be defined such that when feasible, they will extend all the way to delivery of a project requirement. When iterations get real deliverables into the hands of clients early on, the inevitable "aha" moment (whether for clients when they see what's possible, or for designers when they see client reactions) brings requirements changes out earlier.

- **Expecting too much**—Because integration projects are different from traditional software development, some confusion can exist about how to delineate their goals and scope. It can be easy for an integration project to become the "saviour" project that collects all the odds and ends for other projects or that people don't know where else to deposit. Integration projects need clear goals and specific deliverables that are used to manage the expectations of project sponsors.

- **Expecting too little**—On the other hand, integration projects can be underestimated and limited to platform integration only, or minimized unnecessarily. Clear goals must be defined to demonstrate the reasons for undertaking an integration project. They should be substantial enough to justify the investment.

Summary

This chapter has introduced what it takes to build an environment for integration modeling. It has reviewed the differences between integration projects and software development projects, and looked at the criteria for selecting a project approach where organizational and technology factors both come into play. It has looked at the role of the integrator in the larger context of the organization and the role of integration modeling in the business context.

Integration models don't eliminate other types of models, but complement, organize, and extend what other models can provide while placing them in context more clearly. The operating model for integration pulls together new approaches for the virtual workspace, from new styles of teamwork to the partnership model for integration. Implementation strategies for integration projects include the concept of "early returns" to build the perception of a project's value to a company. They utilize sponsorship, allies, prototypes, and approaches that help to manage the chaos of enterprisewide projects.

Armed with new approaches, the integrator is now in the best position to benefit from the catalog of integration models. Neither a technique nor a notation, integration modeling represents an arsenal of means to ensure that your project not only survives but survives gracefully.

II

Catalog of Integration Models

The Cycle Template

Template Description

The Cycle template depicts a life cycle or cyclical process, which is characterized by repetition, evolution, and the features of self-reinforcement and self-correction. The template is shown in Figure 4.1.

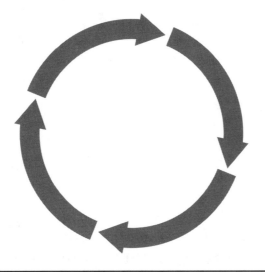

Figure 4.1 The Cycle template.

Template Discussion

Cycles occur in nature as patterns across time and help to organize our experience of time. Growing seasons occur in cycles and the stars mark cycles of celestial events.

The business goals for this pattern include the desire to reduce cycle time, improve the quality of output of the process, and reduce the cost of process execution. The Cycle template can be used to model activities in cases where traditional linear or workflow models fall short.

The core of this pattern is the repetition of activities or process steps, and the periodic interval of the cycle. For example, for a company interested in achieving CMM certification (an evaluation based on the Carnegie Mellon Software Engineering Institute's Capability Maturity Model) [4.1], a project was undertaken to bring the company's development process up a notch in the CMM-defined system of levels. We used the Cycle template to model application development life cycles, where traditional linear and waterfall models fall short.

Linear models imply non-repeatable, ad hoc processes (the lowest level in the SEI Capability Maturity Model), because they indicate project starting and end points with no support for iteration. The cyclical pattern accommodates the features of a mature software development process, which must be repeatable, defined, managed, and optimized. It removes the project design process from operating on a case-by-case basis and defines the ideal generic process, which any project can follow.

When the Cycle Template Applies

The Cycle template can be applied to business processes that occur on a cyclical basis, such as financial reporting or product development cycles. It is reflected in program code in loop processing constructs, such as the pseudo-code `do while` and `do until` forms. It applies when you want a structure for repetition of specified activities that occur in a particular sequence. Use the Cycle template when you want to depict

- An iterative process
- Recurring phenomena
- Time-dependent activities

Iterative Process

The Cycle template can be applied when you want to model a process that repeats iterations indefinitely or until some criteria for completion is met. It can help tune a process to produce a faster cycle time and improved service cycles. For example, product development processes can be modeled with the Cycle template, and then fine-tuned and optimized for greater efficiency. When the model is clear, other templates can be applied to increase the improvements, such as the Seed. Representing the shared database model, the Seed can be applied to a cyclical process to facilitate the sharing of project deliverables.

Recurring Phenomena

Apply the Cycle template when an event occurs on a regular schedule or intermittently. Business drivers, such as political, regulatory, or seasonal events, qualify as recurring phenomena (for example, tax time for an accountant, political elections for candidates, and vacation season for the hotelier). The key is that it be a predictable event that affects business processes as enabled by computer systems.

Time-Dependent Activities

When cycles of time act as initiator or terminator of an activity, the Cycle template can be applied. Many business activities occur on a monthly, weekly, daily, or hourly basis. Computer systems must capture and enact the rules of such time-dependent cyclical behaviors.

For instance, management reporting occurs on predefined intervals of daily, weekly, and monthly reports, with special runs occurring at end of quarter and year-end. Using the Cycle template to model reporting activities taking place at specific intervals helps clarify the required automation of those activities.

Examples

Some examples of applications of the Cycle template include

- The product selection process.
- The application development process.
- A self-managed team.

Product Selection Process

A software vendor needs a defined process for bringing in tools and techniques for automating their application development process. It is determined that they require a process that takes into account previous expenditures for tools, and allows them to capitalize on those previous expenditures without starting over every time the needs change.

Time is a consideration, so the process to be adopted must allow the company to generate requirements quickly and then try out a solution, rather than conducting an exhaustive search that would be too time-consuming. It must allow for both market screening and ongoing monitoring so that when new solutions become available they can be considered without having to go outside the process. Provisions must also be made for running pilots and refining the requirements based on lessons learned in the pilots. The model in Figure 4.2 shows the cyclical model that results from this analysis.

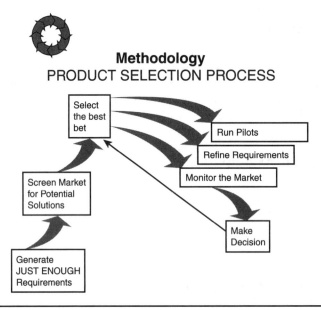

Figure 4.2   A product selection process for a software development vendor utilizes the Cycle template.

An iterative product selection process is designed. As opposed to traditional sequential processes, this approach systematically uses, reuses, and refines requirements and all relevant information. The process defines "just enough" requirements to screen the market for potential solutions. Borrowed from the paradigm commonly known as "just in time" in both training and inventory arenas, "just enough" is defined as sufficient requirements to be able to canvas the market, but no more. Detailed requirements are deferred until after the screening process. The information that becomes available as a result of screening, in turn, influences and enhances the detailed level of requirement definition.

To give an example of how the product selection process is implemented, the following describes its application to the selection of a development methodology:

The first cut of requirements for the methodology is defined on the basis of analysis of the following:

- Current technology center processes as described by the re-engineering team
- Experiences of MIS departments in other organizations
- Commercially available methodologies

Today's market offers a wide array of methodologies with different underlying philosophies and approaches. *Open* methodologies give users a choice of implementation among tools, methods, and techniques, as opposed to *closed* methodologies that are already integrated with a pre-defined suite of products. *Process-driven* methodologies focus on process, whereas *data-driven* methodologies emphasize data modeling, with many vendors re-evaluating their original one-sided approaches in order to better reflect and respond to changing market conditions. Various principles are followed as far as automation of a methodology is concerned: from paper intensive to paperless. Some methodologies focus on development for the newest platforms, others are designed for object-oriented development or for distributed environments, and yet others address mainframe application development only. One can find on the market out-dated methodologies, mature methodologies, and experimental methodologies, "old-timers" and "the new kids on the block."

The company selects the product that offers flexibility, range, and customization opportunities combined with state-of-the-art presentation. This product is brought in on a trial basis. Pilot projects are identified, the product is installed and introductory tutoring is offered to pilot projects managers. Consulting is provided on an as-needed basis, as the pilot project managers become more familiar with the tool.

Meanwhile changes on the market are monitored and analyzed to ensure that another candidate is identified quickly in case of dissatisfaction with the performance and offerings of the first selection. (Should that happen, familiarity with the first methodology by several of the technology center's people serves as an asset for the next iteration.) In this process the requirements are finalized and an understanding of the adequacy of the product is formed. Based on this acquired knowledge, recommendations are formulated and presented for adoption.

Application Development Process

An Internet development methodology (see Figure 4.3) incorporates the Cycle template in its development life cycle. The process starts with gathering business information, and then moves to clarifying the site vision and requirements. It identifies and integrates the needed components, and then builds technical design and design templates. The next step is to develop and test the site, and then publish and provide the ongoing support for the site.

The process incorporates a component strategy, characterized by the use of reusable components that allow us to benefit from prior experiences on similar projects. It also uses templates for accelerated design, and it centers on the release strategy for multiple iteration. The site release strategy, detailed in a separate document, provides

- Limited exposure for technical risk and business risk.
- Early customer feedback that saves time and dollars on future releases.

- Feasibility tested every step of the way.
- Opportunity to take advantage of rapid advances in technology solutions (we wait until it's cheaper).

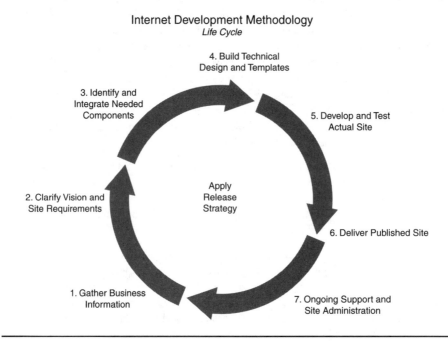

Internet Development Methodology
Life Cycle

4. Build Technical Design and Templates

3. Identify and Integrate Needed Components

5. Develop and Test Actual Site

Apply Release Strategy

2. Clarify Vision and Site Requirements

6. Deliver Published Site

1. Gather Business Information

7. Ongoing Support and Site Administration

Figure 4.3   Internet development life cycle utilizes the Cycle template for an iterative process.

The accompanying development methodology specifies deliverables from start (strategy and design) to finish (delivery of published site and ongoing support).

Self-Managed Team

A software development company utilizes the Cycle template to design the case team that facilitates its project prioritization and approval process. This self-managed team integrates representatives from Business Planning, IT Leadership, and IT Project Management, as shown in Figure 4.4.

Next, the supporting structures required for implementation of the Project Planning and Prioritization Process are spelled out, as shown in Figure 4.5. This model becomes the basis for defining the roles of the CASE team and specifying the requirements for computer applications that enable the newly redesigned business process.

From the model, the following roles and requirements are defined to guide the implementation:

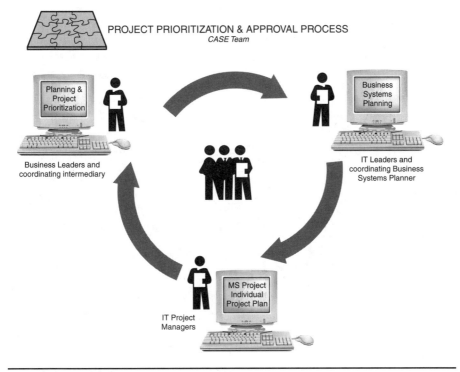

Figure 4.4   A self-managed Case Team carries out the project prioritization and approval process.

Business Systems Planning:

- Coordinate project planning
- Ensure methods, procedures, policies are followed
- Implement or administer measurement program
- Project management controls

Facilitation/Methodology:

- Administer methodology implementation
- Provide facilitation services
- Maintain process library and custom templates
- Support business modeling function

Operations Measurements:

- Support reliability assessment of district production
- Implement data collection process
- Record and report reliability information

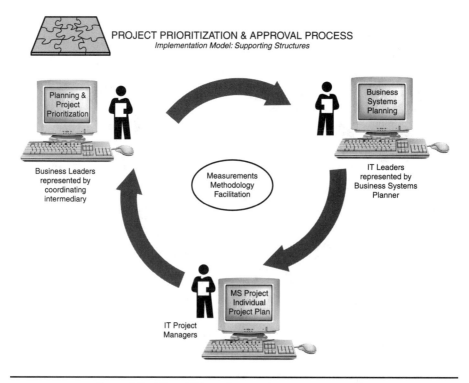

PROJECT PRIORITIZATION & APPROVAL PROCESS
Implementation Model: Supporting Structures

Planning &
Project
Prioritization

Business
Systems
Planning

Business Leaders
represented by
coordinating
intermediary

Measurements
Methodology
Facilitation

IT Leaders
represented by
Business Systems
Planner

MS Project
Individual
Project Plan

IT Project
Managers

Figure 4.5   The addition of supporting structures provides
the basis for specifying requirements.

Subsequent steps involve acquiring and developing the required systems for methodology and measurement automation.

Benefits and Consequences

The following benefits and possible consequences should be considered when selecting the Cycle template as a solution:

- Promotes containment and quantification of ongoing requirements
- Structures reuse so that nothing is lost
- Supports variations in the path of a process

Promotes Containment and Quantification of Ongoing Requirements

When a process is seen as a linear one-time event, it doesn't make sense to document and improve on the process. All you have to do is get it done and forget it. On the other hand, when a process is seen as recurring and cyclical in nature, it makes sense to look for ways to improve future repetitions.

To rethink a seemingly linear process and to start treating it as a cyclical one, it often helps to break requirements up into releases. This helps establish priorities because if no future release is expected, then all requirements must be delivered now. If future releases are expected, you can prioritize and deliver the most important features first and others in later releases. The Cycle template helps you position the process within the constraints of time schedules and fit the requirements into that structure.

Structures Reuse so That Nothing Is Lost

In addition to saving requirements for future delivery, you can also save partially completed work and let it accumulate for future deliveries. The Cycle template provides a structure that implies the potential for reuse, and helps you act accordingly.

If you were using a linear model, you would be more inclined to release all resources at the end of the line, rather than reserving the ones you expect to use next time. If you want to free up resources, maybe you want a linear structure, but if you're trying to create repeatable processes that can be completed more quickly on subsequent iterations, you'll find that the cycle is a better choice.

Supports Variations in the Path of a Process

Complex processes can incorporate many pathways for their completion. Integration requires that you consolidate those pathways into one overall process that can be navigated with many variations. For example, in the typical organization's application development life cycle, multiple types of software development must be accounted for. They include classic development, Internet sites, object-oriented, maintenance, and rapid application development, to name a few. The integrated development process shows an overall cycle of development steps, and provides templates which indicate how different types of software development would traverse the steps of that process.

Template Realization

Models based on the Cycle template are translated into both technical and business models. Because the implementation model for integration projects is middle-out, we will be translating from the template in both directions, into other types of models.

In the technical direction, we might define the functions of a cyclical process, which then will be modeled with the aid of process modeling and collaboration diagrams. For example, the cyclical model seen in Figure 4.6 was developed to help a marketing department automate the process of new product development.

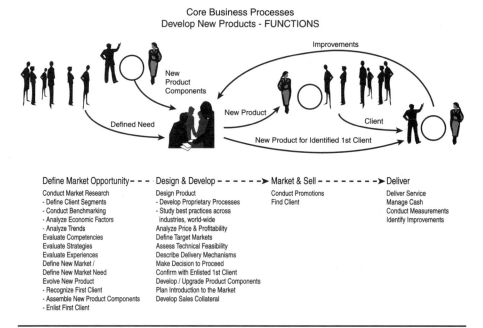

Figure 4.6   New product development uses the Cycle model
to depict the development process.

The next model (see Figure 4.7) defines the process flow at the business level.

The first level technical model (see Figure 4.8), a collaboration diagram, models the steps of the process and the required flows between steps of the process. The reader will perhaps notice that this diagram is more cryptic because it is a more technical type of diagram. It is introduced here to show how the business-oriented model in Figure 4.7 is translated into the technical, tool-supported diagrams required for detailed systems design. Processes and external agents on the business model become components and actors, respectively, on the collaboration diagram. Flows are translated into links and link messages carried between objects.

Subsequent technical models would include the class diagram for the client and competitor databases to focus on analyzing the objects, their attributes, operations, and associations, and the activity diagram for the detailed analysis and design of tasks. Or we might have identified the need to build a prototype to test and refine a set of requirements. As we take an individual look at each step in the cycle, we define how it can best be prepared for technical implementation.

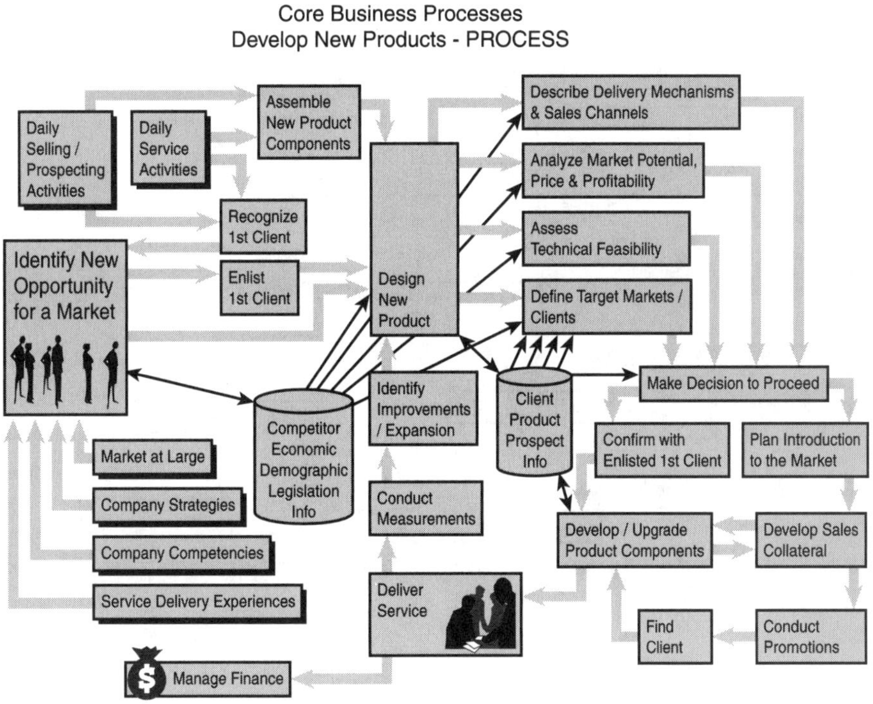

Core Business Processes
Develop New Products - PROCESS

Figure 4.7 Process flow for new product development.

In the direction of the business side, we might generate an action plan based on the new steps in the cycle for actions that the business team must take to improve the business process. For instance, in the earlier example, the new product development process uses client and competitor information for the mass customization of products. This use calls for increasingly detailed knowledge of the market, its segments, and actual customer and competitor behaviors. The action plan, presented to the senior vice president of marketing and supported by the CIO, required that the following two steps be taken:

1. Introduce a client database, which would allow the business to do the following:

   - Capture product usage information for the upgrade of product components
   - Support new product design
   - Describe delivery mechanisms and sales channels
   - Analyze market potential, pricing, and profitability
   - Assess technical feasibility and define target markets and clients

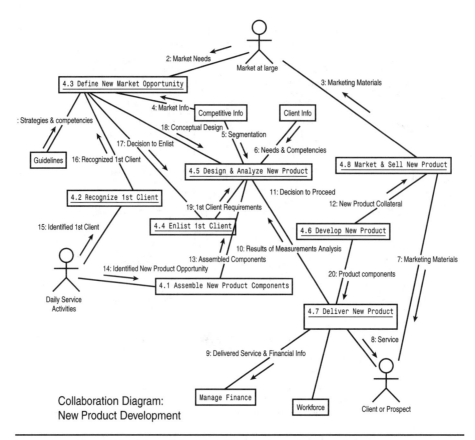

Figure 4.8   The collaboration diagram shows the steps of the process and the required flows between the steps.

2. Introduce a competitor database, which would allow the business to do the following:

   - Define new opportunities for a market
   - Describe delivery mechanisms and sales channels
   - Analyze market potential, pricing, and profitability
   - Assess technical feasibility and define target markets and clients

Later, the action plan provides the basis for a project schedule or, as in this case, several projects are defined and the project schedules developed accordingly.

Based on the Cycle model, we can also generate updates to an existing business process that is represented in business process models. Several technical or business initiatives can be required to implement the new business model.

EAI Applications

The Cycle template is about timing. The Cycle template is used to direct the timing and to orchestrate business events. EAI projects can surface many issues of timing. Internal cycles of reporting, revenue recognition, and other events based on the business drivers of a company affect the ability of systems to share data and function seamlessly. External cycles of investing, regulatory reporting, and the monitoring of economic indicators, also influence the requirements defining EAI projects. EAI identifies business cycles to direct how software interfaces with business events.

The Cycle template has been used to model iteration in

- Data warehousing methodology.
- Rapid application development approach for an EAI team.
- Target business process in an ERP implementation.

Iterative Data Warehouse Methodology

The Cycle template stresses repeatable processes, making it useful when you want to highlight the iterative nature of a process. In Figure 4.9, the data warehouse methodology incorporates the Cycle pattern to show the highly iterative process of data warehouse development.

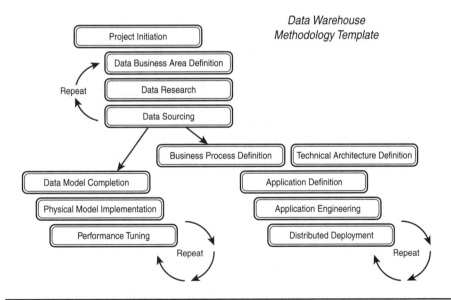

Figure 4.9 Data warehouse methodology incorporates the Cycle template to show the iterative nature of warehouse development.

One early issue in data warehouse design was the tendency to try to build data warehouses according to traditional development approaches. Spectacular failures forced the move to a more iterative approach, which allowed the warehousing project to test assumptions as it proceeded, and continually renew the scope, data research and sourcing, and technical implementation choices. The model shown in Figure 4.9 highlights the importance of iterative approaches in data warehousing.

A Rapid Application Development Approach for EAI

Rapid application development (RAD) relies on four principles:

- **Economy of speed**—Quick response to user needs
- **Prototyping**—Ensures quality
- **Iterative development**—Prioritizes needs
- **Reusability**—Benefits from experience

The Cycle template provides the pattern for a model (see Figure 4.10) showing the give and take between user and development team in a RAD project.

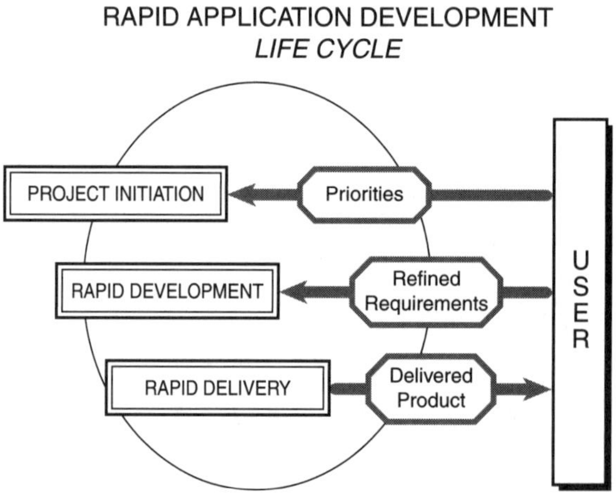

Figure 4.10   The RAD life cycle model applies the cycle template
to an iterative, repetitive process.

In this model, technical components are identified using a release strategy. User priorities are factored in to the design of the initial prototype. Rapid development of a working prototype enables the user to make refinements to the requirements, and delivery of the first release starts the cycle over again for the next component of the system.

Target ERP Business Process

To carry the Cycle template into the business process redesign effort, one project used it to help define the target process for the future. This effort produced a series of models showing the cycles of business processes that must be supported by an ERP initiative. The model in Figure 4.11 shows one of the newly designed processes, a service delivery process for temporary help staffing.

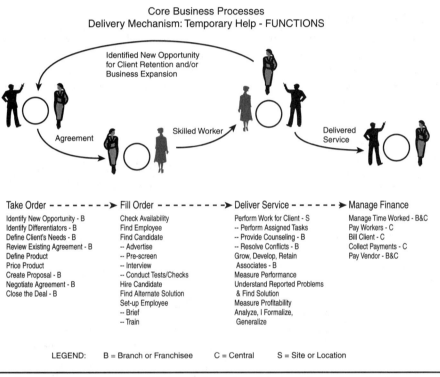

Figure 4.11 A business model depicts the cycles of service delivery through taking the order, filling the order, delivering service, and invoicing the client.

This model indicates the cyclical nature of service delivery processes, and maps the steps of the process into those cycles. It helps company executives get a birds-eye view of the overall picture and place minor components in context. Gaining these kinds of perspectives allows managers to move past some of the differences that stand between them and integrated systems.

Templates That Work Well with the Cycle Template

The Cycle template can be combined with any other template, depending on the needs of a project. This section gives some of the most common combinations and advice on how to combine them.

The Flow Template

The Cycle template is often combined with the Flow model when defining the steps involved in an iterative process. The Flow template allows you to depart from the Cycle template if some steps occur in linear fashion before or after the repeated steps. When these two templates are combined, they provide greater flexibility than would either one on its own.

The Seed Template

The Cycle template can be combined with the Seed template for the introduction of a coordinating intermediary such as a CASE team. The model in Figure 4.12 shows an example of this combination.

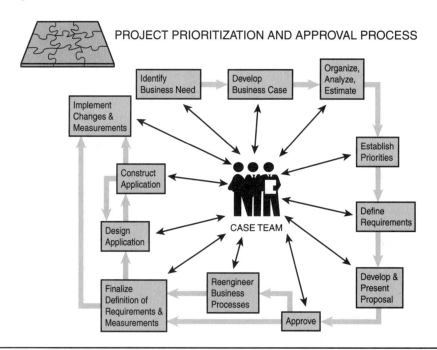

Figure 4.12   The Cycle template is combined with the Seed template in this model showing the introduction of a coordinating CASE team in a cyclical process.

This combination of templates allows the coordination of diverse activities and helps eliminate wasted effort on redundant process steps. The cycle-based model depicts the recurring process by which this company initiates, justifies, and quantifies technology projects, beginning with the business identification of a need. It shows the steps involved, including prioritization, requirement analysis, and reengineering, if required, and carries through to design, construction, and implementation of the desired computer systems.

5

The Seed Template

Template Description

The Seed template is a generator or transformer structure depicting a situation where a core component produces or collects and contains an array of results. The Seed template is shown in Figure 5.1.

Figure 5.1   The Seed template.

Template Discussion

The Seed is about growth, extension, and expansion. It is a structure for building through rapid growth and is also suitable for depicting growth by acquisition or alliance. It can help us to structure the extensions of our reach through alliances and partnerships.

The Seed is also a mechanism of containment. Seeds gather and store, until the time is right for germination. They store resources and feed them into the selected channels of growth. They take in resources and transform them through patterned growth. Thus they can be used to model value-adding processes that take in inputs and add value by performing actions on them, which qualitatively improve the resulting outputs.

The integration goals of the Seed pattern include the sharing of resources and the introduction of a coordinating intermediary to integrate a diverse set of experts and complex activities. For instance, consider a business process involving several steps that flow through various business departments. An example might be a loan application that flows from the customer to the initial contact with an information agent, to a customer service representative who helps fill out an application, to a branch manager who approves the application, to a loan officer who actually grants the loan. Figure 5.2 illustrates the steps required to carry out the loan approval process.

The Seed template can be used to model a solution which introduces a case manager to act as intermediary, expediting the progress of a loan application through the many steps (see Figure 5.3).

Other integration objectives that utilize the Seed pattern include analyzing how we interact with a range of alternatives. The Seed will allow us to contemplate reducing the range, to sacrifice precision for simplicity and convenience, as shown in Figure 5.4. Such an approach helps us to streamline an existing process, bypassing unnecessary steps by simplifying the choices. Simplifying a process before we attempt to automate or integrate it with other models can enhance integration.

We can also use the Seed template to model increasing the range of alternatives to provide increased precision (see Figure 5.5). Sometimes we want to provide greater precision in selecting alternatives, as in the case of one-to-one marketing or mass customization of products. Enterprise application integration supports both these new business models by providing the ability to share information and seamlessly integrate functions.

Loan approved process
From:

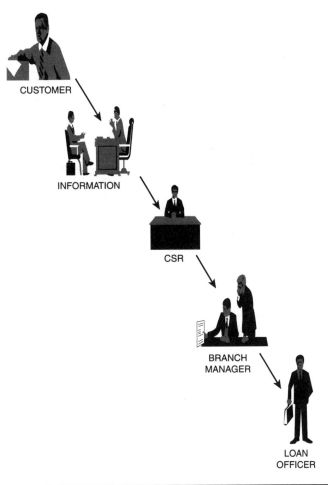

Figure 5.2   The loan approval process involves complex activities
carried out by a diverse set of experts.

Integration: coordinating intermediary
Loan approval process
To:

CASE MANAGER

Figure 5.3   The Seed template models the newly integrated process, which utilizes a coordinating intermediary to expedite the loan approval process.

Integration Models
Decreasing the range of alternatives and coordinating
the activities via a core component

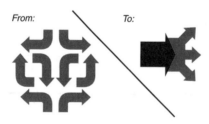

From: *To:*

Figure 5.4   Integration objectives can include decreasing the range of alternatives.

The core function of the Seed model can be either the generation of results, the collection of inputs, or both. Inputs collected can be transformed for value-added outputs. The Seed template also represents extensions of all kinds, whether through rapid company growth in a market or through alliance partnerships.

Integration Models
Increasing the range of alternatives to provide
greater precision

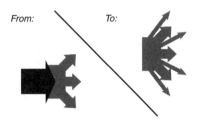

Figure 5.5   Integration objectives can dictate increasing the range of alternatives.

When the Seed Template Applies

The Seed template can be applied when coordinating a collection of diverse experts to eliminate duplication of effort. It can be applied to reduce the number of outputs for a given process, reducing the overhead spent on information specification and production. Or it can help you design for improved resource utilization by specifying multiple process inputs that vary in their input modes. Some specific applications follow:

- Generating multiple outcomes
- Collecting a range of inputs
- Creating multidimensional design
- Managing inputs and outputs

Generating Multiple Outcomes

When the logic of a program contains multiple *if/then/else* structures or a *depends* clause, it can be said to produce multiple outcomes. The Seed template is a useful construct in modeling the range of possible outcomes, the factors the choices depend on, and the transformations required.

For instance, the design for a component of middleware software called for the remote accessing of several legacy applications and their databases. The job of the middleware was to gather information, compile it, and return results to the user, who would interpret the information presented. The Seed template was used to model the desired outcomes from multiple legacy applications that were accessed.

Collecting a Range of Inputs

The repository-based automation of software engineering provided by modeling tools can be taken as an example. The tool encyclopedia (see Figure 5.6) shows how a process can produce deliverables that are passed along from one step to the next and stored in a repository for easy synchronization.

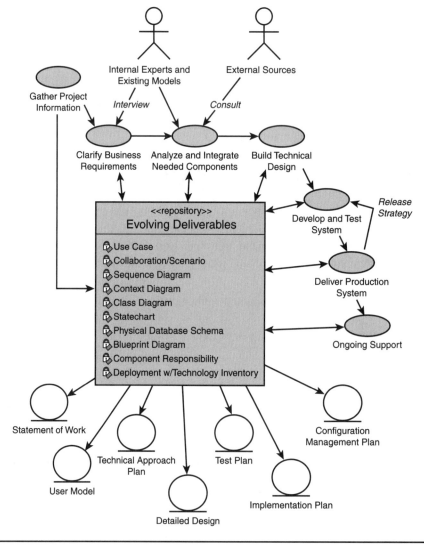

Figure 5.6   The development process model depicts evolving
deliverables, stored in a repository.

In this example, each step of the process creates inputs to the repository and performs transformations on them to produce outputs. For instance, the first step, Gather Project Information, is also modeled with the Seed template, as shown in Figure 5.7.

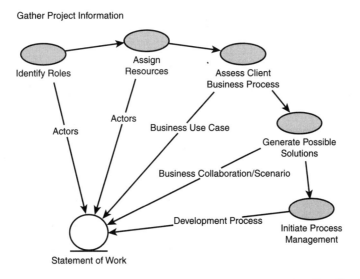

Figure 5.7   The first step of the development process is modeled by the Seed template.

Subsequent steps treat the outputs from initial steps as inputs, enhancing and transforming them to create new outputs. The entire repository reflects the current state of changes applied along the way. Thus, changes in later steps can be propagated back to deliverables from earlier steps, providing the synchronization of change throughout the process. Any process that collects a range of inputs can benefit from use of the Seed structure to clearly define the required components.

Creating a Multidimensional Design

The Seed can be used to specify the design of multidimensional databases for a data-warehousing situation. In the multidimensional model (see Figure 5.8) developed for a decision support system for an insurance company, the core of the Seed represents the fact table.

The fact table houses summarized and categorized facts about the data entities in question, in this case, auto insurance applicants. The facts for this company include the amount of the premium the customer pays for each vehicle insured, the total amount for all vehicles, and the premium paid to the previous insurance carrier.

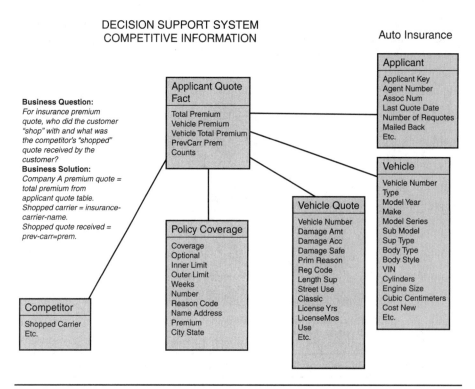

Figure 5.8   This multidimensional design uses the Seed pattern to model fact and dimension tables for an auto insurance company.

The branches of the Seed represent the dimensions against which those facts are measured and reported. This company's dimensions include applicant, vehicle, the insurance quote for that vehicle, policy coverage, and competitor information. Facts are aggregated and stored at the level of the various dimensions so they can easily be reported on request.

Managing Inputs and Outputs

The Seed is a natural structure for components that help other (client) programs handle the tasks of accessing data. For example, I/O routines are software programs that are called by other programs for the purpose of opening a data store, accessing the records stored there using read, write, or update instructions, and closing the data store when finished. I/O routines have evolved from called modules to Object Request Brokers and Information Brokers to messaging and middleware products. The core of the function they provide can be modeled by the in-transform-out pattern of the Seed template.

Examples

Examples of applications of the Seed template follow:

- Hub and spoke routing design for a distribution network
- Switch systems interfaces for a wireless network
- Middleware controller

Hub and Spoke Routing Design for a Distribution Network

Hub and spoke models are an implementation of the generator/transformer structure that is utilized in the transportation and communications industries to design logistics networks and provide the basis for technical architectures. They are also used extensively to define organizational structures for business, particularly in the area of alliance networks.

Airlines utilize the hub and spoke architecture (see Figure 5.9) to define city pairs participating in transportation routes. They allow a carrier to define the precise timing of banks of arriving flights to offer a seamless transfer to banks of departing flights. The use of the hub and spoke design also helps maximize the number of attainable connections for incoming passengers and keep, at the same time, the connecting times within defined and acceptable limits.

AIRLINE ROUTING: DEFINITIONS   Hub and Spoke Network

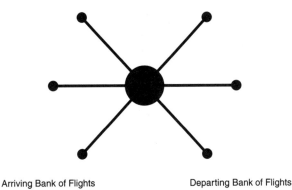

Arriving Bank of Flights   Departing Bank of Flights

Figure 5.9   The airline routing model uses the Seed template
to define a hub and spoke network.

Variations on the hub and spoke theme help companies increase their geographic reach and supplier management efficiency, as well as providing brand, format, and technology leverage. By entering into product distribution alliances with partners defined as spokes on a company's hub, or sometimes as fellow spokes in a cooperative synergy, companies can reduce overhead costs and, by making better use of an existing distribution infrastructure, raise revenues.

Switch Systems Interfaces for a Wireless Network

A wireless network is modeled (see Figure 5.10) using the Seed template to depict the application systems interfacing with the Mobile Telephone Switching Office (MTSO). Subsequent architecture models added platform information to the diagram to define the technical architecture.

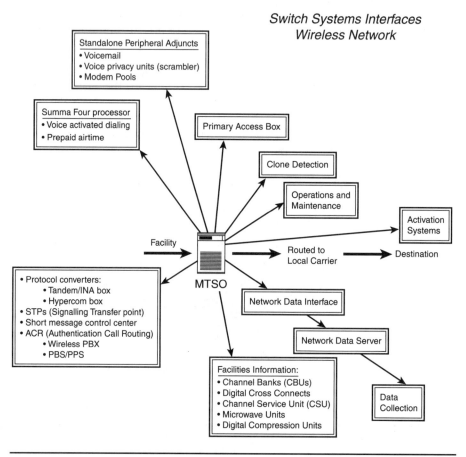

Figure 5.10 The Switch Systems Interfaces model defines the application interfaces to a MTSO switch in the wireless network, using the Seed template.

On the switch systems interfaces model, the Seed pattern helped to break out the multiple interfaces talking to the MTSO switch so they could be included in a Y2K analysis. Technical architecture was also documented, so that all platform and operating system versions could be evaluated along with the equipment itself. After all the interfaces and supporting infrastructures were clarified, responsibility for Y2K analysis could be assigned and compliance progress could be tracked and reported.

Middleware Controller

On a project for Synergistic Solutions, Inc. (SSI), a vendor of EAI software for telecommunications services companies, the team was developing a system to provide a unified interface to data from legacy systems. SSI's product, NetLocate, incorporated a middleware controller that was defined and modeled using the Seed template. Figure 5.11 shows the collaboration diagram that modeled the functions of the controller, and the remote systems to which it controlled access.

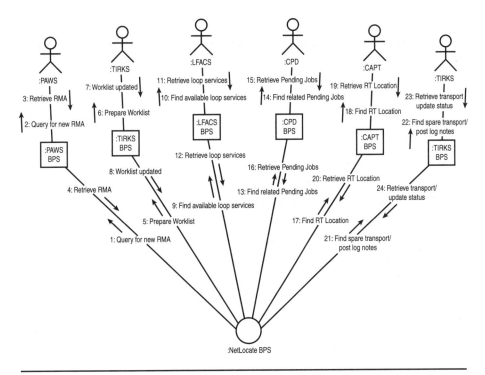

Figure 5.11   The Seed template was used to model a controller function in a middleware collaboration diagram.

The controller object became the core component of the model, and associations modeled each leg of the Seed. Associations are the conduits for the link messages, which specify the data packets involved in accessing a remote system. Intermediate objects that were introduced along each leg specified the behaviors to be applied to access the remote systems. They also handled the receipt of metadata instructions for data access.

Benefits and Consequences

The following benefits and possible consequences should be considered when selecting the Seed template as a solution:

- Allows distribution and accumulation of information, goods, and services
- Specifies a variety of behaviors
- Consolidates multiple functions

Allows Distribution and Accumulation of Information, Goods, and Services

A flexible structure for distribution using network, alliances, or other means, the Seed template represents the main thrust of the pathways for distribution. The Seed template helps you model the factors involved in distribution:

- Extent of reach
- Coverage of the range of alternatives
- Distribution of functionality
- Centralization versus decentralization
- Standardization versus diversity

The Seed template can also help you represent the collection and accumulation of inputs of any kind. It supports the analysis of multiple inputs and their transformation into discrete outputs.

Specifies a Variety of Behaviors

In cases where you need to model behaviors that vary according to some criteria, the Seed template is appropriate. It enables you to specify the range of behaviors and the triggers that initiate the behaviors. Nested *if* logic and the *depends* clause can be modeled by this template.

Consolidates Multiple Functions

When consolidating a diverse set of functions under one coordinating intermediary, the Seed template helps clarify the range of functions. It can help you factor out duplication in functionality, creating a single point of control. In business processes, the lack of control of process steps leads to poorly managed processes with long processing times. One goal of EAI software is to drastically reduce these processing times by automating process steps and minimizing the number of human interventions a process requires.

Template Realization

In the case of the collaboration diagram for the middleware controller (refer to Figure 5.11), the template is already applied in a technical model, and subsequent models are developed according to the usual object-oriented principles:

- Class diagrams define the objects in greater detail, specifying their attributes, operations, and associations.
- Use Cases clarify and summarize the usage scenarios that the collaboration diagram models.
- Component responsibility diagrams define the technical components that must be developed in the target programming language to deliver the desired functionality.

The airline model defining network routing using the hub and spoke diagram is used to provide the groundwork for defining strategic measures and building a data warehouse to store and report against those strategic measures. Business models were developed analyzing the definition of strategic measures, and dimensional models were used to specify the database design for the components of the data warehouse. Entity relationship diagrams for physical database design followed.

For the decision support database, a high-level model uses the Seed pattern to place the database in context with the core business process of decision support. As shown in Figure 5.12, the Seed model captures inputs, core repository, and outputs within the context of their business use.

In this example, the inputs from sources internal to the company are combined with inputs from external sources such as the Internet. Information is housed in a data warehouse repository and is used to respond to queries and produce reports showing news and supporting in-depth analysis. Other business models specify the steps involved in decision-making and strategic use of the information.

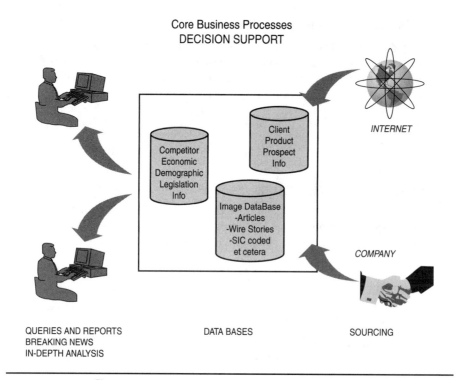

Figure 5.12   The Decision Support process shows a core
database within its business context.

EAI Applications

EAI requires centers of focus, which act as information sources, clusters of activity, and
places where activities coalesce. The data warehouse is a central data source, with data
marts generated from its core of business information. The caseworker or coordinating
intermediary is a center of activity. These focal points help organize the chaos that can
occur when projects span the entire enterprise. Integration focal points include such
structures as business process centers, Web portals, information filters and switching
hubs.

When the Seed template is used to model redistribution of functionality among alternatives, it is supporting typical EAI objectives. Warehousing uses the Seed template for
multidimensional design of information, and middleware can use the Seed construct in
designing core components that perform multiple actions. Some specific EAI applications follow:

- Decision support design
- Middleware component diagram
- Provisioning process optimization

Decision Support Design

Decision Support Systems (DSS) and Executive Information Systems (EIS) are two types of systems that typically utilize the data stored in data warehouses. They provide a user front-end to data warehouses, usually for marketing, finance, and executives needing high-level and summarized information for decision-making purposes.

The Seed template is the core pattern used for multidimensional design of data storage for decision support purposes. Tables aggregating and summarizing facts about key business information are represented by the Seed, with the required dimensions represented by the arms of the template.

Middleware Component Diagram

One function of middleware systems is to provide a unified interface to diverse legacy systems. One telecommunications company used the Seed template to help model the components required for an integrated test management platform. The information broker's role was to provide access to a very large inventory database, encapsulate selected data objects, and pass them on to client programs that required the data.

Component diagrams modeled the function of each UNIX sub-process that performed the data manipulation. Associations between objects carried the link messages that passed required data from one object or step of the process to the next.

Provisioning Process Optimization

In one example, we have seen a telecommunications business process for customer provisioning reduced from 90+ days to a matter of hours by the introduction of a coordinating software intermediary. The original provisioning process involved many steps that were executed by passing control documents from one design engineering group to another. When the document arrived at any destination along the way, lengthy research was required into convoluted legacy systems, causing long delays.

The EAI software that was supplied consolidated all the research into legacy systems and automated the steps the design engineers would have performed manually. It then compiled that research and presented proposed solutions to the design engineers for their approval and selection. What once took months to achieve was now done by EAI software in a fraction of the time.

Templates That Work Well with the Seed Template

The Seed template combines well with

- The Cycle template.
- The Web template.

The Cycle Template

The Seed template can be combined with the Cycle pattern to incorporate the dynamics of repetition and recurring activities. The Seed provides the growth dynamic, and the input-transform-output pattern. The Cycle provides the directional cycle. Together, they can be used to model transformation processes that repeat at intervals.

One telecommunications company used the combination of Seed and Cycle to model the process of ordering equipment and entering the equipment into inventory. In the model shown in Figure 5.13, the Seed provides a repository for the document required by the ongoing business process, and the Cycle provides the framework in which the process takes place.

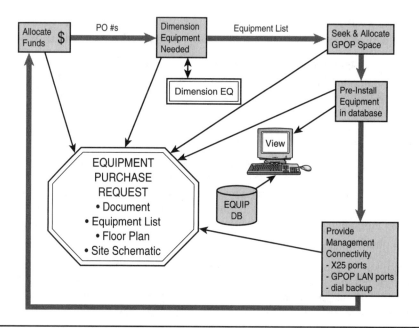

Figure 5.13   The equipment update process combines the Seed and the Cycle templates for a recurring update process.

The steps of the process specify the detailed information that is captured and entered into the required subsystems. Subsequent models drilled down into more detail on the systems as needed.

The Web Template

When dot.com organizations turn into true networks using alliances, partner collaboration creates ties where isolation once existed. Market strategy always involves understanding competitors, locating suppliers, and defining target customers. Internet strategy, perhaps more than other arenas, blurs the lines between these three agents and requires that we collaborate with all three in new ways. The Internet enables the business process that

- Identifies companies operating in niche businesses that can work collaboratively with yours.
- Stratifies the market in ways that enable competition to generate business for all.
- Joins networks to establish strength and size, rather than building it all in-house, enabling your business to stay focused on core competencies.
- Invites customers to perform significant components of your business process for themselves.
- Enables suppliers to share in performing portions of your business process for themselves.

In an initial model, shown in Figure 5.14, the Seed template is used to define the alliance program for a health-oriented Web site.

The natural extension of this model is to combine it with the web template to depict a network of affiliate and channel partners that create new channels of access to the Web site. The resulting model (see Figure 5.15) makes a clearer statement of the advantages of networking and can be extended through a network map to study the extended reach of each alliance partner and affiliate.

This model shifts the emphasis from a focus on entities to a focus on their connections. How we connect, when we connect, and where connections are planned are all questions that can be answered using the Web template. Based on this model and others like it, plans can be laid for contacting the desired partners and soliciting their participation.

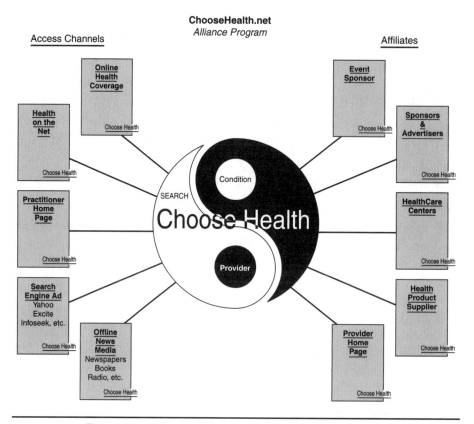

Figure 5.14   The Choose Health Web site uses the Seed model to define its Alliance Program.

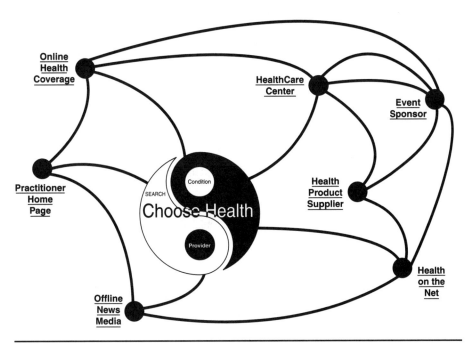

Figure 5.15   The Web template is combined with the Seed template to create
a hybrid model that emphasizes the Seed (the hub Web site), and places it in
the context of the networked model of alliance partners.

$$6$$

The Web Template

Template Description

The Web template depicts a network of nodes (or endpoints) and connectors (or arcs). It is useful in modeling network routing and for performing complex path analysis and optimization. The template is shown in Figure 6.1.

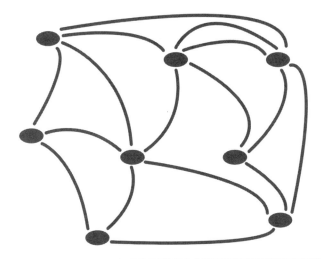

Figure 6.1 The Web Template

Template Discussion

Webs are woven in an asymmetrical manner. Their multiple connections lend strength to weaker strands. They can be built quickly at a high level and detailed later. They provide a durable structure for intermittent, episodic growth. The web structure can help organize irregular growth and provide a sense of control.

Webs can be built anywhere, with connections built on an opportunistic basis. As the opportunity presents itself, you attach a strand of your web. Whenever you get another opportunity, you attach another. The web is useful in unstructured approaches, mimicking the style of the social network.

Webs provide a habitat that can be constantly renewed and also deconstructed. You can add on from all angles. You can build local variations and produce pockets with distinctly unique features. Pockets where you can experiment are useful when applying the pragmatic approach.

The integration goals of the Web template include networked communications design, optimal path analysis, and any process requiring a relational, non-hierarchical structure. The Web is the most relational of the templates, with its capability to add and change nodes and connectors without retooling the basic structure of the network.

The core of this pattern is the ability to build a multipoint web of connections. Telecommunications depicts circuits for providing bandwidth to customers with the Web network model, and of course the Internet is a well-known example of a web implementation. Communications of all kinds are increasingly facilitated through web-like networks, whether in the form of communications networks, internal corporate email connections, Internet bulletin boards, or online communities sharing information.

When the Web Template Applies

Use the Web template when you want to depict

- Networked devices
- Design of routing algorithms
- Online networks and communities

Networked Devices

Network topologies are depicted with nodes and connectors, showing one or multiple potential paths through the web. Anywhere devices must be connected, the Web template will be useful for building the design. Its focus on connection, without the required symmetry of the grid, makes it ideal for complex networks where multiple connections exist. A simple path of connected elements is modeled in Figure 6.2, using the Web pattern.

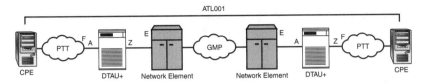

Figure 6.2   This site model uses the Web pattern to show the IDNX services and circuits for a telecommunications provider.

Design of Routing Algorithms

Q. Sun and H. Langendörfer, in a network management research group paper, say "The rapid development and deployment of high-speed networks in recent years have given rise to many new distributed real-time applications such as videoconferencing, teleteaching, video-on-demand, computer visualization, etc." [6.1]. The Web pattern is regularly employed to model the routing problems for supporting these applications. The goals of routing for supporting real-time applications include computing paths that satisfy the quality requirements of the applications while managing the network resources efficiently.

Routing algorithms are also needed for the routing of messages through communications networks, such as the satellite links forming global communications networks. Their optimization requires efficient routing to achieve high data throughput and low latency.

Network simulation modeling tools such as MIL3's OPNET software [6.2] employ Web models to represent the highest level in the hierarchy of models that is used to simulate the dynamic message routing algorithms that determine routing based on network topology and network load. Overlaid on the geographical background of networks, these models resemble the physical systems they depict, so that mapping from the model to the system is intuitive. Other models in the hierarchy provide drill-down to processing that occurs in nodes, and include the details of network protocols and APIs.

Online Networks and Communities

Mapping online resources for learning networks, special interest groups (SIGs), and other shared information sources is becoming more important in today's networked organizations. High tech professionals are exchanging formal training for online educational centers that provide just-in-time training to employees on the job. The Web template is useful in providing a visual overview of available sites for these educational purposes.

Examples

The following examples explore the applications of the Web template:

- Telecom—provisioning configuration
- Airline routing definitions
- Internet project

Telecom—Provisioning Configuration

The Web template was used to help define the organization supporting the provisioning process at a telecommunications company (see Figure 6.3). Modeling the devices and facilities in the network that provides services to customers helped illustrate the roles of the organizations while clarifying the boundaries of responsibility.

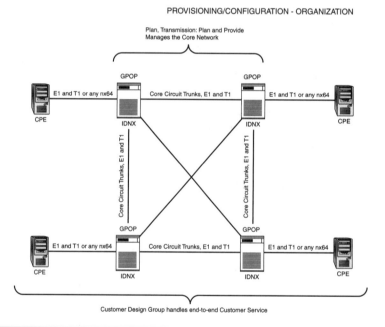

Figure 6.3   The Web template models the configuration of the service network for a telecommunications provider.

This model helped the team to understand both the roles of the organizations involved in customer provisioning and the scope of their responsibility for the process. It also gave a high-level view of how the platform was configured so those team members unfamiliar with network configuration could better envision the network.

Subsequent process models defined the steps of the business process that performed customer provisioning.

Airline Routing Definitions

In the course of building a data warehouse for an airline, the business intelligence team assigned to develop the requirements had to capture definitions for the specialized terminology of the industry. They particularly needed to arrive at a companywide consensus on the terms used to define the business information that the data warehouse must store. This information was critical because it provided the basis for calculating performance measures that would be reported from the warehoused data. As is the case in many organizations, multiple definitions existed for terminology that was specialized and cryptic to the uninitiated.

Thus the job of the business intelligence team was twofold. One objective was to learn about the disparate meanings of the terminology and to understand the reasons for the differences in those meanings. The other objective was to synthesize the information into definitions that the project stakeholders could support. The model seen in Figure 6.4, building a common ground for the data warehouse, presents a representative fragment of the resulting dictionary of terms.

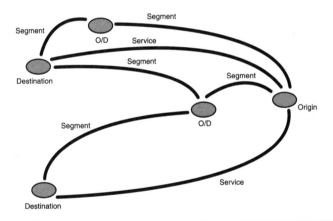

Figure 6.4   The Web template defines segments and
services in the transportation industry.

The segments and services model supported reconciling the definitions of terms for this revenue data warehouse. The model illustrates that

- Flights are composed of segments.
- Segments represent the flight from one airport to another, which is sometimes referred to as a *leg*.

- Segments combine to make up services, which are the overall itinerary booked by a customer, whether composed of one or many legs.
- A service extends from the customer airport of origin to the customer's final airport destination.
- Origin and destination are based on the customer's point of view.

Without clarifying the terminology, it was impossible to share data or accurately quantify the data required to report on measures that are commonly reported in the industry (for example, load factors, plane miles, seats available by O&D market, and so forth). After these definitions and others like them were established, processes could be designed for sharing the data in order to compile strategic measurement statistics.

Internet Project

An Internet architecture plan used the Web template to define network connectivity for the Web site's development team. Figure 6.5 shows the Technical Architecture Plan that outlines connections between a variety of project resources that must exchange information electronically. This model provides a scalable environment for Web development, where the site owner can start with minimal investments, utilizing the Web for connectivity, and upgrade components of the plan as the online business grows.

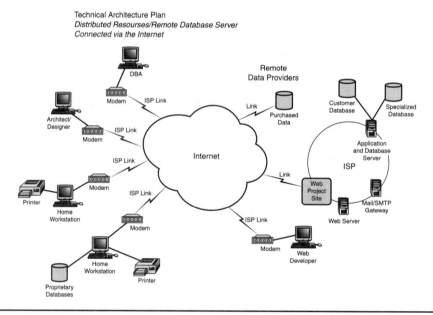

Figure 6.5   The Technical Architecture Plan is based on
the Web template for flexible connectivity.

Team connectivity is provided through a project site, which is housed at the hosting service provider. Team members connect with dial-up and modem connections for access to the Internet. The project site allows for iterative development, with security set up to keep the site private during development stages.

Check-in and check-out of site components can be controlled through the development software's version-control features. An on-site administrator controls installation and update procedures for the team, managing the architectural tiers of Web server, application server, and back-end databases. Some of the site's data is purchased and updates are sent electronically through the Web, with a database update strategy put in place for the synchronization of data-oriented events.

Benefits and Consequences

The following benefits and possible consequences should be considered when selecting the Web template as a solution:

- Relational—Enables flexibility for changes
- Analysis of complex network routing
- Enables services to choose more than one possible path
- Webs are sensitive and encompassing

Relational—Enables Flexibility for Changes

One asset of integration templates is that they enable us to transport valuable integration patterns into organizational forms so they can be supported fully at the organizational level. For instance, the Web is the most relational of the templates. Relational design has been providing benefits to technical design for some years now by enabling flexible design and rapid adaptation of changes.

However, these benefits can be curtailed so that the application of relational technology is not as helpful as we might think. When relational technology is managed within a hierarchical structure, that structure tends to defeat the purpose of the relational technology. In such cases, the managerial process of changing a database is highly structured and formal, with layers of approval and signoff required. Thus, the flexibility in the database design is severely limited by much lesser flexibility in the organizational design.

The Web integration model can be applied to the design of support organizations so that the process followed by those groups is as flexible as the technology they support. Then the time it takes to modify a relational database won't be inflated by the time it takes to process a change request (acquire the needed approvals and signoff, and so forth) and users can enjoy the rapid response times promised when investing in new technology.

Analysis of Complex Network Routing

Models utilizing arcs and endpoints give us the graphical means of developing designs for handling complexity. Network routing algorithms can be both complex and volatile, requiring the ability to change configurations on-the-fly. One source of EAI issues is the inflexible way that configuration of routing paths is embedded in legacy systems.

At one client's site, the EAI project had a goal of enabling the provisioning of high capacity services to better flow through the automated provisioning processes. The flow had been interrupted by network element configurations that were outside the capacity of the operational support system to manage. These configurations were considered incorrect by the software, but in the real world, for various reasons, they were implemented all the time. Some examples included the hardwiring of connections between cable pairs, repeaters, and multiplexers located in fiber hubs, controlled-environment vaults, remote terminals, central offices, and some customer premise locations. The resulting system storage of incomplete information caused unnecessary rework by various system designers in the provisioning of services to customers.

The EAI systems designed to pull out and correct network inventory so that the legacy systems could manage it, relied on integration models using the Web template for their pattern. With the visual representation of the complex connections and configurations of network elements, members of the software development team who were not well-versed in telecommunications concepts could better understand the requirements.

Enables Services to Choose More than One Possible Path

Rigid hierarchical models and those locked into grid formats don't enable the fuzzy selection logic of multiple paths. The Web template enables asymmetrical joining of nodes and connectors. One of the requirements of network design is the redundant support of connections, so that if one path fails, another can be substituted to provide uninterrupted service. The asymmetrical modeling capabilities of the Web template enable us to represent this redundant support.

Webs Are Sensitive and Encompassing

This point can be both a benefit and a drawback. Webs can tend to amplify the effects of occurrences in one portion of the network so that they affect the entire network. Computer hackers take advantage of this reality, navigating between networked devices to carry out vandalism across multiple connected sites. The connectivity actually facilitates their activities, giving them access to sites where they can interrupt customer service or steal information.

On the other hand, one well-placed connection can transform all the other connections. Alliance marketing programs utilize this benefit of networked connectivity. The addition of one new connection extends the reach of all the existing points in the network, and can lead to rapid growth through distribution.

Webs can grow to encompass and surround; thus they can be supportive, or you can get caught in them. They can generate a unified field of resonance, and they can amplify the positive or the negative of that resonance.

Template Realization

In the case of the organizational analysis shown in Figure 6.3, the goal of the project was to build an integrated test management platform, automating the configuration of all test equipment through the access to an equipment inventory database. This very large Oracle database stored equipment inventory information down to the level of IP address for each element. Therefore it could be used to provide address and port information for equipment configuration using vendor-provided software.

The team went from the Web template-based organization model to using the Flow template to model the processes that were performed by each of the organizational units defined in the model. Data flows were analyzed, CRUD (create, read, update, delete) matrices developed, and data requirements versus sources were established. Then data elements could be defined for each of the databases that supported the flow-through of data. The team was able to provide a comprehensive picture to the database administration group for fields to be added to the inventory database.

The information gathered in process designs was also used to create models that illustrated several possible options for implementation of the automated process. As the options were clarified, the implementation models formed the basis of a vendor request for proposal. Vendors benefited from having a clear picture of the requirements, specified in detail, and the company benefited from receiving very specific estimates based on the detailed requirements.

In the later example of the Internet project, the Technical Architecture Plan became a deliverable in the business plan and estimate for building the Web site in question. Resource plans were tied to the architecture selection, including both human and technology resources such as servers, workstations, and ISP hosting.

EAI Applications

The web is a stabilizing connector. Stabilization allows for local variations without demanding standardization. EAI operates outside the usual structure by crossing application boundaries, political boundaries, and vertical divisions. Without the support of the usual structure, it is important to find mechanisms to bring stability and strength.

EAI introduces webs as stabilizing connectors in such forms as the social network, an online bulletin board, and a listserv or community of experts. Learning networks, alliances, and partnerships are also utilized by EAI projects to introduce support.

The Web template, with its applications in network and platform configuration, is ideal for the EAI purpose of providing a unified interface to legacy systems. It can help sort out the tangles in the web of connections, modeling the platform configuration in use by legacy applications for clarity. The Web template's capability to manage the complexity of multiple connections also makes it useful in illustrating difficult concepts for data and process definitions. Some specific EAI examples follow:

- Legacy systems model
- Online learning networks

Legacy Systems Model

A payroll services bureau needed to streamline their existing systems environment before applying a massive software upgrade. The first objective was to get arms around the existing systems and to understand how they could all be brought up to the new standards. The location of these legacy systems affected the company's capability to support their integration, and a way was needed to analyze the infrastructure across the geographic picture.

The team collected data on attributes such as operating system release, local software modifications, and specific applications supported locally. All these factors had consequences for the project's goals of integrating the disparate applications. The Web model seen in Figure 6.6 was used to design a survey of the legacy systems and their attributes.

The survey collected data to scope the integration project and direct development of the project's action plan. A sample of the narrative survey that accompanies the Web model is shown here:

Location: State name

Operations center name

Operations center ID

Type of system (check one):

Supports infrastructure   ___

Supports doing business   ___

Services customers   ___

Enables external communications   ___

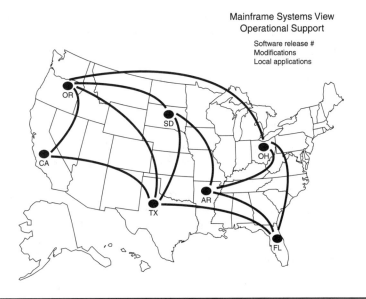

Figure 6.6 The Web model supporting a survey of legacy systems and their attributes for an integration project.

List the following:

- Hardware
- Firmware
- Operating system
- Packaged software
- Software modifications
- Application software
- Data bases
- Archived data
- Data aging criteria
- System interfaces
- Electronic data exchanges
- Screen display & reports
- Electronic commerce protocols
- Serial number

A redesign phase sought out best practices and propagated them across the sites. Using a combination of a map like that shown in Figure 6.6 and the narrative survey, EAI projects can better understand the scope of the effort involved and develop plans for upgrades and introduction of unifying software applications. When the networking exists for an intranet implementation, a map such as this can be utilized, with Web technology, to provide a clickable front end to the survey form, with the ongoing maintenance process facilitated by the company intranet.

Online Learning Networks

Online learning networks are revolutionizing education. In his book, *A Pattern Language*, Christopher Alexander anticipates this development in his section on the network of learning: "In a society which emphasizes teaching, children and students—and adults—become passive and unable to think or act for themselves. Creative, active individuals can only grow up in a society which emphasizes learning instead of teaching" [6.3]. He goes on to recommend a radically decentralized network that provides access to all the resources for learning. Writing before the Internet had made his vision a reality, Alexander envisioned the possibilities that today are beginning to unfold.

The model in Figure 6.7 is part of the business case for an online portal providing education on health care choices. It utilizes the Web template to build a model of access to resources for educational purposes.

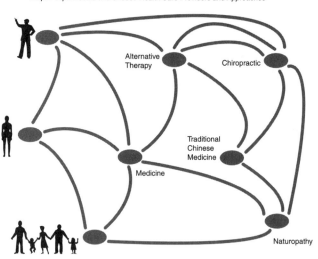

Mapping Health Care Systems and their Relationships
Helps People Locate and Choose Health Care Providers and Approaches

Figure 6.7   An online health care portal uses the Web template to build a model of access to resources.

The use of the Web pattern places the emphasis on the interconnections between health systems. This emphasis supports an active approach of individual and ongoing learning as opposed to the passive approach of teaching. The online portal helps to provide the main ingredient for active learning approaches—the access to a dynamic, ever-growing and expanding network of resources.

Templates That Work Well with the Web Template

The Web template combines well with

- The Ring template
- The Cell template

The Ring Template

The model in Figure 6.8 shows the Web template combined with the Ring template to model data warehouse access both internally through an intranet and externally for customers and suppliers through a gateway to the Internet. New integration models like this one depict the architecture for implementing customer access and supply chain management strategies.

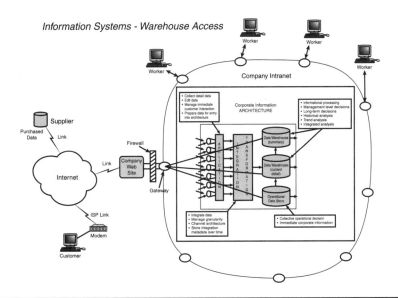

Figure 6.8   This model combines the Web template and the Ring template for giving all parties integrated access to a company's data warehouse.

Other reasons to combine the Web and Ring templates include depicting how a company will tie local area networks to the overall data network, and hybrid designs where some connections are established using a decentralized ring of devices and some connections are Web based. Hybrid centralization and decentralization strategies are useful in combining functions to achieve economies of scale, where identical or analogous processes or equipment in multiple versions exist.

The Cell Template

The Cell model supports modeling of categorization and compartmentalization, especially in the analysis of distribution systems. Whereas the Cell models the compartments, the Web template can depict their distribution through a network or any mapped terrain. Combining these two templates provides for both the separation and the combining of categories such as subject areas, channels, and data subsets.

7

The Flow Template

Template Description

The Flow template is utilized by process and flow analysis to trace the course of information, goods, services, and communications. The template is shown in Figure 7.1.

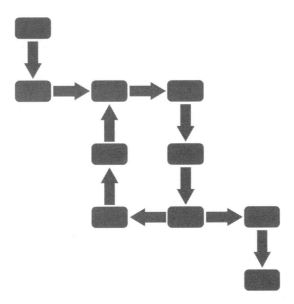

Figure 7.1 The Flow template.

Template Discussion

Flow tends to gain momentum, picking up resources as it goes along. The flow of water carves a path, which becomes broader and deeper over time. In the study of traffic flow, governing structures become important. The application of triggers and devices that manage and streamline the flow of processes are introduced.

The integration goals of the Flow template include the reduction of complexity and reconciliation between multiple steps. Flow analysis can help to minimize the number of interconnections and interfaces in order to reduce cost. It can support the reconfiguration and reordering of process steps to reflect concurrent process execution and dependencies. Flow analysis can also surface the need to eliminate or relocate intermediate steps that add little value to the process.

For example, in a data-warehousing environment, the aggregation of data for reports can become a bottleneck that slows query and reporting time frames to unacceptable intervals. A flow analysis might suggest that the aggregation of data be removed from the time frame in which that data is selected using queries and accessed in reports. The model in Figure 7.2 shows that analysis.

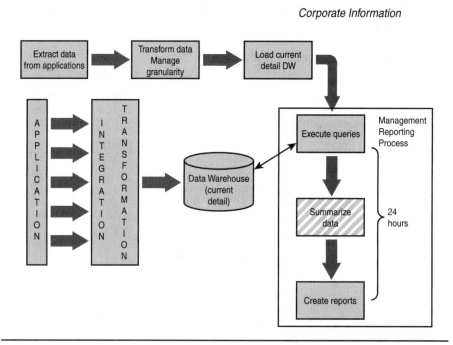

Figure 7.2   An analysis of corporate information flows reveals that data summarization slows query and reporting time frames.

The desired changes can be accomplished by building summary tables at an earlier point in the processing cycle. Figure 7.3 shows relocation of the data summarization step.

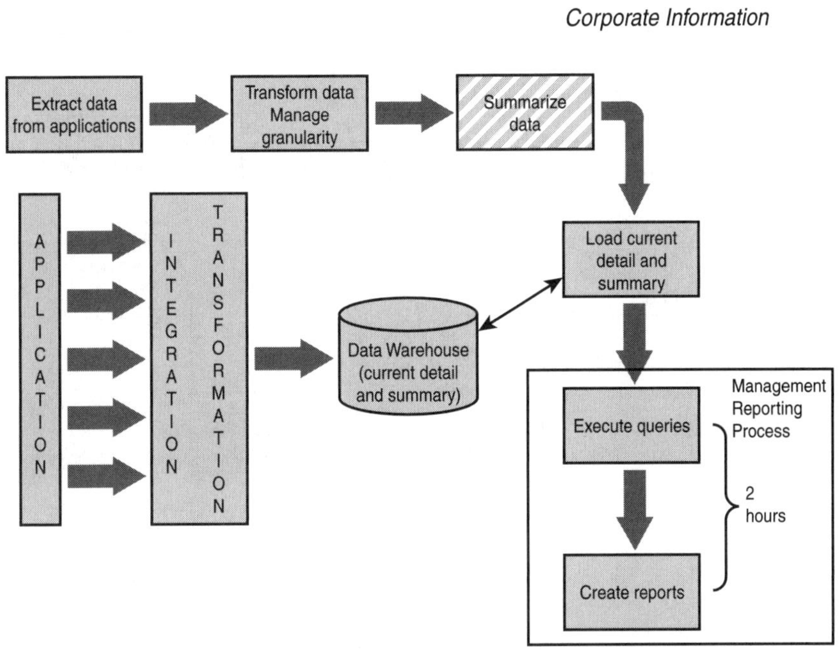

Figure 7.3   Data is summarized earlier in the processing cycle to shorten the time frame required for queries and reports.

Relocating the activity of summarizing data for reporting from the query and reporting time frame to the earlier step in the overall process removes it from the critical path of management reporting. Response times for database reporting are also shortened considerably by this improvement.

When the Flow Template Applies

The Flow template can be applied to the following situations:

- Workflow analysis
- Data Flow analysis
- Business process improvement
- Customer scenarios
- Identification of variances

Workflow Analysis

Workflow analysis is a specialized application of the flow template. With the addition of defined notation to depict specific information about a workflow object's characteristics and metrics, it can be the basis for mapping the activities in a given flow of tasks. The sample model shown in Figure 7.4 shows the analysis of a telesales operator's workflow.

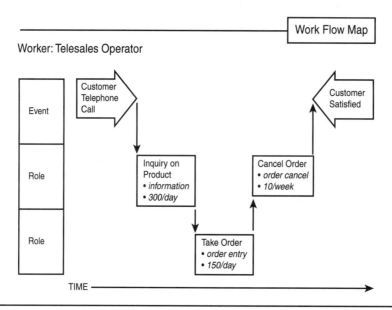

Figure 7.4   This Work Flow map uses the basic Flow template
with additional notation for workflow analysis.

The objective of workflow analysis is to gather and organize relevant information about activities. This information is used to define application requirements and to redesign the core process or business function.

Workflow analysis is performed after an overall core process has been defined, but before the new application is designed. Its purpose is to capture the essential features of each activity as quickly and economically as possible, noting the complexities and redundancies of the way the activity must be performed with the current business process.

Data Flow Analysis

The Data Flow diagram (DFD) is a familiar part of the necessary process modeling for application development. It allows you to capture business rules for data entities and the dependencies between data entities. Data Flow diagrams model the inputs to an activity, its outputs, and the information that is stored at various points in the process.

They show the flow of data between processes from the point of view of the data, including the possible paths for navigating that flow between data entities. They do not show the path that will be selected, the flow of control, or the start and end points. Data Flow models are developed to model the following views:

- Business activities from the point of view of the business process owner
- System requirements from the view of the owner of the automated system
- System implementation from the view of the designer of the automated system

Data that has been defined through data flow diagramming is then represented in the entity relationship diagram for database design and development. Processes are clarified by the use of data flow diagrams, and subsequent models break them down into defined components and activity diagrams.

Business Process Improvement

A process improvement project at an employment services firm used the Flow template to redesign the business process for one of their core processes, the outsourcing of project staffing. The resulting business process model is shown in Figure 7.5.

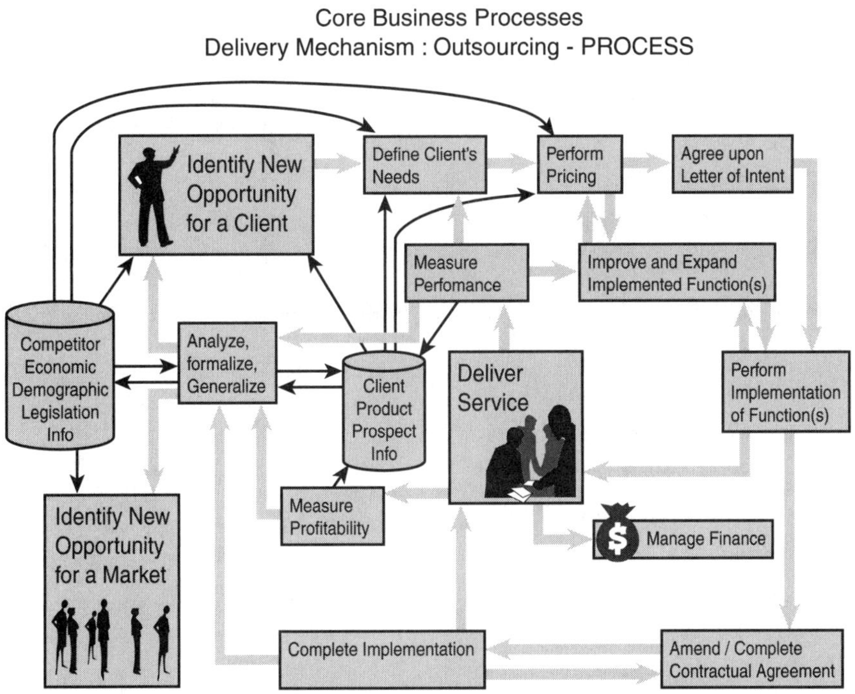

Figure 7.5 The target model for outsourcing uses the Flow template to depict the core business process.

To surface and formalize the "best practices" in this company's outsourcing business, the Flow model does the following:

- Describes the flow of activities
- Defines information needed for decision support
- Describes tasks that must be performed

The high-level Flow model is utilized to avoid leveling issues in order to improve presentation of the concepts involved in supporting this core process. The redesigned processes will be propagated throughout the company's franchise.

Customer Scenarios

The design for an alternative health care Web site utilizes the following visitor scenario, which details the demographic profile for one type of customer who is expected to visit the site. The scenario lists a set of typical visitor actions for this type of customer. Scenarios such as this one are helpful in usability design of Web sites.

Visitor Scenario #1:

Visitor Profile:

Baby Boomer—Professional (living anywhere)

Visitor Actions (Session 1):

Typically logs on at work during lunch break.

- *Read email.*
- *Check stocks.*
- *Read WSJ Online.*
- *Visit Excite!*

Any of the above could be a *point of entry*, bringing the visitor to the *Choose Health* Web site.

- *Enter Choose Health Web site.*
- *Check on current news.*
- *Search for specific health concern.*
- *Perform search in California, at the state level.*
- *Get list of providers.*
- *Visit provider home pages.*

- *Go to provider selection questions.*
- *Return to provider home page.*
- *Find out which health topics have news.*
- *Go to the provider's discussion group.*
- *Return to provider page.*
- *Select a provider for a particular health issue.*
- *Add provider name to his/her personal health plan.*
- *Save health plan (will return and add more later).*
- *Bookmark site and return to work.*

Visitor Actions (Session 2):

Logs on in the evening, at home computer.

- *Return to Choose Health Web site.*
- *Retrieve personal health plan.*
- *Continue to next portion of the health plan.*
- *Visit provider's home pages.*
- *Check provider's calendar of events.*
- *Select an event.*
- *Go to site of event sponsor.*
- *Exit.*

The visitor scenario provides the basis for the flow analysis captured in the customer scenario model shown in Figure 7.6.

Using the Flow template to develop a visual model helps the designer to focus on the dynamics of the customer scenario, and to determine which steps of the process should be facilitated with navigational cues. It also helps determine the desired path to encourage the visitor to stay and interact with the system. The undesired path is the one that leads to premature exit, and indicates a need for visual cues to the visitor that remind him to bookmark the site or give instructions for returning without interruption.

Other Flow models will help the designer identify actions a visitor can take that will require special controls to provide for session continuity (state management). Session controls will be activated when the visitor wants to save the work accomplished in one session and return to it at a later date. The model in Figure 7.7 shows the requirements in visitor scenario #2.

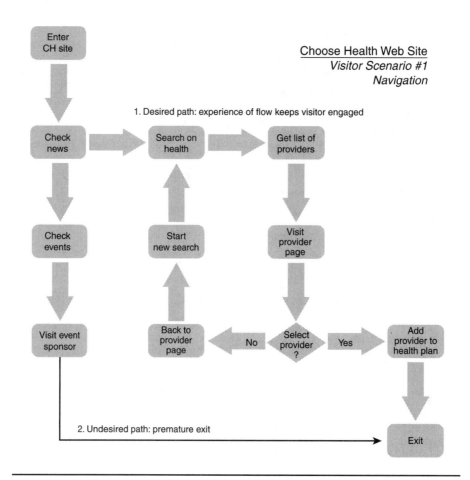

Figure 7.6   This Web site used the Flow template to model a customer scenario as the basis for usability design.

Visitor Scenario #2:

Visitor Profile:

Baby Boomer—Professional (living anywhere)

Visitor Actions (Session 1):

Typically logs on at work during lunch break.

- *Read email.*
- *Check stocks.*
- *Read WSJ Online.*
- *Visit Excite!*

Any of the above could be a *point of entry*, bringing visitor to the *Choose Health* Web site.

- *Enter Choose Health Web site.*
- *Search for specific health concern.*
- *Perform search in California, at the state level.*
- *Get list of providers.*
- *Visit provider home pages.*
- *Go to provider selection questions.*
- *Return to provider home page.*
- *Find out which health topics have news.*
- *Go to the provider's discussion group.*
- *Return to provider page.*
- *Select a provider for a particular health issue.*
- *Add provider name to his/her personal health plan.*
- *Is personal health plan complete?*
- *If yes,*
    - *Save health plan.*
    - *Print health plan.*
    - *Exit.*
- *If no, does visitor want to continue?*
- *If no, save health plan.*
    - *Bookmark site and return to work.*
- *If yes, return to Choose Health Web site.*
- *Choose next action.*

In this case, the Flow model depicts decisions the visitor can make that will activate the need for session control actions such as saving files, storing visitor information, updating cookies, and so forth. A decision to leave without completing a personal health plan will result in actions that allow the visitor to resume his research where he left it when he returns for another visit. When the plan is complete, the visitor can save the plan for future reference and optionally print a copy, an action that transfers him to a printer-friendly version of the plan. The visitor can also decide to continue interacting with the site even though a plan is complete, in which case the scenario closes on the "choose next action" step.

Models such as these provide the business requirements which are the basis for technical design documents that take the specifications to more detailed levels.

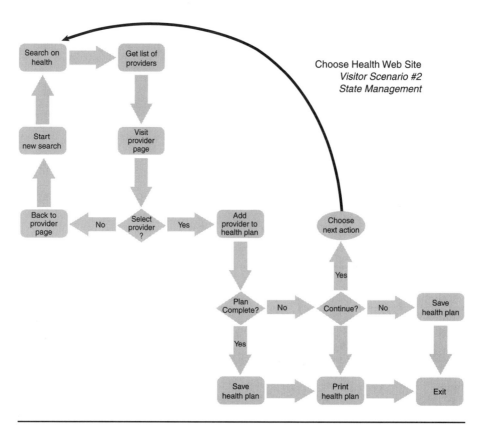

Figure 7.7   Another Flow model helps the designer focus on
the requirements for state management.

Identification of Variances

One purpose of charting the flow of a process is to turn up the variations in the
process. These can be necessary variations on a theme, in which case they will be provided for by integration, or they can be variances, which are unnecessary departures.
In the case of variances, measures can be put in place to ensure they are discontinued.

Often, the identification of variances gives us a clue as to where integration efforts
need to focus. Local variations on a process can point up actual differences in the
requirements. If the views that create the variances are strongly held, they can indicate
new requirements. That possibility should always be considered, especially when the
differences seem to defy resolution.

For example, a quality project undertaken at a bank a few years ago turned up differences in the development process as conducted by two different teams in the IS

department. One team, the Deposit Transaction Accounting (DTA) team, was responsible for supporting the systems that store checking accounts, and the other, the Marketing Information Systems (MIS) team, was responsible for the marketing applications. The two teams had a significant difference in their definition of the precision required to pass the Quality Analysis (QA) review step of the system installation process.

The DTA team held that nothing short of 100% accuracy was required for QA approval and passing the review step. The MIS team felt that 97% or even 95% accuracy was sometimes an acceptable margin for installing a system to production. As it turned out, both were right. For checking accounts, every penny must be accounted for at all times. But for the purposes of marketing, 95% of the desired information delivered today was far superior to 100% of the desired information that might be delivered six months from now (which is how long it would have taken to achieve 100% accuracy).

The difference in doing business between DTA and MIS became the basis for a significant requirement in the new quality process. That requirement stated that the methodology selected to support the quality process must be customizable to meet the needs of differing applications.

Examples

The following examples explore the applications of the Flow template:

- Service delivery process
- Provisioning process
- Document Imaging applications

Service Delivery Process

The Flow diagram is used to model the steps involved in one of the core business processes for an employment services firm. Service delivery was analyzed for the purposes of building requirements for the enterprise resource-planning package that would support the process in the future. The model shown in Figure 7.8 depicts the steps of the process for delivery of temporary help to client companies.

The target model builds in information about data required by the processes, and introduces performance and profitability measurements according to a separate measurement plan. One innovation discovered in producing this model is that services delivered in the field should be mined for new market opportunities on an ongoing basis. Captured in the model shown in Figure 7.8, this practice was propagated throughout the organization with the help of the Flow models.

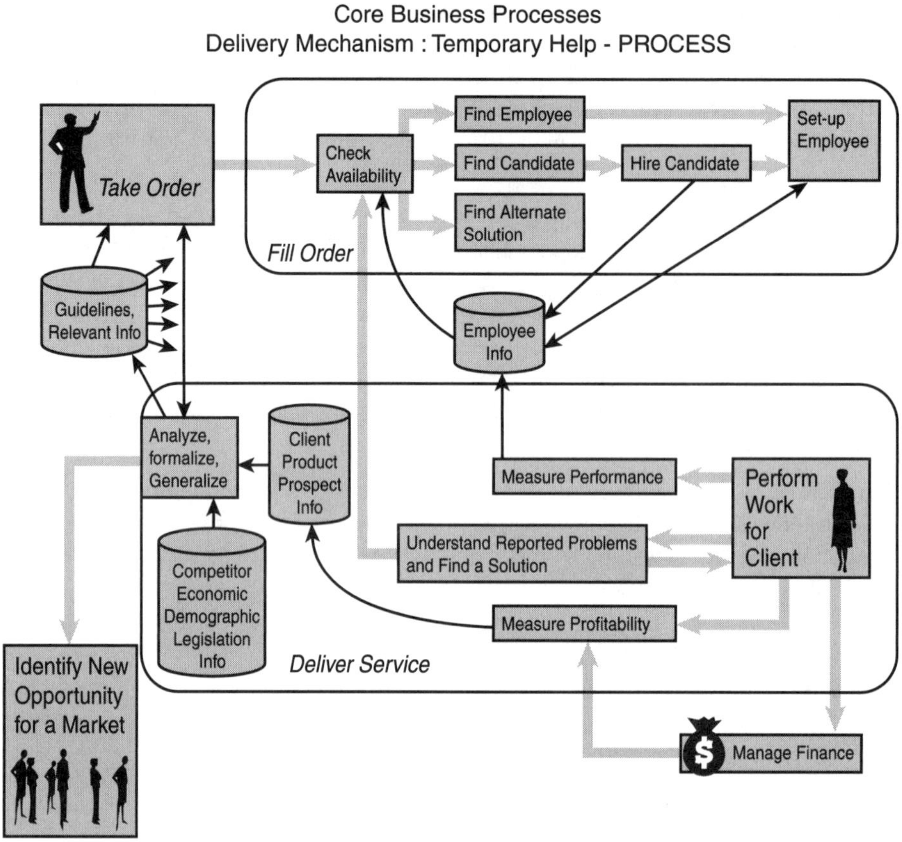

Figure 7.8 The Flow template is used to define the steps of the temporary help service delivery process.

Provisioning Process

Shown in Figure 7.9, the Flow template models the business process of provisioning at a telecommunications service provider. This information was utilized by the project developing an integrated test management platform. The integrated platform required that all components of the information needed to configure a piece of equipment into the network be available online and stored in a database for automatic retrieval. The process analysis was used to determine the content of each component of data, based on how it was used in the process.

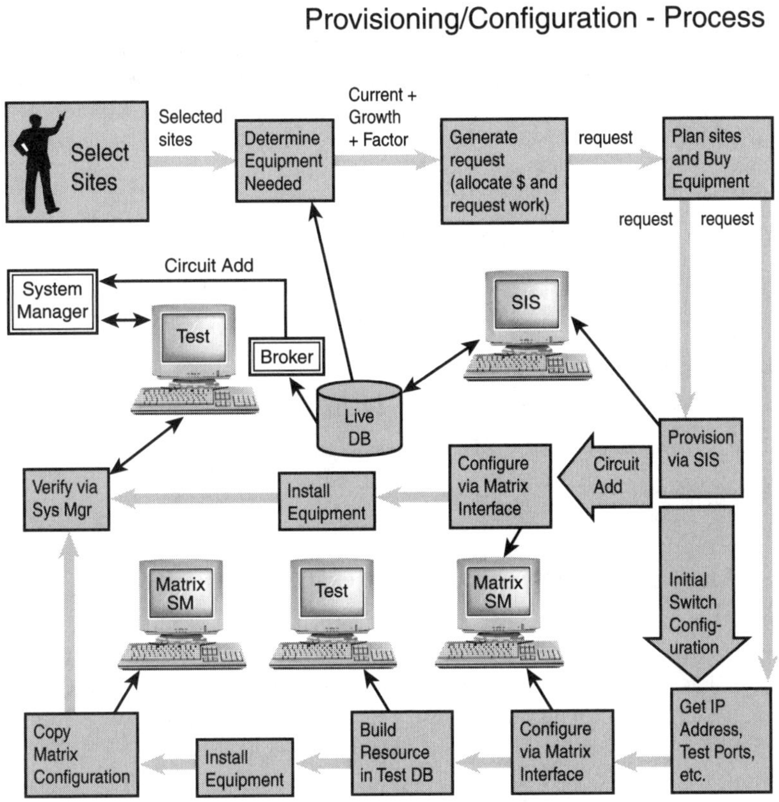

Provisioning/Configuration - Process

Figure 7.9   The Flow template is used to clarify the steps of the provisioning process for the design of an integrated test management platform.

After all the occurrences of data updates, changes, and deletes were identified, the information could be consolidated and entity relationship diagrams produced for database design updates. Changes were then requested from the database administration group, so that the inventory database could support the requirements of the improved process.

Document Imaging Applications

Two basic steps exist in document imaging for storage and retrieval. The simpler step is the reproduction of current document filing systems in electronic media. This procedure relies upon scanning technology and storage systems for its successful implementation. The other step, typically occurring after the electronic duplication of files, involves intervening on existing business process to integrate document management software. The configuration of document management software depends on first gaining an understanding of the flow of documents in the context of business process.

For instance, in an insurance agency, the storage of policy files represents a basic requirement fulfilled by electronic reproduction. Claims correspondence and new policy handling are processes that can be modeled to support the integration of document management. The Flow template helps to map the steps required, with its focus on sequential process.

Benefits and Consequences

The following benefits and/or possible consequences should be considered when selecting the Flow template as a solution:

- Linear analysis for discrete steps
- Clarifies duplication or proliferation of unnecessary steps
- Clarifies interfaces and use of related repositories
- Suggests streamlining options

Linear Analysis for Discrete Steps

When a linear analysis is called for, the Flow template provides a format for defining the step-by-step activities of a process. Linear analysis is the mainstay of computer system design. Flow charts are one of the oldest techniques for breaking out the components of a system and charting their chain of command. Sequential processing is at the heart of many programming tasks, applying program logic one step at a time. The Flow template supports the visual modeling of this chaining of activities so that the activities can be studied, realigned, compartmentalized, and so forth.

Clarifies Duplication/Proliferation of Unnecessary Steps

When the Flow model is used to analyze a process flow, it helps illustrate which steps can be eliminated or combined to make a more concise and integrated process. Figure 7.10 shows this use of flow modeling.

The example shows a flow analysis indicating that a number of steps could be consolidated to make a process more efficient. Flow modeling is used to illustrate the concept of this solution to certain integration problems.

Clarifies Interfaces and Use of Related Repositories

When you chart the steps of a business or system process with Flow models, you make their structure explicit and therefore available. As you gain a clear picture of that structure, you can begin to fit in the other components that are required to make it operational. The interfaces between functions become clear, and the use of related repositories is spelled out in detail at each step of the process.

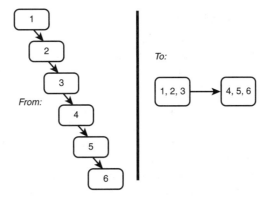

Figure 7.10   The Flow template is used to model the consolidation
of steps for an integrated process.

Suggests Streamlining Options

Flow models can be used to analyze process steps and to determine when some steps
can be run in parallel and what dependencies exist between steps. For example, in
Figure 7.11, the flow is redesigned from sequential to concurrent processing.

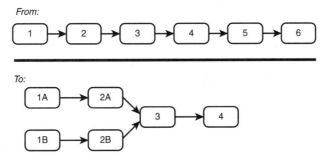

Figure 7.11   The Flow model is used to help streamline a process
by running certain steps concurrently.

Concurrent processing models shorten the time frames for system execution, development cycles, and other situations where running steps in parallel is feasible. Streamlining processes, combined with automation of the resulting steps, can lead to major
reductions in business process cycle times, which translate to retained customers and
significant cost improvements.

Template Realization

Flow models can be translated into technical models such as data flow diagrams, activity and collaboration diagrams, and entity relationship diagrams. Customer scenarios such as those seen in Figures 7.6 and 7.7 provide a basis for technical requirements documents, which lead to program specifications.

When Flow models are used to depict business process improvements, they can be implemented on the business side by changes that are applied to market positioning, business models, and action plans. Because flow models implement linear analysis for breaking out the components of a process, it is advisable to couple them with other integration models that support synthesis and are more context-oriented. Depending on the goals of a project, the separating influence of the Flow model can need to be tempered by the unifying properties of other templates.

For example, when the Flow model is combined with the Seed, it describes a process facilitated by a coordinating intermediary. Introducing that coordinator pulls the steps together and gives them a focal point for a much more integrated process.

EAI Applications

Flow is about developing channels. Flow smoothes and carves the landscape as it introduces changes gradually. It is a structure of incremental improvements and the occasional radical shift. One way to build a flow is to put the supporting pipeline in place first, and then allow data to flow through. Another, more organic way to build a flow is to start with the flow of data and let it carve out a path, which is then reinforced and institutionalized. Ad hoc reporting combined with analysis of the requests follows this style of operating when it monitors user requests for ad hoc reports and identifies the requests that are repeated, indicating a favorite report or shared data reporting requirements. It then moves those favorite and repeated reports into production as canned reports and delivers them on a predetermined schedule. The flow of reporting, in this case, is allowed to precede the definition of the reporting structure.

Governance mechanisms are introduced by flow analysis to harness the flow of information, goods, and services. EAI requires new channels that occur outside the box. Sometimes information must flow outside of the company, to customers and suppliers. At other times, new information flows into the company, such as customer information gathered online. Flow analysis can help determine how to secure both internal and external information in an increasingly complex environment.

EAI introduces flow in customer scenarios for Web design, resource flow in supplier management, and building secured channels of information. Its marketing applications include the modeling of market channels, new market analysis, and customer retention (stopping customer runoff). Some specific EAI examples follow:

- Marketing Data Mart
- Enterprise Resource Planning

Marketing Data Mart

A marketing department used the Flow model to define the process for developing and marketing products and services. The model in Figure 7.12 defines the requirements for the marketing data mart, based on how the business process will use the information.

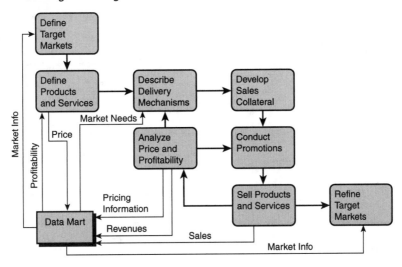

Business Functions: Develop and Market Products and Services
Utilizing Marketing Data Mart

Figure 7.12   The Flow model helped identify the requirements for a Marketing Data Mart by modeling the process of developing and marketing products and services.

As the control flows from one step to the next, the data requirements are clarified by data flows that depict the information required by the business process. Subsequent models will drill down for more detail on the steps of the process, and technical models will be developed to specify the data attributes and their relationships for the data mart. The required data will then be extracted from the corporate data warehouse on a regular basis to be housed in the marketing-specific data mart.

Enterprise Resource Planning

The Flow template was used to help determine requirements and significant integration challenges for an ERP implementation in a staffing company. The model in Figure 7.13 depicts the flow of steps involved in recruiting workforce professionals.

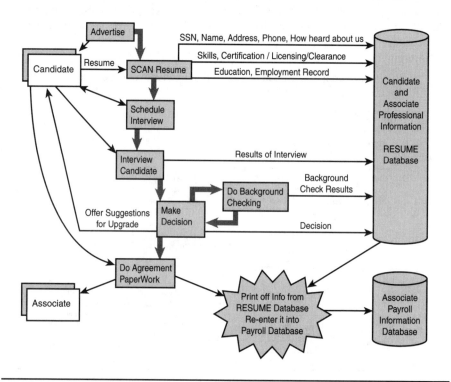

Process Breakdown Map for Staffing Business Functions
RECRUIT WORKFORCE - Professionals - Current Challenges

Figure 7.13   The Flow model defines the steps involved
in recruiting workforce professionals.

Use of flow analysis helped this ERP redesign and planning team determine the variances in process and the current challenges for workforce recruiting. Data integration analysis indicated that under the current process, employees had to print information from one database and re-enter it into another database. Data sharing became a significant requirement for the ERP implementation.

Templates That Work Well with the Flow Template

The Flow template combines well with

- The Cycle template.
- The Seed template.
- The Tree template.

The Cycle Template

Flow combines process steps with similar content. When flow analysis is applied to the study of circulation of goods, services, and data, it can be combined with the Cycle template to factor in timing considerations. It also supports the repetition of certain steps within a process, for iterative processes.

The Seed Template

When the steps of a process can be coordinated by a caseworker or by a shared database, the Seed template combines with the Flow template to model their integration. Process steps produce deliverables that flow into the core component, which collects and transforms them for later use in subsequent steps.

The Tree Template

Flows can come together to create channels, or separate to create a distribution tree. When a flow multiplies into a range of smaller flows, the resulting decomposition can be depicted by a combination of Flow and Tree models.

8

The Wave Template

Template Description

The Wave model (see Figure 8.1) is used to describe the layers of a system, environment, or network. Separating the layers helps manage their complexity. Waves occur at intervals and with frequency and modulation. Waves ripple out, and can carry information, impulses, and messages. Waves are a medium of transport. In nature, waves wear away the rough edges; they erode and soften.

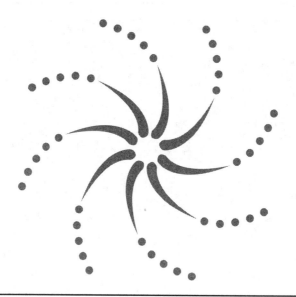

Figure 8.1   The Wave template.

Template Discussion

The integration goals of the Wave template include supporting layered architectures, tiered access strategies, and product versioning. Waves can help integrate identical or analogous processes that occur in multiple versions in order to achieve the combined benefits of economy of scale and customer focus. They can help delineate the boundaries of business processes in order to evaluate whether or not to move them. A company might choose to move a boundary to encompass a customer or supplier, allowing them to be included in the company's process in new ways. Such inclusion can help eliminate errors because of miscommunication and can prevent or lessen delays and service capacity problems. Or a company might want to take on work for customers or suppliers that they would normally perform for themselves. The company can add more valuable services in this way, such as consulting or product delivery, and thereby optimize the overall process for both parties.

For example, the traditional shopper performs the following steps:

1. Go to a store.
2. Select articles for purchase.
3. Complete a purchase transaction.
4. Convey the purchased items back to the home.

In this four-step process, the store is responsible for interacting on the second and third steps, and the customer carries out the first and fourth steps independently. When a store provides delivery services, it extends its boundary on the fourth step of the process, and if the store goes online, shoppers can visit from home, thereby extending the boundary on the first step as well.

On the other hand, in some cases the customer will take responsibility for more of the steps in a business process, alleviating the need to wait in line or interact extensively with service personnel. A familiar example is the self-service automated teller machine (ATM) at a bank. Banking institutions have lessened their customer service overhead extensively by providing self-service ATMS on every corner. Customers can lessen their wait in the teller line by visiting a convenient ATM.

When the Wave Template Applies

The Wave template can be applied to the following situations:

- N-tier architecture
- Specification of product versioning
- Design for cooperation and synergy

N-Tier Architecture

The Wave model is useful in depicting any number of architecture tiers. It helps separate out the layers and assign technical components and component responsibility accordingly. In n-tier architecture, it is possible to have many configurations of physical tiers. An example might include a desktop client PC, Web server, application server, database server, and access to legacy systems residing on the mainframe or other platforms. The model in Figure 8.2 shows a typical layering of n-tier architecture.

In this model, every layer of the Wave model is assigned to a role or function. Within each layer are the mechanisms employed to deliver that role or function. The client PC delivers the presentation layer. An application server delivers application functionality, and data management is provided by the data server. Mainframe systems provide access to legacy applications. The Wave model provides a visual representation that pulls the various mechanisms together as one.

The Wave template is carried forward into subsequent models to depict platform and technology decisions by component and layer, clarifying the planned deployment of the required technology.

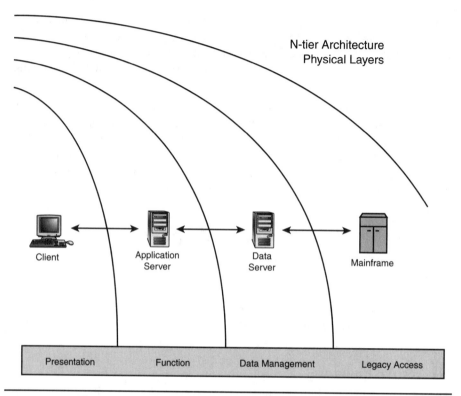

Figure 8.2   The Wave template provides the basis for modeling the n-tier architecture with multiple physical layers.

Specification of Product Versioning

Product versioning is the practice of offering successive versions of a product, ranging from a bare-bones model to premium versions that incorporate additional features. Some producers start with the basic model and add on, whereas others start by building a full-featured model and subtracting features for customers with fewer needs.

The Wave model, where layers indicate the version and specify its parameters, can support the analysis of features to include at different price points. The modeling helps you handle the complexity of product versioning by presenting the entire spectrum on one page. For example, Figure 8.3 shows the versioning scheme for Web hosting services for a typical commercial Internet service provider.

The first wave on the Hosting Categories model illustrates the features and pricing included in basic shared services. Second are those for premium shared, and then dedicated server and dedicated server with extra options. This instance of the Wave template utilizes the familiar table-like structure to organize the content of the model. However, the Wave is a flexible structure that can be used to illustrate more complex information in addition to the straightforward application shown here, as subsequent examples will show.

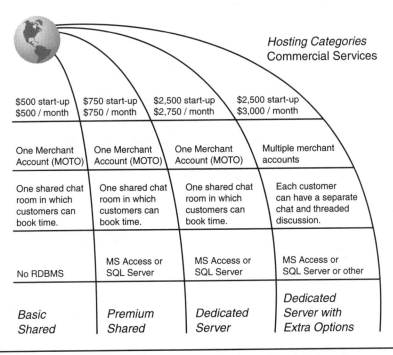

	Hosting Categories		
	Commercial Services		
$500 start-up $500 / month	$750 start-up $750 / month	$2,500 start-up $2,750 / month	$2,500 start-up $3,000 / month
One Merchant Account (MOTO)	One Merchant Account (MOTO)	One Merchant Account (MOTO)	Multiple merchant accounts
One shared chat room in which customers can book time.	One shared chat room in which customers can book time.	One shared chat room in which customers can book time.	Each customer can have a separate chat and threaded discussion.
No RDBMS	MS Access or SQL Server	MS Access or SQL Server	MS Access or SQL Server or other
Basic Shared	*Premium Shared*	*Dedicated Server*	*Dedicated Server with Extra Options*

Figure 8.3   Hosting Categories model illustrates the versioning scheme of a typical commercial Internet Services Provider.

Design for Cooperation and Synergy

The model in Figure 8.4 was developed during a reengineering project for a software vendor. Its layers consist of the approaches and attitudes that must change in support of the new way of doing business that the reengineering project will introduce.

This plan was part of the company's design for cooperation and synergy between not only the technical components but also between people in the cultural arena. Integration projects, like reengineering projects, often introduce significant waves of cultural change that must be managed if the overall project is to succeed. The Wave template can help to map out the expected waves and set out strategies for handling them.

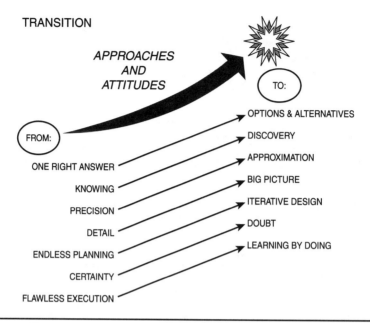

Figure 8.4   The transition model lays out the changes in approach and attitude that a reengineering project will introduce.

Examples

The following examples explore the applications of the Wave template:

- Data network layers
- Spectrum of services
- Tiered access plan

Data Network Layers

As you saw in Chapter 2, "Introduction to Integration Models," a cellular company used the Wave model to define the layers of a data network for the Y2K inventory analysis. The model is repeated in Figure 8.5 for the sake of convenience.

Use of the Wave template in this case allowed the data engineers to use their own terminology to describe their environment, and then to organize the information so that other non-engineering groups could understand it as well. This example illustrates the difference between the accommodating Wave model and the inflexible Table (which is also a type of layered model). The Wave could be said to be a free-form Table structure, providing greater flexibility.

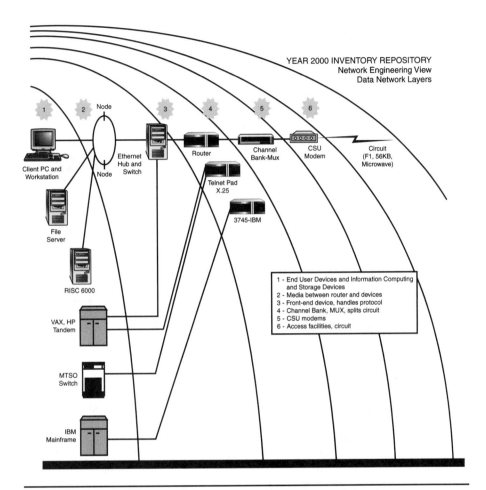

Figure 8.5   A cellular company's Y2K analysis used the Wave template to define the layers of the data network.

Spectrum of Services

The marketing group at a staffing firm agreed that their service offerings could be better understood when placed in a model that shows the spectrum of services, from single temporary workers to full outsourcing. The Wave template is the basis of the model shown in Figure 8.6, where the spectrum of services is expressed in a layered way.

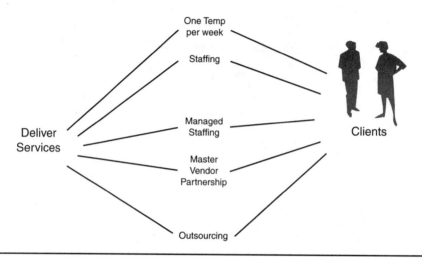

CREATE AND IMPLEMENT PRODUCTIVITY IMPROVEMENT SOLUTIONS

One Temp
per week

Staffing

Deliver
Services

Managed
Staffing

Clients

Master
Vendor
Partnership

Outsourcing

Figure 8.6   The Wave template is used to break out the layers
of this company's spectrum of services.

This model serves as the executive summary, which is accompanied by documents
defining each service level in detail. It makes up one component of the definition of a
product. Combined with other product models, it is used to help the team arrive at
consensus on the meaning of data and terminology.

Tiered Access Plan

An Internet reseller of Web-hosting services utilizes the Wave template to model the
required tiers of access shown in Figure 8.7. It defines both online access for visitors,
members, and customers and offline access to databases and the computer programs
running behind the scenes.

In this example, the Wave template provides a visual way of expressing the layers of
security that must be supported. It is accompanied by a detailed security and backup
plan covering the disposition of all equipment related to the project, whether at the
client site, hosting service provider, or at the work site of project resources.

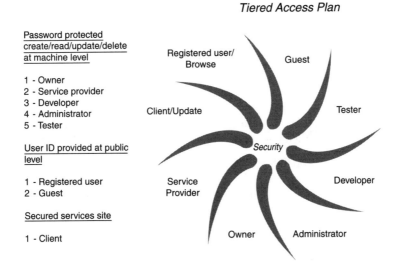

Figure 8.7 The Site Security Tiered Access Plan provides a map for securing an online reseller of Internet hosting services.

Benefits and Consequences

The Wave template provides the following benefits and possible consequences:

- Allows inspection of cross-section
- Clarifies application of architectures
- Supports assignment of responsibility

Allows Inspection of Cross-Section

Computer systems introduce layers of complexity, which can be difficult to navigate. For example, a programmer who is called to resolve a problem in a production system must decide where to look for the source of the problem. It might be the program code itself, which has an error in its logic, or it might be the database that is storing bad data. If neither of those is the problem, it might be in the communications layer, or the way the operating systems is functioning. In advanced technology, such as systems distributed through the Internet, additional applications, browsers, transport mechanisms, HTML coding, and databases must be considered.

For the uninitiated, it's hard to even imagine what the layers might be. Wave models make it possible to factor out those layers, creating a cross-section of all the possible places something could go wrong. The team can then inspect each layer in turn for a more thorough understanding of the potential issues.

Clarifies Application of Architectures

When architecture is defined using the Wave model, the template helps to clarify how that architecture can be applied in the technology deployment. It shows the tiering of components that interface and cooperate to deliver requirements. Each tier is broken out and its requirements are detailed. These layers contain the components of the architecture, which are then covered in detail in deployment models.

In the case of a Wave model developed in UML or another tool-supported language, it becomes very simple to reuse the components as entered at the architecture level in subsequent diagrams for component responsibility and execution.

Supports Assignment of Responsibility

Using the Wave template to separate out the layers of technology can support the assignment of management responsibility or component responsibility. For example, a Y2K analysis uses the Wave template to define management responsibility at a high level. A middleware product uses it to define the initial layers of components. After the components are defined, the functions they are responsible for can be modeled in a component responsibility diagram.

Template Realization

Tool-supported architecture models developed in UML or other notations contain reusable components that can be dragged directly into component responsibility and other technical diagrams. These models represent the implementation and deployment decisions on a project, and are utilized for standards reviews and for implementation planning.

Models that express product versions and tiered-access strategies require action plans that initiate projects, depending on their goals. For example, the Site Security Access Plan in Figure 8.7 was the basis for developer specifications that directed the development of program code for applying the password protection. The service analysis (refer to Figure 8.6) was used to help create rigorous definitions of products so that supporting systems could be configured properly.

EAI Applications

EAI uses waves to regulate the fluctuations of a process or object between two or more extremes. For instance, product versioning enables a product's definition to range between two poles, such as the following:

1. The basic or introductory version of an EAI product that reads data from legacy systems as a single "BLOB" and delivers it unparsed to the viewer, through the use of a unified GUI interface.

2. The deluxe or advanced version of an EAI product that reads data from legacy systems as a "BLOB," parses it, interprets the data, and recommends specific actions to the viewer through the use of a unified GUI interface.

Other versions of the product would fall in between these two extremes in the functionality they deliver. Using the Wave template to regulate the fluctuations in product definition clarifies their progression through the addition of types of functionality, while keeping them within the defined boundaries. A situation displaying the wave dynamic can also provide the impetus to extend the boundaries.

EAI also uses waves to delineate the differences between functionality included in each product version. It can also help to mediate between opposites, converting antagonistic opposition into a continuum encompassing both possibilities. The spectrum of services seen in Figure 8.6 provides an example of mediation between opposing categories. In that example, there existed a rivalry over resources between the single-staffing department and the managed service team. Expressing the spectrum of services as a continuum helped the company resolve that rivalry and clarify decisions of resource allocation based on revenue projections for each layer of the spectrum.

Waves amplify and provide a medium for carrying messages and information. Wave forms utilized by EAI projects include architecture layers, network layers, and layers of management. Tiered security access schemes are Wave forms, as are product versioning and spectrum of services. Some specific EAI applications follow:

- Middleware architecture
- Product component layers
- Shared data architecture

Middleware Architecture

Synergistic Solutions, Inc., a vendor of EAI middleware systems, uses a layered UML model to depict the system blueprint diagram for its NetLocate product. The model in Figure 8.8 helps the client purchasing this system to understand the intended architecture and what will be required to deploy the product in a particular environment.

The NetLocate system blueprint diagram organizes the components of the system into layers, including

- **Application specific**—Oracle-stored procedures that are used to access the Oracle database and the database belonging to certain remote systems from which NetLocate retrieves data
- **Application general**—Web browser and HTML coding used to provide user access to the retrieved data

- **Middleware**—Components specific to the NetLocate product such as application and Web servers and program DLLs and executables required to provide system functionality
- **System software**—Operating system and Oracle database management system

NetLocate System Blueprint Diagram

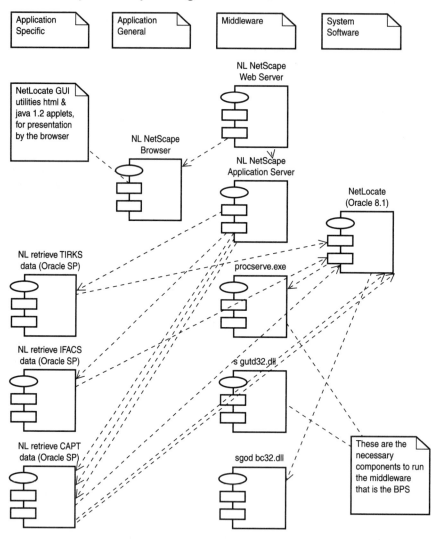

Figure 8.8   Synergistic Solution's NetLocate product uses the Wave template to model the system's architecture in UML.

The layered model shows the required components from the architecture viewpoint. Subsequent models, such as the component responsibility model, reorganize the components according to their interaction and the functionality they collaborate to deliver.

Product Component Layers

Another software vendor uses the Wave template to clarify the product and service layers required to deliver payroll services to their clients. This vendor started out as a service bureau, receiving data tapes from customers and executing the payroll processing required to deliver data and check-processing services to client companies' employees. As the business grew, it developed in two directions.

On one hand, the core payroll engine, coded in assembler programs, evolved into a packaged product which some customers purchase and install in their own back-office application areas. On the other hand, the company still provides service bureau functions to many of their customers. Both the packaged product and the service bureau operate from the same core software engine. As customer requirements and technological advances made their core product's technology and features obsolete, this vendor found that a major upgrade would be necessary to keep their products and services viable.

After an attempted technical re-architecture of the product failed, the company decided to purchase a competitor company that produces a high-end packaged solution for payroll services. This strategy of improving processes by acquisition established that they would become the acquired company's biggest customer. The software vendor effectively would replace and re-architect their core payroll engine by installing the package from the acquired company.

To support the rollout of this major upgrade to their systems, the tiers involved in the rollout are broken out and depicted in the model shown in Figure 8.9.

Shown in the lower-left corner of the model, this vendor's product incorporates a central engine, which performs the core of the required processing for payroll applications. Their product has undergone major revisions in order to keep up with customer demand for features and functionality. It includes the core functions traditionally provided in their payroll services, plus the custom functionality requested by varying customers. The software also comprises both in-house developed features and those that are included in the purchased package intended to increase the level of product performance.

Next, the services layer includes customer service, technical and production support, account management, and product installation. A layer up and to the right, the output engine handles user products including reports, files, and interfaces that are delivered to customers. At the next layer, front-end products provide automated interfaces and enhancements to the service, and in the final, outer layer, training precedes product installation.

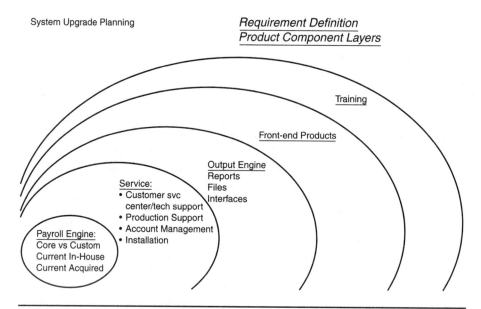

Figure 8.9   The System Upgrade Planning model depicts the layers of product and service required to roll out an upgrade.

The use of the Wave template in this analysis allows the project team to clarify the product and service components across the enterprise. Implementation of the upgraded product requires the collaboration of multiple organizations, each of which must update their piece of the overall service. This and subsequent models help to orchestrate the massive resources (two thirds of the company's resources were eventually diverted to this effort) required to complete the rollout of the upgraded product.

Shared Data Architecture

A staffing firm must develop shared definitions of product identifiers in order to automate key product development functions for the marketing department. The Wave model shown in Figure 8.10 separates the categories used to identify a product so that each can be defined and encoded for automated support.

This model separates the categories of product identification at the highest level for data sharing objectives. Subsequent models provide more detail in entity relationship diagrams and physical database design documents.

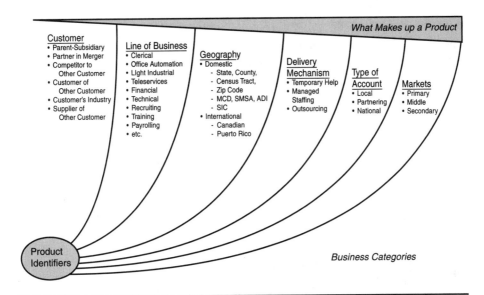

Figure 8.10 The Wave model defines what makes up a product so that the enterprise can define core business categories for process automation.

Templates That Work Well with the Wave Template

The Wave template combines well with

- The Cell template.
- The Seed template.
- The Ring template.

The Cell Template

The Cell template breaks out categories and compartments of data and processing information. It can be combined with the Wave template for the analysis of communications layers and layers within a category or compartment.

Whereas the Cell template focuses on the compartment and its contents, the combined Cell and Wave templates focus more on the interfaces between cells, which act as communications layers. In computer systems, messaging and middleware components can be clarified by the combination of the Cell and Wave structures.

The Seed Template

The Wave template can be combined with the Seed template, because layers are sometimes organized around a repository, controller, or other seed structure. The model seen in Figure 8.11 shows the use of both Seed and Wave templates to depict requirements for a network data collector at a cellular company.

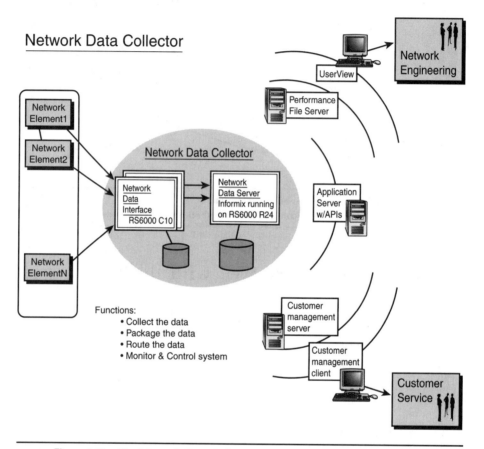

Figure 8.11   The Network Data Collector model combines the Wave and Seed templates to depict the functional requirements for the collection and dissemination of information about network elements.

The NDC collects data from multiple network elements or mobile telephone switching components across a cellular network, through network data interfaces (NDIs) running on an RS6000 machine adjacent to the switch. Data from the NDIs is compiled and stored on the Network Data Server (NDS), which makes it available to the application server with application programming interfaces. Individual application servers pick up the data from the generic application server and serve it to their respective client interfaces.

The Ring Template

The Wave template can be combined with the Ring template to show the layered architecture within the distribution mechanisms pictured by the Ring template. The model in Figure 8.12 depicts the layers of architecture that are required for the repository utilized by a model management strategy.

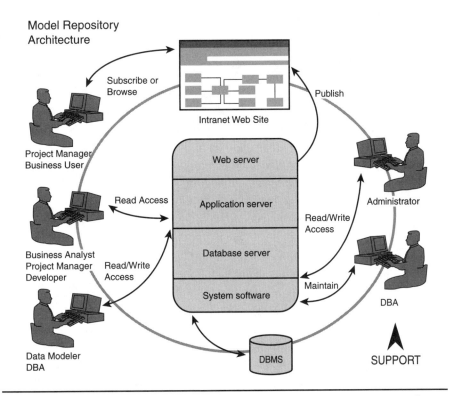

Figure 8.12   The Model Repository Architecture utilizes the Wave template in combination with the Ring template to show layers of architecture for a modeling repository.

The model repository architecture defines the layers of architecture including

- Web server to support intranet access to the stored models
- Application server for access to the modeling software itself
- Database server for the database management system that stores model components
- System software that underlies all three of the other layers

This model establishes the requirements for the technical components of architecture. Subsequent models assign technology inventory to the architecture layers discussed in this chapter.

9

The Ring Template

Template Description

The Ring template (see Figure 9.1) is useful in depicting chaining of events, people, devices, or network addresses. Although the Cycle template models directional processes, the Ring template models non-directional, non-hierarchical connections. Rings are useful in evaluating centralization versus decentralization of business function, and determining which activities and resources should be managed locally and which would benefit from a global perspective.

Figure 9.1   The Ring template.

Template Discussion

Rings are about leveraging resources for economies of scale. They provide inclusion and exclusion, as witness the term "in the loop" to describe someone enjoying the inclusion of a ring. Exclusion refers to the use of rings for handling issues of security, privacy, and disclosure.

Integration goals of the ring include connection and realigning resources for global deployment or for local saturation. Rings allow you to focus in on a target or plan an expansion.

When the Ring Template Applies

The Ring template can be applied to the following situations:

- Network topology
- Decentralization versus centralization
- Modes of connectivity

Network Topology

The Ring template is a common type of network topology that has often been applied to LAN specification (see Figure 9.2). Token rings interconnect nodes in a circle for a directional use of the Ring template.

Applying the Ring template to network topology helps you to visualize the physical network implementation. It gives you a medium in which to assign tasks to specific machines in the loop, and to assay protocols for passing packets around the circle.

Decentralization Versus Centralization

Rings suggest options for decentralizing resources through networking. They can be used to depict how those resources will be allocated, and to design their network connections. For instance, a service bureau running the same core software engine in 20 different states needs to streamline its process for new software releases. The old process is lengthy, requiring over 45 days to roll out any significant upgrade. The situation is complicated by the fact that different locations run different versions of the operating system and run on different platforms, making each installation unique to its location.

The upgrade team does an analysis of the software, operating system, platform, and steps required for installing a new release in each location. It is then possible to determine which steps will continue to be decentralized to the branch locations and which ones can be centralized for better coordination. Based on that information, the team creates a generic process for all locations to follow, using the Ring template to model the intranet-based solution, as shown in Figure 9.3.

Ring Topology

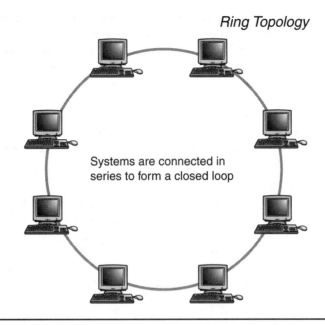

Systems are connected in
series to form a closed loop

Figure 9.2   Network topology uses the Ring template to
depict systems connected in a closed loop.

Software Release Process

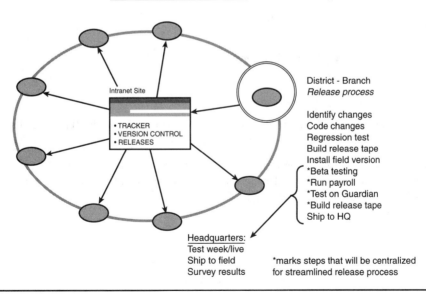

Figure 9.3   The Software Release Process model uses the Ring template
to model decisions about centralization and decentralization.

The team then generates project plans for the necessary local upgrades to make it possible. Though portions of the generic process are still implemented locally, its standards, tracking, version control, and final releases are determined and controlled centrally from headquarters. Subsequent software release timeframes are reduced significantly.

Modes of Connectivity

The Ring template can be used to depict a variety of different modes of connectivity, from physical network structures to organizational structures to communications plans. The Ring model implies non-hierarchical connection.

Ring models are useful when working with an integration strategy which requires new and improved connections. Many of the goals of integration revolve around introducing connections where there haven't been any. For example, customer relationship management, an EAI objective that many companies need, relies upon introducing connections between the branches of a network and sharing information through those new connections. Without this sharing, we cannot get a picture of the whole customer relationship. That whole picture is used to leverage our knowledge into 1:1 marketing strategies.

Examples

The following examples explore the applications of the Ring template:

- Y2K inventory analysis
- Model management strategy
- Connectivity plan
- Customer relationship management

Y2K Inventory Analysis

The cellular division of a telecommunications provider utilized the Ring template to model end user computing resources for a Y2K inventory analysis (see Figure 9.4).

Local area networks and the business units they supported were identified and quantified for this Y2K inventory. Management responsibility for compliance is assigned and tracked based on this previous model.

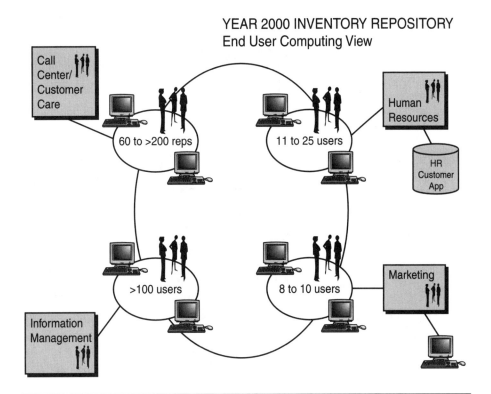

Figure 9.4 A Y2K inventory analysis uses the Ring template
to model the end user computing view.

Model Management Strategy

The data management group at an airline uses the Ring template to define a model management strategy for the entire company. They use it to capture and display information about the following:

- Tool components
- Roles and responsibilities
- Permission to perform specified functions

The model shown in Figure 9.5 puts them all together for a visual guide to the company's strategy for model management.

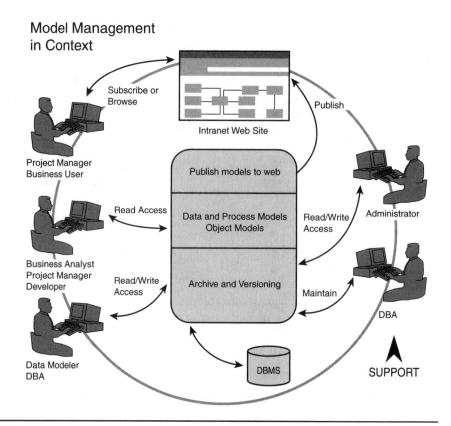

Figure 9.5   The model management strategy shown here is based on the Ring template.

Used in this way, the Ring template helps establish the context for the required components. Based on this model, the data management group can define how projects will implement the strategy. Project plans are developed for installing the required tools, and for rolling out access to developers, modelers, business analysts, project managers, and business users. This model is also used to provide an introductory overview to all intended users.

Connectivity Plan

The Ring template is applied in an employment services company to produce a consolidated connectivity map for all the different configurations that exist in branches in the field. Figure 9.6 shows the Office Connectivity Map that will be explored in greater detail in the case study provided in Chapter 12, "Case Study: Enterprise Resource Planning (ERP)."

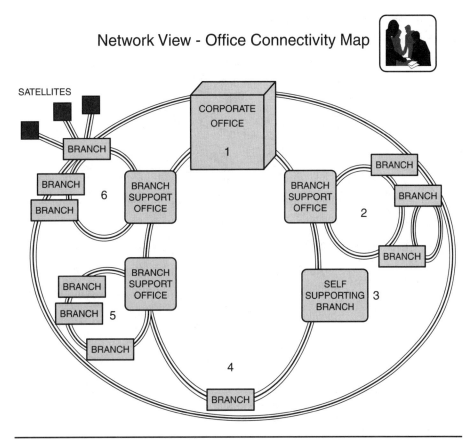

Figure 9.6   The Office Connectivity Map uses the Ring template
to analyze branch configurations.

The Office Connectivity Map shows the variety of available models for networking branches together and shows how they are connected to both field support and headquarters.

Customer Relationship Management

The Ring model is used to define business requirements for a client relationship information database. Shown in Figure 9.7, the Ring provides network connections so that all of the customer activities conducted at any company branch can be captured and included in the customer database.

Customer Database Realtionship
Data sourcing

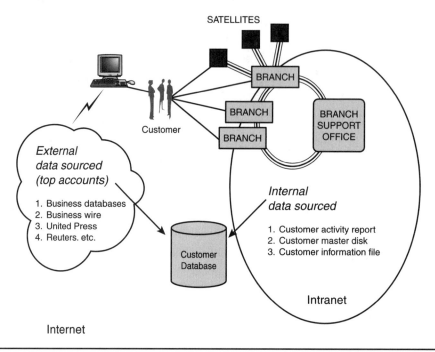

Figure 9.7   The customer relationship is captured through network connections as shown in this Ring-based model.

This model focuses on data sources for the customer relationship database. It incorporates both internal and external sources to provide the widest possible coverage and understanding of the relationship with the customer. Data extracts will capture profitability and performance information, support identification of new opportunities for an existing customer, and support definition of the customer's needs.

Benefits and Consequences

The benefits and possible consequences of using the Ring template include

- Inclusion and exclusion.
- Non-hierarchical structure.
- Support of scalable perspective.

Inclusion and Exclusion

The Ring template can bring greater inclusion through the connections it provides. For instance, the Internet gives an increasing number of people access to information by providing public access to materials that used to be confined to government and educational institutions. It creates greater democracy through access to the information. However, it can also create and intensify the "digital divide," a situation the U.S. Commerce Department calls "falling through the net" [9.1]. The Commerce Department reports on technological "haves and have-nots" as those with access to new technology and those who lack basic access. Critics of the new techno-economy see the potential for a greater divide between those who are Internet-connected and those who are not.

Models that use the Ring structure can be highly inclusive or they can exclude non-members of the circle. Therefore, they are appropriate when modeling democratic structures, and useful to draw lines of demarcation for security planning.

Non-Hierarchical Structure

Select the Ring template when you want to model a non-hierarchical structure such as a network, or a circle of peers sharing information through email, bulletin boards, or other electronic means. Although rings can include layers for versioning, so that an outer layer doesn't have all the access that an inner layer does, they are essentially inclusive structures. The Ring is utilized in academic circles for the model of interrelated colleagues sharing discoveries and research. This collegial relationship is very different from the controlled hierarchical pathways of the typical "chain-of-command" in many corporations.

Support of Scalable Perspective

The Ring template suggests the perspective that can be gained by either focusing in, as in targeted interventions, or expanding out, to encompass the larger picture. For instance, the model in Figure 9.8 is taken from the shared data strategy for a Department of Defense information infrastructure plan named with the acronym SHADE (Shared Data Environment)[9.2]. It shows how the Ring can be used to define a target and all the supports necessary to focus on delivering the targeted component.

In other cases, the Ring serves to incorporate and expand, as in sales models of territories covered by a company's sales force. The circle of inclusion depicts the current coverage and the planned expansions.

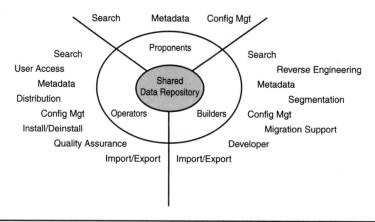

Figure 9.8   The Tools for Requirements, Build, Operate Process Ring model depicts a core component and the necessary supports.

Template Realization

Ring network models are realized by network configuration plans and charts; these give specifications for network details such as protocol, media, signaling, and data transfer rates. They are accompanied by fault management and reliability schemes. The model management Ring model discussed previously spawned several action plans for installing and supporting the tools that the plan called for.

Integration planning realizes Ring models through connectivity plans, organization models for cooperation, and the action plans for implementing them.

EAI Applications

EAI uses the Ring template to provide connections in a non-hierarchical structure. Many EAI applications rely on Internet connections for the infrastructure to provide front-end access to integrated systems. Modeling those systems and their relationships in a circular pattern supports the integration goal of connectivity.

Integration also requires analysis of centralization versus decentralization decisions. EAI relies on such analysis when determining the focal points of integration strategies. The

Ring model helps you to depict these decisions visually. Some specific EAI applications follow:

- Internet Front-End GUI
- Virtual Centralization
- Coordinated Decentralization

Internet Front-End GUI

Many EAI applications use the infrastructure of the Internet or Intranet to provide a common graphical user interface to integrated applications. One company used it to give managers access to their repository of application information in a Y2K analysis. Another uses Web-enabled access to deliver integration of legacy systems through middleware solutions.

Data warehouses often utilize the Internet and intranets to distribute access to corporate information resources. The Ring is the structure that ties together these repositories and the enterprisewide access strategies that they support.

Virtual Centralization

The virtual corporation, popularized in recent years for distributing the traditional components of an organization, relies on Ring-based technology to provide virtual centralization. Employees reside in virtual offices, whether by telecommuting, hoteling (utilizing virtual office space that's assigned on a temporary basis) or by the use of rolling office carts that comprise a portable office and allow employees to set up shop anywhere in the building. Shared virtual offices are furnished with GroupWare systems for electronic brainstorming and electronic whiteboards connected to videoconferencing equipment connect employees working at a distance.

Virtual communities spring up on the Web and become the audience of the future—a target for Web designers, financial backers, and content creators strategizing to deliver techno-media over the Web. Network and cluster organizations model themselves on the Ring model to define boundary-less organizations where resources are connected across vertical, horizontal, hierarchical, and geographic obstacles.

Coordinated Decentralization

Decentralization strategies foster decision-making at the local level. Applied with the Ring model, they emphasize the optional local variations, while coordinating the strategic aspects of a system that can be centrally managed. Policy decisions remain centralized, but non-policy is allocated to the local level. Local cultures are allowed broad influence over their particular area, without losing the benefits of overall coordination.

Templates That Work Well with the Ring Template

The Ring template combines well with

- The Wave template.
- The Web template.
- The Seed template.

The Wave Template

Some Ring models combine effectively with the Wave pattern to express levels of domain or layers of access to resources. The model in Figure 9.9 shows a combination of the Ring pattern with a leveling structure for domains of measurement. It was introduced during a reengineering of software development process to depict the goals of a new measurement program.

Measurements
LEVELS OF MEASUREMENTS

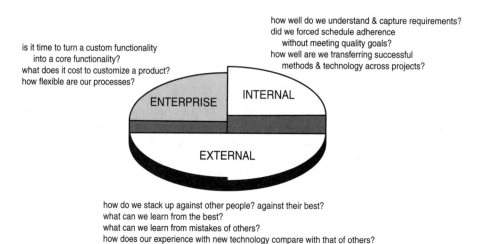

how well do we understand & capture requirements?
did we forced schedule adherence
without meeting quality goals?
how well are we transferring successful
methods & technology across projects?

is it time to turn a custom functionality
into a core functionality?
what does it cost to customize a product?
how flexible are our processes?

ENTERPRISE   INTERNAL

EXTERNAL

how do we stack up against other people? against their best?
what can we learn from the best?
what can we learn from mistakes of others?
how does our experience with new technology compare with that of others?

Figure 9.9   The Measurements model combines the Ring and Wave templates to define the levels of measurements required.

The Measurements model shows that for both effectiveness and efficiency, it is helpful to introduce different levels of measurements such as *internal* (for example within a department), *enterprise* (for example across an enterprise), and *external* (for example within an industry or across industries). Each level provides a different perspective and useful insights.

On the internal level, the following questions are asked:

- How well are we transferring successful methods and technology across projects?
- Did we force schedule adherence without meeting quality goals?
- How well do we understand and capture requirements?

On the enterprise level, contributions to business value are measured in order to understand the following:

- How flexible are our processes?
- What does it cost to customize product?
- Is it the time to turn a custom functionality into a core functionality?

External benchmarking will help to answer questions such as

- How do we stack up against other people?
- How do we stack up against the best?
- What can we learn from the best?
- What can we learn from mistakes of others?
- How does our experience with new technologies compare with that of others?

The Measurement model uses the Ring and Wave together to organize levels of measures that a company can evaluate as part of the redesign of their development process. Other combinations of Ring and Wave can result in the use of concentric circles to describe tiers of access to resources or sphere of influence.

The Web Template

The Ring template combines well with the Web template for depicting extended network connections. It enables one to add one or many nodes of equipment to the ring of connection. The Network Data Collector modeled in Figure 9.10 uses the Ring in combination with the Web to depict the architecture that combines an IP Network with feeds from network elements and the distribution of data through the network data server.

The Network Data Collector utilizes network data interfaces at the cellular switch (a network element) to collect and route information through the IP network to a server environment. From there, an Operational Data Store (ODS) compiles and stores statistical data on call traffic across the wireless network.

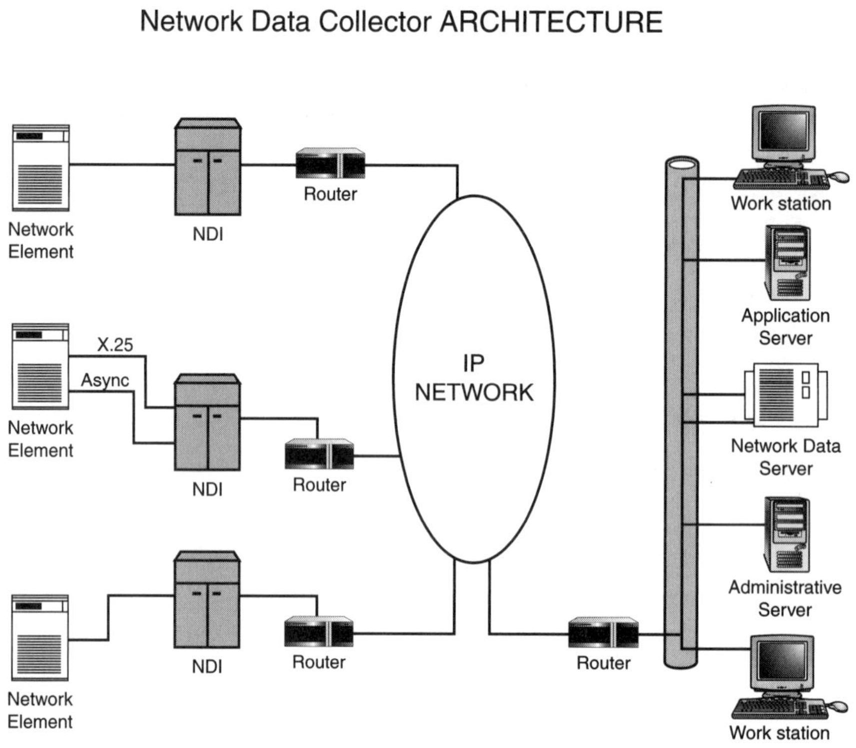

Network Data Collector ARCHITECTURE

Figure 9.10   The Network Data Collector model uses
the Ring template in combination with the Web template.

The Seed Template

The Ring can be combined with the Seed for applications that employ a central database or access unit along with devices chained through a network ring. The Star-wired Ring Topology, shown in Figure 9.11, represents a hybrid network topology combining a multistation access unit with the token Ring.

Distribution of seed-generated results can be depicted with the combination of the Seed and Ring templates. Other uses include shared resources such as a shared printer for a ring-enabled work group.

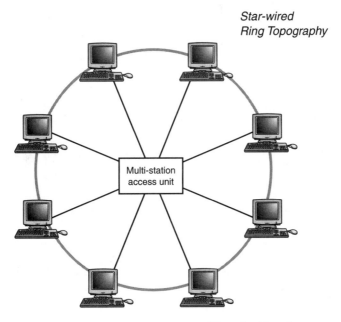

*Star-wired
Ring Topography*

Star-wired topology uses
the multi-station access unit

Figure 9.11   Star-wired Ring Topology combines the Ring
template and the Seed template for a hybrid structure.

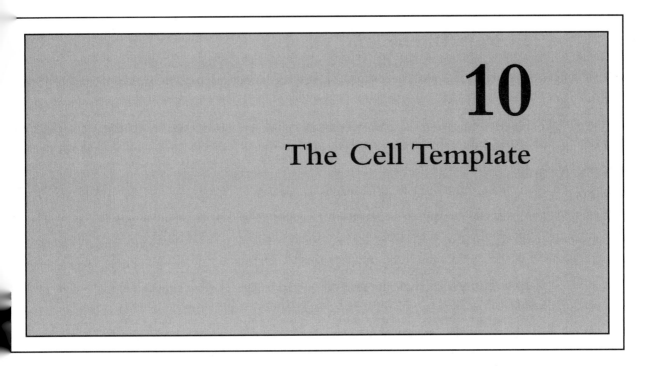

The Cell Template

Template Description

The Cell model (see Figure 10.1) supports modeling of categorization and compartmentalization. Cell models are useful for analysis of distribution systems, geographical division, and behaviors at the local versus global levels.

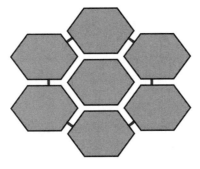

Figure 10.1 The Cell template.

Template Discussion

Cells are self-contained, with layers of communication mechanisms between them. Cells are building blocks. They are distributed. Cells can store components of functionality and can house a map to activate that functionality (such as bit-mapped indexes do). That makes them useful in modeling non-sequential processing that relies on set processing. For instance, consider the data processing model applied to RDBMS access. It handles data non-sequentially through selection of data subsets, or cells, which are managed as a group. Cellular modeling of these data subsets allows you to group and manipulate types of data on the model in a way that's similar to how you group and manipulate data through database access tools.

Subsets of cells can operate simultaneously and independently. They are also used to isolate and separate, so that only the top level knows what goes on in each cell.

Integration goals of cells include the categorization required by data architecture for data sharing. Departmental data analysis and design provide detailed definition of data elements, but enterprisewide sharing of data requires a higher level of analysis. The Cell pattern helps deliver the structure for data architecture that breaks out subject areas across the enterprise and provides a "city plan" for mapping data entities into subject areas. When informed by a holographic map of the data such as that used in bit-mapped indexing, the Cell provides a high level of integration where each cell holds a space for all the other cells within itself.

When the Cell Template Applies

The Cell template can be applied to the following situations:

- Analysis of interfaces
- Replication, encapsulation, and inheritance
- Categorization and compartmentalization

Analysis of Interfaces

For integration to be successful, interfaces between application systems must be seamless. The Cell model can help you define the components and the layers of communication that are required between components. By allowing you to focus on each component separately, cells divide functions out and help you arrange them coherently.

By focusing on each component in detail, you can define the similarities and differences between data elements that are exchanged and shared. Database normalization ensures that data occurs only once within a database, relieving the overhead of maintaining the data multiple times for multiple occurrences, and ensuring data persistency.

Cell analysis supports the goals of normalization by clarifying where data belongs at the business level, which simplifies the process of normalization at the detailed level of technical design.

Cell analysis also supports the de-normalization of database designs. De-normalization occurs when speed of retrieval is prioritized over the requirement for data persistency and state management. Systems designed to support analytical processing often require that data be de-normalized to improve the performance of data access against large volumes of data. The Cell template supports this goal in the same way that it clarifies requirements for normalization. It provides a visual analysis of the business segregation, aggregation, and categorization of data, so that subsequent technical design modelers have a better understanding of these business needs.

Replication, Encapsulation, and Inheritance

Data replication enables users to easily and seamlessly move and share data in real-time among mixed system environments. It requires the definition of components of data to be moved through replication technologies. *Encapsulation* refers to the practice of enclosing data using one protocol within the messages of another protocol. To make use of encapsulation, the encapsulating protocol must be open-ended, allowing for arbitrary data to be placed in its messages. Another protocol can then be used to define the format of that data. *Inheritance* is the practice of developing classes that can be reused from one application to the next, without rewriting the required code or method for accessing and manipulating data.

By enabling the design of layering within cells, the Cell template gives you a way to clarify which aspects of a data entity will be universal, local, and application specific. This provides the integration-oriented basis for determining the desired encapsulation, inheritance, and replication schemes for various requirements of packaging and transporting data.

Categorization and Compartmentalization

The Cell provides a visual pattern for categorizing business information and compartmentalizing business events. Thus it serves as a high-level pattern which incorporates some of the design concepts of object-oriented approaches. Object-oriented approaches generally apply to implementation models, so having a means of depicting events and objects at the business level is valuable.

The Cell allows you to separate discrete categories of data, focusing on each in turn while still holding the space for all the others. It asserts that all the categories have something in common, while showing their variations through the separate cells.

Compartmentalization allows you to define a business event and all the information that is related to it. As you define multiple compartments, you assemble a model of general theme and local variation.

Examples

The following examples explore the applications of the Cell template:

- Measurement program
- Shared data architecture
- Functional responsibility map

Measurement Program

A software vendor must establish a measurement program as part of a reengineering of the development process. The model in Figure 10.2 helps vendors understand the categories of things that can be measured in their technology product's environment, from product features to business impact. A description of the model and its definitions follows.

Measurements
CATEGORIES OF MEASURES

EFFICIENCY:
Doing Things The Right Way

EFFECTIVENESS:
Doing The Right Thing

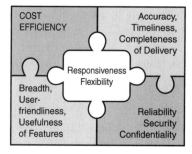
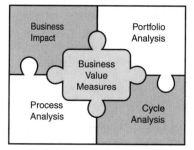

Figure 10.2   The Cell model is used to establish categories of measures for a software vendor.

To define measurements for performance delivered, it is beneficial to consider two independent dimensions of measurements: efficiency and effectiveness.

Efficiency—Doing Things the Right Way

Efficiency measures the ability to produce a desired effect with a minimum of effort, expense, or waste. In other words, measurements of efficiency help one understand whether things are being done the right way. Cost efficiency is a measure that can be obtained relatively easily. Examples of cost efficiency measures are

- Cost per function delivered.
- Cost per check issued.
- IT expenditures as percent of revenue.

Non-cost oriented efficiency measures focus on customer/client perception and satisfaction with the use of quality characteristics, such as

- Accuracy of deliverables.
- Timeliness of deliverables.
- Completeness of deliverables.
- Responsiveness.
- Reliability.
- Access and availability.
- Responsiveness in problem handling.
- Security and confidentiality.
- Flexibility.
- Breadth of features.
- Usefulness of features.
- User-friendliness of features.

To formulate specific measures of customer satisfaction the following questions are asked:

- What is to be counted?
- How often should it be counted?
- Where is it captured?
- What information do calculations, comparison, and so forth derive?
- What is to be reported?
- What is the target audience for the report?
- Who else might benefit from this information?

Customer satisfaction measures user contentment with products and services by the following:

- Establishing feedback mechanisms to obtain solicited information
- Analyzing the findings

Business process owners, line-of-business executives and application end users make up the audience for customer surveys and evaluation questionnaires, following up each delivery of a product or service. Customer forums, focus groups, and user groups also can be used.

Effectiveness—Doing the Right Thing

Effectiveness addresses the need for doing the right thing in order to fulfill the business objective. Different categories of measurements of effectiveness can be introduced:

Business impact measures are used to evaluate products and services in terms of the following:

- Contribution to competitiveness
- Contribution to profitability
- Contribution to flexibility

Business impact measures can include

- Business value of ability to support new markets
- New revenue streams enabled by a product or service
- Additional revenues from customized products
- Decreased customer service costs

Portfolio analysis concentrates on trends in product and service quality over extended periods of time. Portfolio measures can include

- Annual trends in product quality.
- Annual trends in delivery cycle time.
- Trends in services offered, such as
  - Consulting.
  - Help desk.
  - Product documentation.
  - Product training.

Process analysis measures show whether or not a process is under control. Understanding the dependability of a process calls for

- Ability to answer questions such as
  - Can budget be estimated accurately?
  - Can schedule be estimated accurately?
  - Can product quality be predicted reliably?
- Examination of the rate at which
  - Work flows through each step of the process.
  - User requirements are translated into function delivered to the user.

- Rate of workflow or rate of translation of requirements determines
    - How many errors are detected and corrected during each phase.
    - How well requirements are traced through the process to delivery.

Cycle analysis measures responsiveness and utilizes the following:

- Examination of the rate at which
    - Requests for new products are fulfilled.
    - Requests for enhancements are fulfilled.
    - Requests for services are fulfilled.
- Rate of fulfillment determines
    - Variances between projected and actual completion time.
    - Variances between average and median times to deliver.
    - The rate at which backlog requests are moved into active status.

This application of the Cell template in a development process measurement plan helps to separate the categories of measures and provides a visual depiction of the categories.

Shared Data Architecture

As part of an analysis for a publish-and-subscribe implementation, an airline needs to define the categories of data sharing. Based on the model in Figure 10.3, the team defines principles for sharing data. The team also outlines the properties belonging to specific views and their encapsulation for inheritance at other levels.

The Shared Data and Inheritance model describes the data sharing and inheritance required from three different viewpoints: common view, portfolio view, and application view.

Common View

The *common view* describes the core shared data for a given subject area. Core data objects describe constant data requirements. Customer, employee, and price are examples of core data objects. The core data object contains data attributes and properties that are common to all viewpoints. All common properties are inherited by the portfolio and application views.

Portfolio View

The *portfolio view* adds locally shared data, which is unique to the portfolio in question. Local properties can either add more specific definition to a core data object, or can create extended data objects by combining core data objects. Extended data objects express the relationship between core data objects. For example, revenue expresses the relationship between customer and price.

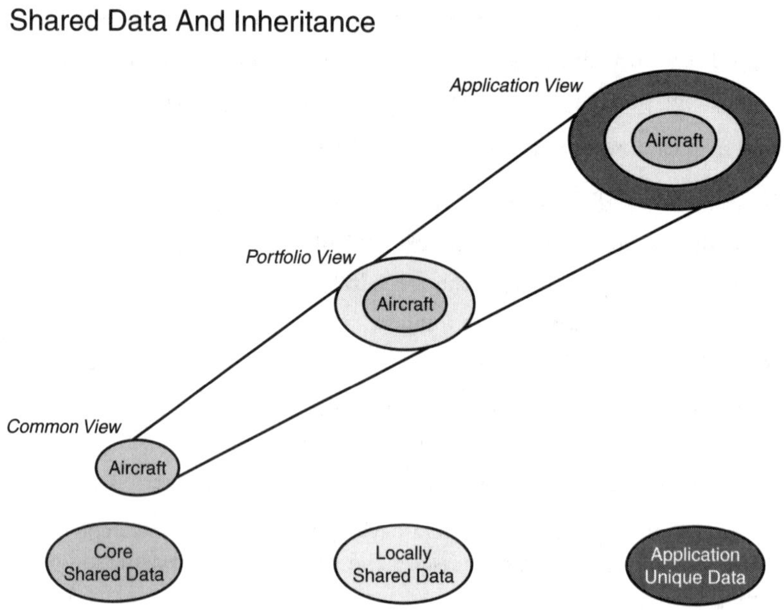

Shared Data And Inheritance

Figure 10.3   The Cell model defines sharing of data and inheritance of data properties from three different viewpoints.

Application View

The *application view* inherits the portfolio properties and adds another layer of metadata, which is unique to the particular application.

Data is mapped into subject areas by logical and physical data models or entity relationship diagrams. The logical data model creates a "city plan" for the subject areas. The physical data model is used as a map to manage the integrity of data subscriptions.

Functional Responsibility Map

The Cell template is the basis for the model in Figure 10.4 to define the Functional Responsibility Map from the viewpoint of facilities at a wireless services company. It assists the team in visualizing the components that must be addressed in upgrade planning, and allows the assignment of responsibility for those components.

Each component on the Functional Responsibility Map represents an area that must be evaluated for upgrade requirements. The model helps the upgrade team to identify the components and assign managers to take responsibility for upgrade implementation.

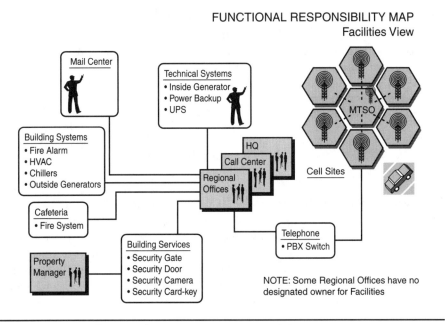

Figure 10.4   The Functional Responsibility Map uses
the Cell template to depict areas in the facilities view.

Benefits and Consequences

The benefits and possible consequences of using the Cell template include

- Analysis and definition of data interfaces.
- Structured analysis of communications paths.
- Design of messaging and middleware components.

Analysis and Definition of Data Interfaces

Data analysis for traditional software development projects focuses mainly on the data specific to the required application. Integration requires a closer look at the interfaces between applications, and creates a need for ways of visualizing the borders and boundaries across which data is shared. Cell models support that visualization by depicting subject areas and high-level groups of data, providing a structure beyond the detailed level. They allow you to focus on layers by separating the significant segments of data and zeroing in on the boundaries of the segment.

Structured Analysis of Communications Paths

Logical and physical data modeling supports the definition of access paths for data grouped into databases. The Cell model provides a mechanism for modeling and testing communication paths for larger aggregations and components of data at the business level. By breaking out the subject areas and analyzing and defining their contents, Cell models help define the channels required for business communications.

For instance, the Internet utilizes the concept of channels to manage subscriptions for users who want to receive information on a particular topic. News groups and push technology utilize channels to organize a subscriber's access to information.

Design of Messaging and Middleware Components

Messaging focuses on the delivery of information packets through dynamically assigned pathways. Middleware components help the requesting system to navigate the process of accessing a data store, packaging selected information, and returning it for viewing at the requesting application. Cell models can help you visualize the packets and packages of information that will be manipulated by these delivery technologies.

Template Realization

The use of Cell templates contributes to the modular design of systems. Cells can be translated to components or data objects and classes. High-level Cell models can contain behaviors and entities or categories, which can be translated into many object classes. They also support the development of state diagrams, which analyze the states that an object can pass through. For instance, a project can use the Cell pattern to develop state diagrams, indicating the required transitions to be supported through a middleware implementation. Cells are also behind the visualization of deployment diagrams, where you break out platform components and assign technology inventory.

Strategic models using the Cell template, such as the business positioning and measurements examples, are translated into tactical plans for actions to be taken. These plans can direct activities for both the business team and the supporting technical team. Each cell on these diagrams can also be broken out into many subject areas, data models, and physical databases.

EAI Applications

EAI utilizes the Cell structure to help manage data and objects, versioning sets of functionality within wrappers, and to build communications infrastructure. It can be used for the propagation of best practices, through sets of employees and/or locations. Marketing uses include the analysis of share of wallet within a given market.

The following sections describe some specific EAI applications.

Data Architecture Design

The Business Strategies Positioning model in Figure 10.5 uses the Cell template to define the data architecture design for an employment services company. Data architectures must establish mechanisms to categorize data at the business level in order to make the data understandable and accessible. The Cell model helps the data modeling team to do that by providing broad categories of data requirements which will later be broken down to data entities and attributes in entity relationship diagrams.

Figure 10.5   The Business Strategies Positioning model uses
the Cell template for data architecture design.

Each of the categories defined by the Business Strategies Positioning model will be researched for data requirements. Then the information categories will be broken down into data entities and logical data models. Subsequent models will define the physical data storage mechanisms for implementing the data architecture plan.

ERP Information Model

An enterprise resource-planning project uses the Cell template to define how the company makes an agreement, or contract, with customers. Terms of agreements are specified according to the criteria depicted by the cell components. Figure 10.6 shows the Business Categories model used to define customer agreements.

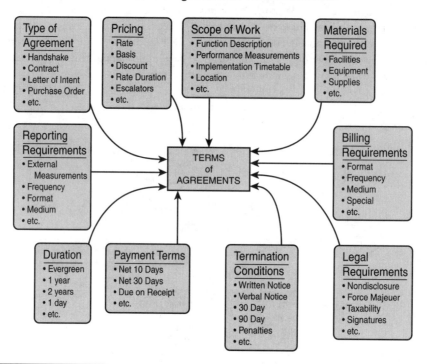

Business Categories
How We Make an Agreement with Consumer

Type of Agreement
• Handshake
• Contract
• Letter of Intent
• Purchase Order
• etc.

Pricing
• Rate
• Basis
• Discount
• Rate Duration
• Escalators
• etc.

Scope of Work
• Function Description
• Performance Measurements
• Implementation Timetable
• Location
• etc.

Materials Required
• Facilities
• Equipment
• Supplies
• etc.

Reporting Requirements
• External
  Measurements
• Frequency
• Format
• Medium
• etc.

TERMS of AGREEMENTS

Billing Requirements
• Format
• Frequency
• Medium
• Special
• etc.

Duration
• Evergreen
• 1 year
• 2 years
• 1 day
• etc.

Payment Terms
• Net 10 Days
• Net 30 Days
• Due on Receipt
• etc.

Termination Conditions
• Written Notice
• Verbal Notice
• 30 Day
• 90 Day
• Penalties
• etc.

Legal Requirements
• Nondisclosure
• Force Majeuer
• Taxability
• Signatures
• etc.

Figure 10.6   The Cell template is used to model how
a company makes an agreement with customers.

Each cell on the model lists the detailed elements of the category it represents, including the following:

- Type of agreement
- Reporting requirements
- Duration
- Payment terms
- Termination conditions
- Legal requirements
- Billing requirements
- Materials required
- Scope of work
- Pricing

All cells contribute to the content of customer agreements that will be supported by the software system under development. Joint application design helps to ensure that all affected parties are in agreement with the components displayed by the diagram.

Templates That Work Well with the Cell Template

The Cell model combines well with

- The Wave template.
- The Web template.

The Wave Template

Waves define layers and Cells define categories. Together, they can depict layers within categories or categories within layers. For example, the Wave and Cell models are combined in Figure 10.7, which defines the activities of recruiters for a redesign project in a financial institution.

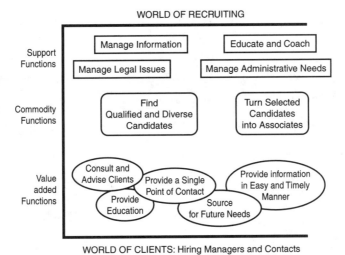

Figure 10.7   The Cell and Wave templates are combined to define the activities involved in recruiting.

Model layers are designated by the three captions running down the left margin of the model:

- Support functions
- Commodity functions
- Value-added functions

The activities performed within each function are depicted by cell components that are grouped by layer.

The Web Template

Webs define connections. Cells define categories and compartments of things that need to be connected. Cells can provide a way to model the contents of nodes on a Web. Figure 10.8 shows the combination of Cell and Web templates to model the single point of entry for incoming data from multiple sources.

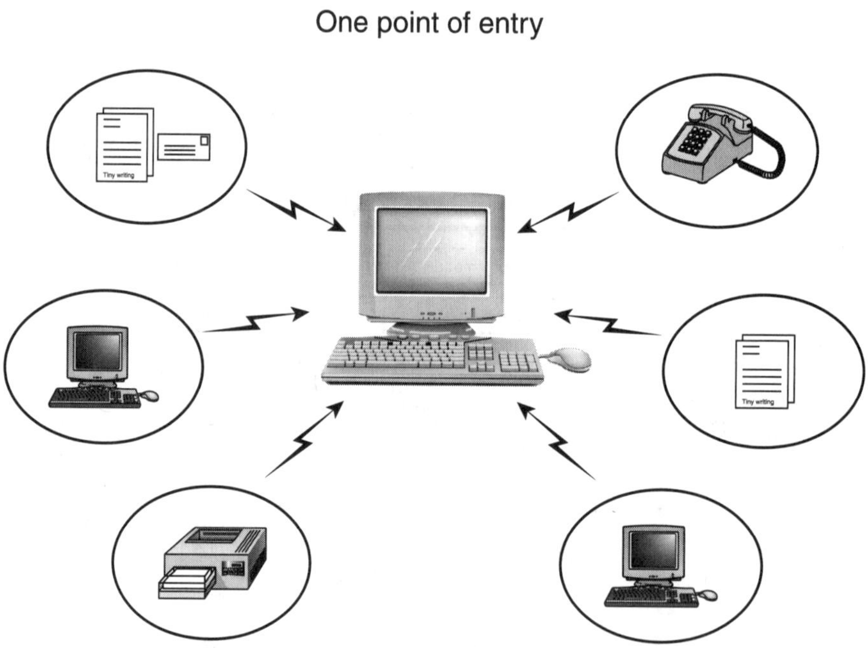

One point of entry

Figure 10.8   The Cell template is combined with the Web template
to depict the single point of entry for multiple data sources.

In this example, the Cell breaks out the types of data sources that are connected to the single point of entry through the Web. Telephones, fax, computer monitors, and paper sources are included.

The Tree Template

Template Description

The Tree template (see Figure 11.1) is a structure utilized to model systems with characteristics that include complex branching, diversification, and the implementation of distribution alternatives.

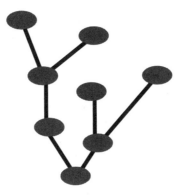

Figure 11.1   The Tree template.

Template Discussion

The Tree template can provide asymmetrical structures with coherence. It models extension and the type of growth required to penetrate a market or to increase market share. Branches are homogenous. Trees provide one-way connections, and are suitable for either breaking down a process or combining several processes.

Integration uses include middleware reliability analysis for error handling and fault determination. Decision trees and stochastic trees use the Tree pattern for predictive analyses. It can also be useful in any situation where a hierarchy of actions is needed.

For example, in the modeling of use-case requirements for software design, the Tree can be used to ensure that coverage of all possible error handling is achieved. Normal processing covers the main branches of the use-case tree and abnormal processing, or error handling, drives the development of an alternate branch of the tree. When the alternate path stops branching, you know that all possibilities are covered.

Similar to decomposition diagrams, the Tree structure provides a more flexible alternative. To recast the decomposition diagram as a Tree model suggests a new direction—from static decomposition to the dynamic growth of branching. It allows the breakdown of components, as do decomposition diagrams, but adds the possibility of composition, consolidation, and unidirectional division. The Tree is a free-form version of the decomposition diagram.

When the Tree Template Applies

The Tree template can be applied to the following situations:

- Composition and consolidation
- Complex branching analysis
- Decision support systems

Composition and Consolidation

The Tree template is used to depict all the components required to compose a higher-level function. In the component marketplace, where component integration is becoming more important than new development, the Tree models the way planning is done to assemble components that deliver specified functionality.

It can also begin at the highest level and break down functions to their logical components. Then you can analyze for specifics and assign out the making of the components.

Consolidation involves integrating function into fewer processes or a single process. For instance, when merging acquired branches, a business can choose to consolidate the operating models in use in those branches and narrow down the options branches are allowed to implement. Such a consolidation of operating models paves the way for implementing common integrated systems to support those models.

Complex Branching Analysis

Variety stems from the complexity of a system's environment. A standalone system can function with the use of a simple, one-sided view of the business information. However, slight variations in the viewpoints of differing departments can cause an entire subset of data to be defined differently or new data sets and processes to appear.

Two systems being developed side-by-side for related project aims can affect each other's growth indirectly. The branching patterns result from complex interactions between systems. The development of components of the growing systems depends on selecting those that are successful in both for reproduction (branching) and replication. This simple principle, combined with the complexity of the environment, is able to generate complex branching patterns akin to those found in nature.

Decision-Support Systems

The design of decision-support systems relies on usage models that employ decision trees encompassing the range of queries that must be addressed. A usage model demonstrates specific examples of how it is expected the system will be used. It provides queries, reports, and examples of the business decisions that will be based on them. The usage model analyzes the criteria for those business decisions, determining what information is needed in order to support all the criteria of a particular decision. The Tree pattern is used to model all the branches of those criteria and the decisions they comprise.

Examples

The following examples explore the applications of the Tree template:

- Analyze spectrum of services
- Process breakdown map
- Data architecture

Analyze Spectrum of Services

The vice president of marketing at an employment services company needed to integrate the spectrum of services that the company offered, understanding it in order to design software automation of the services. The model in Figure 11.2 shows the Spectrum of Services from the client's viewpoint.

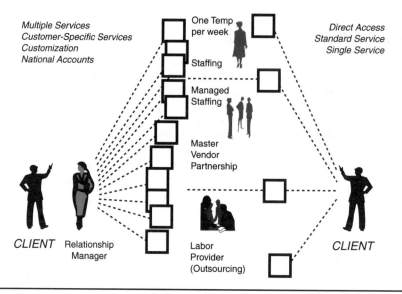

Client View: Spectrum of Services
One-point-of-contact or Streamlined Process

Multiple Services
Customer-Specific Services
Customization
National Accounts

One Temp per week

Staffing

Managed Staffing

Master Vendor Partnership

Direct Access
Standard Service
Single Service

CLIENT   Relationship Manager

Labor Provider (Outsourcing)

CLIENT

Figure 11.2   The Tree pattern is used to depict the
Spectrum of Services from the client's viewpoint.

On the left side of the model, the relationship manager represents the client's needs to the organization, providing a single point of contact in cases where the company provides

- Multiple services.
- Customer-specific services.
- Customization of services.
- National account management.

The customization that is provided by a relationship manager results in a finer level of granularity on the tree (more branches).

Non-mediated access to services creates a streamlined process when clients require

- Direct access.
- Standard service.
- Single service.

Both the access mediated by a relationship manager (managed staffing view), and the non-mediated access (client-managed view) utilize the core spectrum of services, from the provision of a single temporary worker to be managed by the client to onsite managed staffing, and to completely outsourced staffing options. The Tree model helps clarify the relative complexity of the two views represented on the model, including the client-managed view and the managed staffing view. The view that displays fewer branches indicates the situation with reduced complexity.

Process Breakdown Map

The Tree structure is used in Figure 11.3 to break down the processes of core business functions for a staffing business.

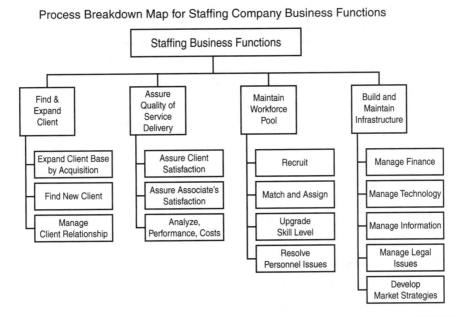

Process Breakdown Map for Staffing Company Business Functions

Figure 11.3   The Process Breakdown Map utilizes the Tree structure to analyze core business functions.

The Process Breakdown Map utilizes the Tree pattern in the form of the familiar decomposition diagram to analyze the activities that comprise key business functions for a staffing business. Four key business functions are identified and expanded through decomposition blocks.

Data Architecture

An auto insurance company used the Tree template to design data architecture for its marketing data warehouse. The model in Figure 11.4 shows the hierarchy of the desired data about customers.

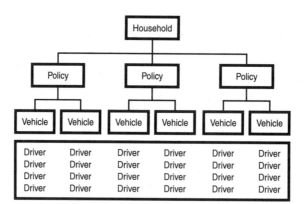

Figure 11.4   An Information Architecture model uses the Tree structure to depict the hierarchy of customer information.

Starting with the household level, the insurance company wanted to store and track customer information about insurance policy, vehicles covered, and drivers covered in the policy. By depicting the hierarchy inherent in the information, the model helped the technical team understand how storage databases should be designed.

Benefits and Consequences

The benefits and possible consequences of using the Tree template include

- Ensure coverage of usage scenarios.
- Support decision set analysis.
- Analyze genesis/diversification.

Ensure Coverage of Usage Scenarios

Tree models show the broad view of the highest level functionality that is being analyzed. They pull together the sub-processes and subordinate activities that must be supported under the umbrella of the Tree structure. Clear-cut breaking down of sub-processes is not always possible without tearing the texture of a business setting. Sometimes activities must overlap and share resources, performers and results. The Tree template accommodates the asymmetries of real-world processes.

Although the Tree helps keep the whole business function in your mind, it also allows you to break it down to numerous levels of detail. This branching can continue all the way to the lowest atomic level, ensuring that all details are examined.

For example, the typical technology project schedule utilizes the work breakdown schedule to break tasks down to very fine levels of detail. A schedule of activities and tasks can be broken down to hours and even minutes if required. Attaining this fine level of detail helps project managers create accurate estimates of time and resource requirements.

Support Decision Set Analysis

Decision set analysis is used in the requirement analysis, design, and specification of decision-support systems. A decision set is the set of information required to enable the formulation of a particular decision. For example, a marketing executive is responsible for product management and must make pricing decisions on financial products. The model in Figure 11.5 shows the information that is required to support pricing decisions, formatted with the Tree structure.

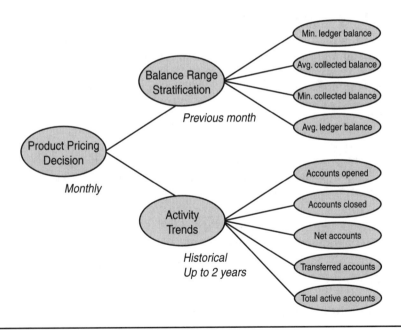

Figure 11.5   The User Decision-Use Case Tree models the set of information that is required to make product-pricing decisions on a monthly basis.

Product-pricing decisions are based on two primary factors. One is the balance range stratification, a report that delivers balance activity by balance ranges, sorted by state, line of business, product category, product, and balance range. The second factor is the activity trend, which is used to view effects of price changes, see cyclical trends, and for ongoing product management. This model clarifies the information sets required and lays the groundwork for more detailed models that will capture field names and calculations against the data that will be required for report design.

Analyze Genesis/Diversification

The Tree template enables the modeling of the originating core process, whether in high-level business requirements or in the more detailed capturing of use-case specifications. Thus you can organize your models according to the business function they support, or other originating core idea, model, or activity. Underneath the umbrella of that core function, you then plan the diversity, branching, and extension of activities.

In this way, the Tree structure helps manage the diversification of resources, distribution coverage, and tactical maneuvers. It enables you to keep up with diversity, while fostering it by planning ways to facilitate it.

Template Realization

Use-case Tree models can be realized into other models in the usual way for object-oriented design. Use cases generally are illustrated by scenario models, which utilize collaboration diagrams to spell out how the related components will interact. Decomposition-oriented models depict activities that can be captured in action diagrams for detailed design. This is the level for making determinations about coupling, encapsulation, and inheritance in component function.

Business models such as the Spectrum of Services model (refer to Figure 11.2) require various actions to implement, from strategic decisions to the action plans for carrying them out. After the Tree model defines the full spectrum, the picture can make managers aware of sections within the spectrum that have been overlooked and need attention. Part of the value of Tree modeling is that Trees enable us to view the sections of the spectrum in context, clarifying the extent of each section and showing whether it is being exploited to its full potential.

Decision sets often drive the requirements for the design of data marts, which present a subset of information from a data warehouse, based on the requirements of the subject area. The decision sets and their trees are detailed with multidimensional modeling techniques for database design.

EAI Applications

EAI uses the Tree to model use cases and schemes of distribution. It can be used in the case where the team develops a prototype of best practices or an experimental technical model and wants to replicate it through a distribution scheme. The Tree provides a pattern useful for driving plans, technology, and services out or down through an organization. The Tree template is useful in organizing use cases for requirement analysis, and helps ensure that all possible cases are covered. It can also be used to model architecture schemes, breaking out the distribution of needed resources.

Some specific EAI applications follow:

- Middleware use cases
- Server architecture

Middleware Use Cases

SSI is a vendor of EAI software for telecommunications companies. They focus on customer provisioning of high-capacity services such as DS1 and DS3, developing systems that provide a unified, GUI interface to legacy applications (Operational Support Systems, mostly). Their systems pull together information from many legacy systems and present it to design engineers so those engineers don't have to deal with multiple systems, because there is a huge learning curve on those legacy systems. NetFlow is a product that helps correct problems in the administration of hardwired elements in the Operational Support Systems (OSS) that are commonly used to administer them. These OSS systems are not designed to handle certain configurations of network elements that actually occur in the field, with the result that there are interruptions to the flow of the process of managing those disallowed configurations. The NetFlow product helps design engineers by identifying those configurations, "fixing" their entries in a special database, and informing the OSS of their existence.

The model shown in Figure 11.6 was developed to capture the use cases that describe the desired functionality of the NetFlow product. It uses the Tree structure to depict the possible branches in functionality, ending in more detailed possibilities on the right side of the diagram.

The highest level of function for this product is the administration of hardwired elements. That function is composed of the following sub-functions:

- Build and maintain the hardwired database.
- Poll and manage the work list that conveys the information from and to the legacy systems.
- Find hardwired elements.

Under the "build and maintain the hardwired database" function, the "build database" function is composed of the following:

- One-time automatic build
- Manual build

NetFlow Use Case Tree

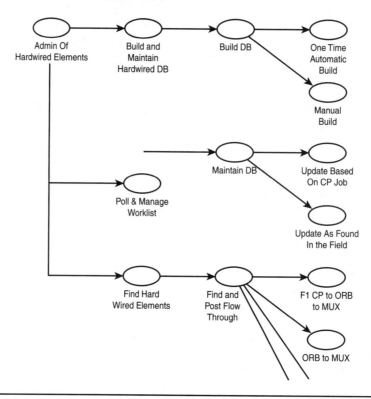

Figure 11.6   The NetFlow Use Case Tree defines the
desired functionality for a middleware product.

The "maintain database" function includes

- Update based on Cable Pairs job.
- Update as found in the field.

Finding hardwired elements consists of finding and posting the service order so that it
flows properly through the process for the variety of possible configurations (F1 Cable
Pairs hardwired to Object Repeater Bay to Multiplexer, Object Repeater Bay to
Multiplexer, and so forth).

The Use Case Tree is subsequently resolved into collaboration diagrams, which depict
one scenario for each significant use case. Scenarios model the objects that collaborate
to deliver those use cases. To show how NetFlow works, the team develops a generic
model of the core middleware that controls processing of NetFlow, which is a product
called the Business Process Server (BPS).

The BPS is a generic support process, which accesses a common database, developed in Oracle, to configure its rules, queues, and external interfaces based on the start-up command line. When running, the BPS spawns the pre-determined number of remote system interface processes, which can interface with remote systems with a number of protocols including EHALAPI, sockets, and ODBC. The BPS loads and executes the pre-determined business rules for its startup defined role.

Class diagrams and collaboration diagrams are used to specify the components of the BPS and show how they collaborate. Then those components are reused in the collaboration diagrams that depict the scenarios for the NetFlow product.

Server Architecture

The model in Figure 11.7 is part of the shared data strategy for the Department of Defense information infrastructure plan for a Shared Data Environment [11.1]. It uses a Tree structure to break out the distribution of server resources according to an overall data architecture scheme.

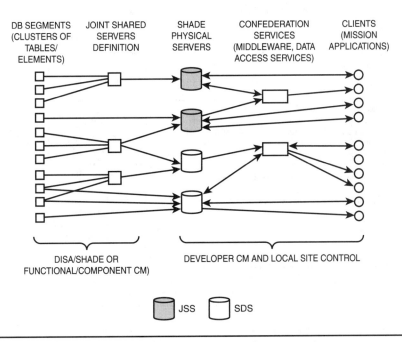

Figure 11.7   The Server Architecture model employs the Tree structure to break out the distribution of server resources.

In the Server Architecture model the distribution runs both directions, centering on the core of physical servers, and then expanding to cover database segments on one hand and client applications on the other.

Templates That Work Well with the Tree Template

The Tree template combines well with

- The Seed template.
- The Flow template.

The Seed Template

Another example from the DOD's shared data strategy shows the combination of the Tree structure and the Seed repository shown in Figure 11.8.

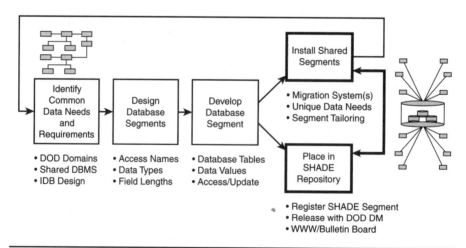

Implementing DOD Data
Standards: A Business Process

Figure 11.8   The DOD Data Standards model combines a Tree model with a repository for the distribution of stored information.

Incorporated into a Flow model depicting the business process, the combined Tree and Seed structure illustrates the database concepts that are employed.

The Flow Template

The Flow template traces the course of information, goods, services, and communications. Combined with the Tree, it can be used to depict versions of a flow, with tree-like branching to incorporate each individual version. Figure 11.9 uses the combination of Tree and Flow templates to depict the Process Breakdown Map for staffing business functions.

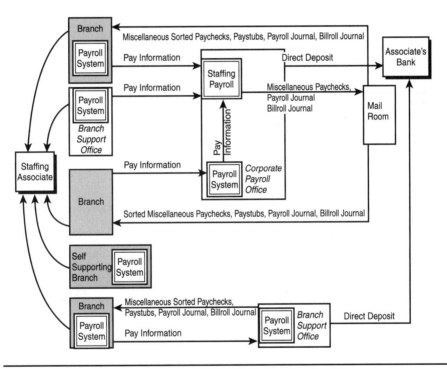

Process Breakdown Map for Staffing Business Functions
PAY ASSOCIATES - Miscellaneous Paychecks

Figure 11.9 The Process Breakdown Map combines the Tree
and the Flow templates to depict versions of a process.

The Tree and Flow templates are combined to model the process of paying associates, breaking out the different versions in different types of branches. The model shows all the possible configurations, including the following:

- Branches that run their own payroll systems with corporate office payroll support
- Branches supported by a regional branch support office

- Branches supported by regional branch support office as part of corporate support office
- Self-supporting branches

The flows of information and goods are traced between all the possible branch configurations. This model is used to develop requirements for the implementation of ERP systems that consolidate payroll processing across the enterprise.

III

Applying
Integration Models

12

Case Study: Enterprise Resource Planning (ERP)

Today's most successful companies understand and practice enterprise application integration through innovative approaches and techniques. A composite story, drawing from experiences applying *Enterprise Resource Planning (ERP)* software with companies in the employment services sector, provides an example of how such companies would apply integration models to ERP objectives.

The packaged software that is provided by ERP vendors such as PeopleSoft, SAP, JD Edwards, and Baan delivers improved enterprise application integration by offering an integrated suite of applications to perform standard business functions. Back-end functions such as accounting, inventory, and shipping are supported, as well as front-end functions such as call-center and sales-force automation. ERP packages are used in conjunction with business process reengineering techniques to upgrade big chunks of a company's supporting systems.

Until recent years, packaged-software vendors concentrated on one application or a suite of applications that they automated without regard to other applications that a company might have in its systems portfolio. Consequently, large corporations that purchased and installed packaged applications found themselves with islands of data and processing that must be bridged to other islands. As these bridges grew, the maintenance of a system and its interfaces also grew to take up more and more resources. In response to this dilemma, software vendors expanded their offerings to include all or many of the related applications that a company would require, delivering them pre-integrated by the vendor.

Companies undertake ERP implementations when they need to integrate multiple systems quickly. Sometimes business competition forces companies to undertake ERP initiatives when competitors, because of tight integration of their own systems, can offer more desirable services and product features. At other times, technological advances require that a company upgrade all its systems to keep up with new opportunities. Yet another reason companies install ERP systems is when outsourcing initiatives have failed and they want to reinstate their own information technology systems support. When bringing this function back inside a company is a good time to overhaul the systems and make sure they're integrated and maintainable.

Background

The new Chief Information Officer's charter was to replace obsolete computer systems with current packaged systems, providing a competitive advantage through technology. This meant using advanced systems to bring more resources to market (that is, filling jobs more quickly with their temporary employees) while at the same time slashing prices by reducing operating margins. The goal was to implement improved business processes by configuring and installing packaged ERP systems according to the results of an enterprisewide reengineering effort.

The sales and service delivery team would be able to fill jobs more quickly with temporary employees by using sales support applications that were configured based on best practices identified and propagated throughout the organization's distribution network. New business acquisition and retention of existing customers would be enhanced through customer management software and customer information reporting.

The field offices would be able to reduce operating margins by using packaged applications that support field office functions such as billing, payroll, time accounting, and collections. The definition of core business processes, flow of activities and decision support needs would ensure the proper configuration of the packaged software to take advantage of reengineered processes with the latest technologies.

The pre-integrated nature of the ERP packaged software would provide a new baseline for all of the company's systems, including those that would not be involved in the initial installation. Those included isolated systems without integration requirements, systems that were not included in the available ERP functions and unique in-house applications and customized applications. Systems would be converted into the new order on a scheduled basis, and new development would target the standards established by the ERP implementation. As all applications migrated into the new systems environment, integration would increase and the company would begin to develop sophisticated knowledge management at the corporate level to be used for decision-making.

The CIO's main problem was the seemingly insurmountable gap between what he knew (the fragmented puzzle of the company's current systems) and what he needed to know (business requirements for the new systems). He had very little information about how the existing systems were actually being used to conduct business. His technical managers, field managers, and the headquarters staff that supported them all wanted the package installation to succeed. All held a piece of the information needed to make it a success, but none could see the whole picture. Without the crucial understanding of the use of current systems as a basis for defining future business requirements, the implementation project risked missing the mark.

Applying Integration Models for ERP

When integration modeling techniques are applied to our CIO's problem, they fill the gap by gathering company intelligence and consolidating it into models that can be taken in at a glance. The models are used to analyze requirements for configuring the new system and to orient the technical team implementing the new software.

Figure 12.1 shows the process methodology followed in the example for ERP integration.

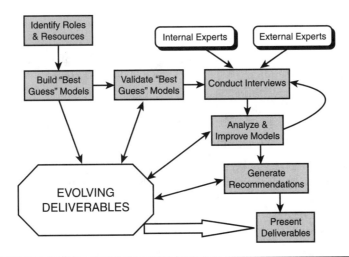

Figure 12.1   The Process model for an ERP integration project specifies the steps that must be taken to complete the project.

The process model for this ERP integration project shows the steps involved in developing the requirements for an ERP implementation. The products from each step of the process are added to the evolving set of deliverables. Deliverables from earlier steps are utilized and refined by later steps. Early steps are completed with the support of the sponsor (in the case of this example, this would be the CIO) and his senior technical advisors, setting up the heart of the process, the serial interview of business area representatives and subject matter experts. Serial interviewing proceeds in iterative fashion with the application of integration models and techniques to analyze and improve on the initial models. The next sections describe the details of the seven steps of the process:

1. Identify roles and resources
2. Build "best guess" models
3. Validate "best guess" models
4. Conduct interviews with internal experts and external sources
5. Analyze and improve models
6. Generate recommendations
7. Present deliverables

Identify Roles and Resources

The first step is to introduce the new roles required specifically for an integration project. The next several sections describe these roles.

Champion

The champion is the process owner and "chief persuader," the overall coordinator and internal PR agent for the project. He performs the following functions:

- Helps build enthusiasm
- Educates others on the project's benefits
- Generates support throughout the organization

In this example, the CIO clearly became the champion for the project. Monthly and sometimes more frequent meetings were held with the champion to provide ongoing updates and mid-course corrections for the duration of the project.

Contributors

Business area representatives from across functions provide a sounding board for the duration of the project, giving input on what works and what doesn't (from the field). Contributors are also responsible for ongoing prioritization of needs. Represented areas include

- **Sales**—This can include the senior executive for the sales area, but it would also include sales people from the field and branch or regional managers.

- **Marketing**—In our example company the vice president of marketing became an important project ally, working closely with the integrators and the project champion to set direction and provide organizational support.

- **Corporate Management**—This includes CIO, president, and vice president levels. Interview results are summarized and applied to help define the goals and priorities of the project.

- **MIS (Senior Technical Analysts)**—Systems managers and senior technologists knowledgeable about the company's systems environment are essential to the success of the project.

- **Product Engineering**—New product development, research and development, managers, and technical specialists are included.

- **Business Planning**—Strategic planners, senior marketing executives, investor relations experts, and sometimes legal counsel can be included, depending on the goals of the project.

- **Service Delivery**—Line managers, customer-service providers and their managers, regional executives, and branch staff can all be included from this perspective.

Integrator

The role of the integrator is flexible and fluid. It requires a tolerance for ambiguity and the ability to provide reflective feedback to project stakeholders. Some of the functions of the integrator include

- Conducting the project
- Conducting open-ended interviews
- Starting outside the box
- Stepping in to define issues
- Identifying candidates to resolve issues
- Getting back out of the box through a phased approach

When the new roles have been introduced and understood, the integrator works with the project sponsors to identify and assign the initial resources required, including

- Internal experts to be consulted, such as subject matter experts and representatives of the business areas affected by the project or business initiative

- External sources, such as industry associations, online information, consultants, and competitors

- Existing models, systems, and information repositories that will be consulted to gather information for the project

As the consultation of the initial resources identified proceeds, additional contacts and sources will surface and can be added to the list. Depending on the time availability and the depth of organizational contacts of the project sponsors, the initial list can be limited or it can be fairly comprehensive. It should not be exhaustive.

Build "Best Guess" Models

The goal of the next step is to develop a starting point for viewpoint analysis models that capture the essence of each significant point of view represented in the project. The integrator will do just enough preliminary research to pull together a straw man, or discussion starter, as a basis for interviews. The straw man is a descriptive model you set up so that people can knock it down and correct it, which is easier than starting from scratch.

Validate "Best Guess" Models

Validate the starting point models by reviewing with members of the technical team and by reviewing existing documents. If necessary, do some external research on the industry to make sure you understand the basic concepts of doing business in the target market space. (See Chapter 13, "Using Integration Models to Synthesize Industry Models," for a discussion of industry research and integration modeling.) Test your models against a brief review of industry norms.

Conduct Interviews with Internal Experts and External Sources

Serial interviewing is the preferred method of gathering information in viewpoint analysis models. The goal is to understand the different viewpoints without having them modify one another, as usually happens in a group setting such as Joint Application Design or focus groups.

Interviews should start by introducing the goals of the project, the point of the models, and the conventions of the models. Interview subjects can depart from the preliminary models and just describe their situation, or they can offer updates to the models. Use them as conversation starters, not as formal controls on where the interview can go. In the same vein, predetermined survey questions are usually not recommended. If desired anyway, send them out ahead of time and collect responses at the interview, only clarifying verbally what's not clear from the written responses.

Analyze and Improve Models

This is the point where you step back, review the viewpoint analysis models, and begin to select and apply the desired integration models. Scenarios and view models typically reveal the integration issues of the project, surfacing the concerns of the business area representatives.

As you begin to identify solutions, you will update the models and return them to interview subjects for their feedback and corroboration. This process is an iterative cycle that terminates when the new models have become clear and project participants understand the responses to their particular concerns.

The following section on integration issues shows how integration models are applied to resolve integration issues in an ERP example.

Generate Recommendations

The outcome of one or more iterations of analyzing and improving viewpoint models is formulated into a set of recommendations for the overall solution. The recommendations should include action items at two levels: near-term deliverables and long-term plans.

Try to identify areas of opportunity where relatively simple, minor, or low-cost improvements can be made in such a way that significant integration benefits are accrued. These opportunities are considered "low hanging fruit" because they are most within reach and available to be harvested early on in the Enterprise Resource Planning project.

The purpose of introducing a tactical element at this time in the project is twofold:

- Early returns in cost and time-savings
- Visible successes from the project early on to build credibility and support throughout the organization

The recommendations presented should provide both interim solutions and long-term or strategic solutions.

Present Deliverables

Deliverables presented should draw on the pool of scenarios, view models, and integration models developed. They are organized to present the recommended solutions in the context of their business setting.

View models and integration model solutions are presented to the project champion and business area contributors. They provide the requirement basis for configuring the ERP package. The integrator will collaborate with specialists knowledgeable in the installation requirements of the package selected.

Integration models solutions provide the basis for subsequent technical models. A subset of the solutions models and subsequent technical models are presented to the technical teams who will carry out the actual implementation of the packaged solution. View models can be presented if the team needs orientation to specific current implementations.

Integration Issues

To integrate applications across an enterprise, as ERP requires, you must understand their origins in the business objectives that define the system requirements. We're not looking for those origins to provide a history lesson, but more of a prime directive. The question is first how to get the prime directive and then how to get it into a context that's meaningful.

Knowledge Gaps

When systems and business functions are managed in isolation, with a manager focused on his or her turf alone, you end up with everyone responsible for a piece and no one responsible for the whole. Furthermore, you create a situation where no one knows what occurs outside his or her own rigidly defined domain. Managers learn to manage upward and downward, but not across the organization.

The result is a gap in just the kind of information that an ERP project requires: knowledge about the relationships between systems and the business objectives of applications, and knowledge about the future requirements for them to cooperate.

Scenarios and Viewpoint Analysis

To bridge the knowledge gap, you introduce scenarios and viewpoint analysis models. These enable you to model current usage of applications across the company, interviewing as needed to understand individual differences in requirements. You then produce a series of models for each viewpoint, gathering an understanding of what is most important to each perspective.

The resulting collection of models delineates the differences between the relative positions of many project stakeholders. Some of the variations identified are minor, whereas others seem irreconcilable. However, you now have the advantage of knowing about them, and knowing them from inside the viewpoint, as they appear to the owners of the system.

On completing this analysis, you are armed with information that no one else in the company has, and that many could use.

On some of the projects from which this example was composed, the scenarios were strictly verbal. They consisted of verbal exchanges of stories, which told us why our interview subjects held the views they did. For the purposes of this example, some of the most significant scenarios have been formalized and written down. In addition, the related view models for those selected are presented below. The selected list includes

- CIO scenario
- CIO view model
- Sales scenario
- Sales view model
- Marketing scenario
- Marketing view model
- Other view models (listed to give an idea of the scope)

The CIO Scenario

The IT department has teams supporting systems in 12 sites across the country, and the only similarity between the 12 is the general function the systems are performing. Different hardware and software configurations are in each site, some PC-based, some midrange, and a couple even running dumb terminals against old mainframes. The software was written at different times by different vendors, some of which aren't even in business anymore. It's a hodge-podge of aging systems, and a big problem is there's no way to leverage resources across that chasm.

No one can provide an overview of all the systems. None of the technical managers can see the forest for the trees, and they spend all their time putting out local fires. What's needed is not just knowledge of all the systems and what they do in technology terms—what's really needed is to know why they do what they do, and whether they need to continue doing it today and tomorrow. Because not only must yesterday's systems and technology be understood, but the main charter is to bring those systems into the new Millennium by installing ERP systems. At the same time, new technologies must be utilized to pay off by supporting re-engineered business processes and the changing demands of a fast-paced marketplace before the competition does it first and puts the company out of business altogether.

The CIO View Model

The CIO view model (see Figure 12.2) shows a broad viewpoint, with high-level information about systems and the end users of the technology represented. It describes the functions of the systems but stops short of employing technical names. Depending on our goals, we could add much more detail on the systems (application names, technical platform, network and facilities types, primary data flows, processing timing windows) without changing the broad view perspective of the model. It would still stand for what the CIO sees when he looks at the technical environment from a top-down perspective. The information could still be taken in at a glance.

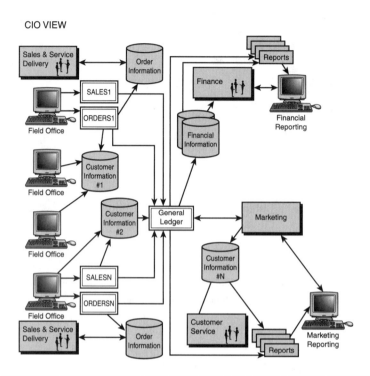

Figure 12.2   The CIO View model depicts what the CIO sees when looking at the technical environment from a top-down perspective.

The Sales Scenario

Mac's scenario from Chapter 1, "The Context for Enterprise Application Integration (EAI)," is repeated below for the sake of convenience:

> *Mac, from Sales, has finally gotten his client Bill Smith to agree to a face-to-face meeting, to discuss follow-on business. He's excited because Bill's company is a big client and a lot is riding on this sale, so he's not leaving anything to chance this morning. He's wearing a $500 suit, he's got all the collateral sales materials the client could possibly want to see, he's even got his laptop with a fancy new calculator program that allows him to generate a price quote on the spot.*
>
> *But as soon as he sits down across the desk from Bill, he suspects something is wrong. Bill's not smiling as big as usual and he seems to be keeping his distance this morning. Mac's antennae are shouting, "Something's wrong!" but he doesn't have a clue what it might be.*
>
> *"So, Mac, your company services a lot of accounts for us all over the country, right?"*
>
> *"That's right, Bill; in fact, that's one of the reasons we're a good fit for you locally. We know your company, how you like to do things; it won't take much to ramp up operations here based on what we're already doing for your company."*

"So what can you tell me about the problems in Denver last night? I understand Tom's still waiting on his morning reports..."

At this point, Mac knows he's dead in the water. It's happened before, and even though he went through the roof last time, it's happening again. Nobody called to brief him, and now instead of making the sale, he's got to pacify an angry client even though he had nothing to do with the problem.

The Sales View Model

The sales view model clearly acknowledges the importance of the customer to the sales representative by placing the customer in a central position at the top of the chart. Field offices support sales activities by sending collateral materials and special offers, and by providing service to customers. The sales representative obtains sales collateral from the field office and pricing information from centrally managed computer systems. Field offices report performance results (and problems) to headquarters using central computer systems. But when that information flows only one way, sales associates struggle with the type of knowledge deficit you read about in Mac's scenario.

As you can see, the data Mac needs (performance and problem information being sent from field offices to the central computer systems) appears on the model shown in Figure 12.3, stored in databases loaded by the central computer systems, but without connections tying it back to the sales representative. In the end, changes to this model, distributing "trouble reports" across districts, provided an early warning system to the sales force, heading off the kind of blindsiding that Mac had encountered from a client.

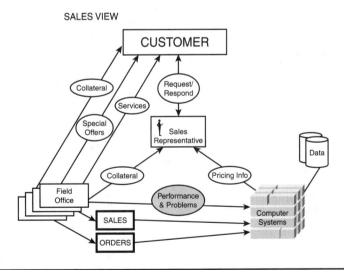

Figure 12.3   The Sales View model depicts what's important to the sales representative.

The Marketing Scenario

> *The VP from accounting is presenting charts and graphs on product performance and recommended price changes for next quarter. Along with marketing, they're in the quarterly meeting with the president of the division, and their teams have put in weeks of hard work, pulling together the numbers to present. Watching the accounting numbers unfold, the marketing representative knows his figures are checked and rechecked, formatted and graphed to perfection, so even a busy executive could follow along.*
>
> *As accounting is summarizing the situation, she pulls out her last chart, and marketing slowly starts to shake his head. "What's going on?" he wonders to himself. "Those numbers can't be right. Somebody's way off. But this is finance, and she ought to know." And the VP from marketing suddenly knows that it's going to be a long weekend, searching back through weeks of work, trying to find the point where this train jumped the track.*

The Marketing View Model

The marketing view (see Figure 12.4) captures the importance of data sharing and reporting for the analysis and presentation of across-the-board information. Requirements for the ERP implementation include the incorporation of data from internal systems, reports, and extracts, as well as from external sources.

MARKETING VIEW

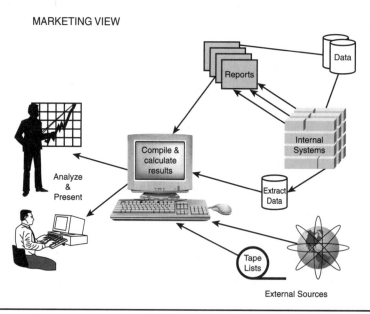

Figure 12.4   The Marketing View model captures the importance of data sharing and reporting to the marketing department.

Other View Models

For the sake of brevity, a few key view models have been included in this example. Some other view models that were developed on typical projects included

- **Current Systems View**—Internal Reporting
- **Current Systems View**—Billing and Payments
- **Provider's View**—Reporting for Clients
- **Financial View**—Billing
- **Financial View**—Payments
- **Sales View**—New Business
- **Field Office View**

Scenarios, some as brief as a descriptive paragraph, accompany each view model.

Specific Integration Issues

Modeling the previous viewpoints defined a clear set of business objectives for the implementation of the ERP software. Based on the models, seven specific integration issues were identified and resolved with the help of integration models:

1. Redundant data and multiple non-matching data sources
2. Significant data-sharing shortfall
3. Poor integration of external data sources
4. Lack of connectivity
5. Lack of internal cost-allocation mechanisms
6. Limited management reporting
7. Limited client reporting

Redundant Data and Multiple Non-Matching Data Sources

The CIO view model (refer to Figure 12.2) revealed that this company was storing duplicate information about the same business subjects, as well as maintaining multiple non-matching sources for that information. They were producing marketing reports from one set of systems and financial reports from another. Little wonder that those reports rarely delivered matching financials to the executives.

Before implementing a new system, the redundant data needed to be consolidated into a shared data repository. The Seed template provides the visual pattern for the strategy of building a shared data repository.

The relevant portion of the CIO view model is redesigned, based on the template, to consolidate sales, order, and customer information into one shared data repository, which can be supported by the packaged ERP solution. The model in Figure 12.5 shows the solution applying the data-sharing strategy.

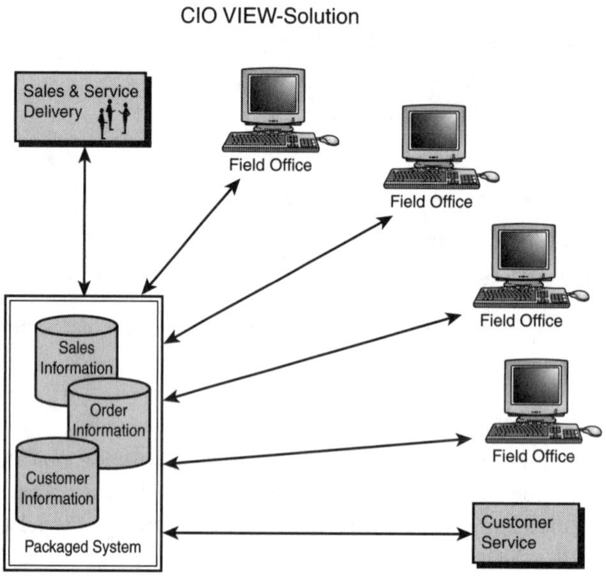

Figure 12.5   CIO View—The Solution model applies the Seed integration model for a core component, which collects and contains an array of inputs.

The newly consolidated database becomes the sending application source for a data warehouse implementation, which is distributed using a local area network for marketing and financial reporting use.

Significant Data-Sharing Shortfall

The view models show sales teams in one location operating from customer information that is unique to that branch and not shared with other branches, even though the customers often visit and do business with many branches. Service delivery processes are also unique depending on location, and therefore cannot share information either. These concerns and the lack of integration behind them must be addressed in the requirements for the rollout of the new packaged systems.

It is important to understand how applications exchange information, and the shortfall of those methods. Many business areas routinely manage failed system interfaces by printing a report from system A, walking it over to system B's input screen and keying in the information. Analysis of the application interfaces should always include all the interfaces, automated or manual. It also should include both the designed interfaces and those that evolve as workarounds.

To resolve the issues that are revealed in both the previous sales and CIO view models, a new model emerges, as shown in Figure 12.6. In the new model, redundant data are consolidated, and multiple data sources are reconciled. Management reporting of both financial and marketing information is centralized into a data warehouse along with "trouble reports" for companywide distribution. Sales and service delivery processes are re-engineered so that information can be shared and customers can appear once in the database with all relevant information available across branches.

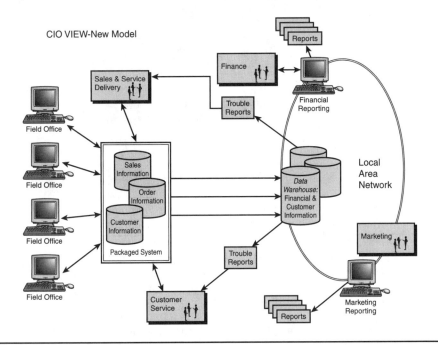

Figure 12.6   CIO View—A New model resolves the issues that were revealed in both Sales and CIO View models.

On closer inspection, models for the financial view also indicate problems in data definitions and subsequent problems sharing data in the process that extends from pricing to customer payment collection. In fact, pricing activities belong to one business area, negotiation of contract agreements belong to another, and service delivery belongs to yet another business area, and so on through accounts receivable, billing, and collections. The definitions of data differ from one area to the next, and this ERP project offers the first opportunity, in many cases, for these areas to work together on common definitions.

To define the requirements for data integration in the shared databases, the Flow template (see Figure 12.7) is utilized.

FLOW
The flow template is utilized by process and flow analysis to
trace the course of information, goods, services, and communications.

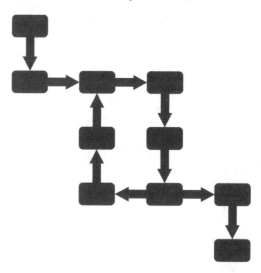

Figure 12.7   Process and flow analysis utilizes the Flow template to trace
the course of information, goods, services, and communications.

The Flow template helps the team depict the steps involved and begin reconciling data definitions. Separating the steps through workflow analysis enables the team to identify variances in data definitions and helps them understand the use and required content of related repositories.

As guidelines providing data flow for the shared database strategy, the resulting new view model (shown in Figure 12.8) provides the solution. Other models and specifications are developed to detail the data entities and relationships encompassed by the Flow template.

Based on the Financial view model, the team understands that it must determine an overall definition of product for the company, and the support of marketing executives is enlisted for this effort. What makes up a product is defined according to key parameters in the following areas:

- Market
- Customer type
- Delivery mechanism
- Investment cost/return
- Business unit

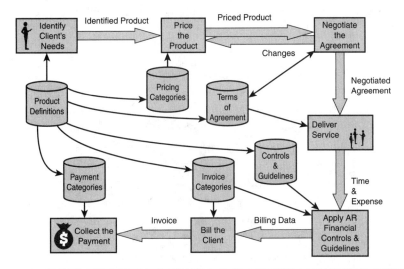

FINANCIAL VIEW: From Pricing to Payment-Process

Figure 12.8 The Financial View model depicts the steps and data involved in the process that extends from pricing to payment.

- Type of account
- Line of business
- Geography
- Performance measurements
- Pricing guidelines
- Competition

The team learned that the pricing categories must lead to the terms of contractual agreements, reflecting their structure. Contracts should reconcile with the invoice categories in use, and all of these must add up to the payment categories. Pricing categories incorporating direct and indirect costs are established and defined. The terms of contractual agreements are defined and categorized. Billing requirements are established, with the invoice to include "the minimum amount of information that the client needs in order to pay." Finally the cost equation for pricing is analyzed and the rules for allocating cost back to customers or to other accounting units is clarified and documented.

Lack of Integration of External Data Sources

The Marketing view model in Figure 12.4 indicates the importance of integrating external data sources into the systems solution. However, many of these sources are amorphous and not well understood. The Cell template helps marketing analyze the subject areas for inclusion, capturing the significant definitions and data sources. The model in Figure 12.9 shows the initial set of subject areas as determined by the business strategies for market positioning.

Figure 12.9   The Business Strategies for Market Positioning model depicts the initial set of subject areas defined by the marketing area.

Cell models enable you to analyze and define data interfaces, initiating the requirements for the shared-data architecture. Subsequent models focus on the data required for each cell compartment, as shown in Figure 12.10, which shows one example of the models developed to depict the next level down from broad subject area definitions to detailed data models.

It is then an easy transition from the previous model to producing use case models for the technical requirement level. Figure 12.11 shows the resulting use case model from which the technical requirements can then be driven down into class diagrams, component diagrams, and so forth.

Lack of Connectivity

One requirement that had to be supported by the ERP implementation was to improve on the company's distribution of information by providing new mechanisms of connectivity.

The Ring template (see Figure 12.12) provides the pattern element for distribution. The Ring template models peer-to-peer relationships in non-directional organization. It is applied here as a mode of connectivity.

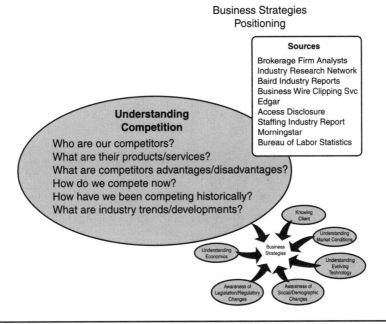

Figure 12.10   Next-level models focus on usage requirements.

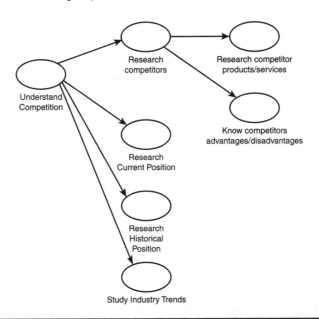

Figure 12.11   The Use Case Tree model depicts the
activities involved in competitive analysis.

RING
The ring template is useful in depicting chaining of events, people, devices or network addresses. Models peer-to-peer relationships.

Figure 12.12   The Ring template is useful for depicting the chaining of events, people, devices, or network addresses. It models peer-to-peer relationships.

With companies employing growth strategies that are powered by merger and acquisition, issues of connectivity are common. One of the less obvious problems is that different acquired companies configure their branch and field offices in different ways. They combine support offices with regional branches, and have different means of tying all the information back to headquarters.

The Ring template is applied to produce a consolidated connectivity map for all the different configurations that exist in branches in the field, as shown in Figure 12.13.

The Office Connectivity Map shows the variety of available models for networking branches together and how they are connected to both field support and headquarters.

In this diagram, the outer ring represents connections to support back-office functions such as payroll, billing, and collection. The inner ring represents enabling decision-support functions, including statistical reporting that goes from branches or support offices to the corporate offices and the compiled summary information that goes back to the branch, such as branch performance, profit and loss, and weekly and monthly job order statistics.

Corporate Office (#1 on the diagram) represents corporate headquarters where back-office functions take place, including payroll, billing, collection, legal, marketing and sales, and recruiting support, technology support, training and human resources, and so forth.

Branch Support Office (configuration #2 on the diagram) shows how main branches operate, with an area manager and support personnel performing administrative support and marketing and sales support in the Branch Support Office, while relying on

Corporate Office to provide other back-office functions. In some instances, branch offices report hierarchically to a regional branch support office, which reports to corporate, and in others, a branch can report to another branch, which then reports to a region reporting to corporate.

Network View - Office Connectivity Map

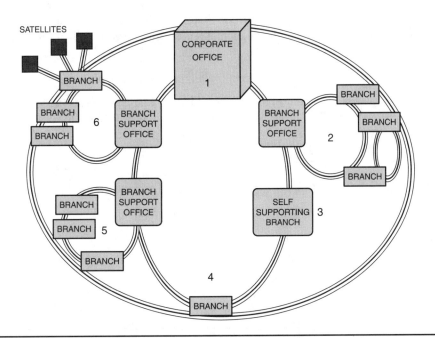

Figure 12.13   The Network View model of Office Connectivity Map shows the different configurations that exist in branches in the field.

Self-Supporting Branch depicts branches where one branch operates as if it were an independent entity, providing all its own front and back office support functions, and relating to corporate only through performance and decision-support reporting.

Branch (#4 on the diagram) depicts a possible target model for the future, where the branch is supported in both front and back-office functions by the corporate office through automation, creating a "virtual office" environment.

Branch Support Office (#5 on the diagram) represents offices where the original corporate headquarters of the acquired company is still providing front and back-office support.

Branch Support Office (#6 on the diagram) shows how branches operate with the original headquarters providing administrative and sales and recruiting support, and back-office functions such as payroll and billing coming out of the corporate office. This example also shows satellite offices, which are employed to extend the reach of a branch and provide a local presence in a more distant market.

Lack of Internal Cost-Allocation Mechanisms

Initial interviews surfaced accounting problems with the allocation of overhead costs, where managed accounts carried an unfair proportion of the burden for infrastructure cost and retail accounts were unintentionally subsidized. The Tree template (see Figure 12.14) was used to explore the distribution alternatives for correcting the internal allocation of costs.

TREE
The Tree is a structure utilized to model systems whose characteristics include complex branching, diversification and the implementation of distribution alternatives.

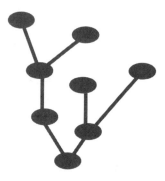

Figure 12.14   The Tree template is used to explore the distribution alternatives.

After the cost of support services is allocated properly over the four market divisions of the example company, the divisions can, in turn, allocate expenses to the field offices (see the Cost Allocation View in Figure 12.15). Feedback mechanisms are also designed for managing projections and year-end overages.

Limited Management Reporting

Another problem that rises to the surface in enterprise-wide efforts is that of comparing statistics from incompatible systems. Within the confines of one system, the numbers can make sense to the recipients of system reports. But as the marketing scenario demonstrated, fragmented information sources can lead to mismatches in management reporting.

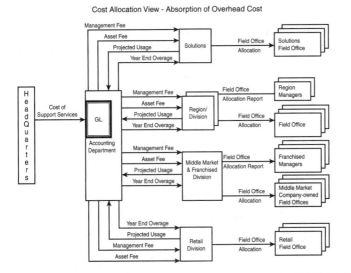

Cost Allocation View - Absorption of Overhead Cost

Figure 12.15   The Cost Allocation View model depicts
the strategy for absorption of overhead cost.

The goal of the corporate information repository is to store data once, updating it only under controlled conditions. The model in Figure 12.16 shows the solution, housing financial and customer information in a data warehouse for reconciled management reporting to all levels.

Management Reporting View - Solution

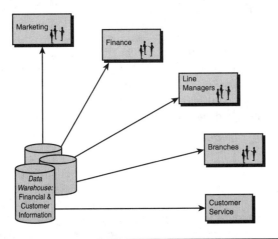

Figure 12.16   The Management Reporting View—The Solution model depicts
the use of a shared repository to reconcile management reporting.

Limited Client Reporting

Client reporting trends in employment services created a demand for extensive reporting of service statistics such as turnover, absenteeism, number of calls, average response speed, skills supplied, staff usage, and reasons for staffing levels. It was important to consolidate these service statistics into shared databases as well, as depicted in Figure 12.17, for distribution to identified types of clients.

Client Reporting View - Solution

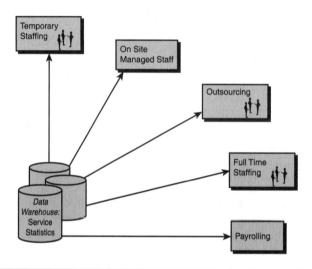

Figure 12.17   The Client Reporting View model depicts
the shared repository solution for data sharing.

Subsequent use-case models and technical specifications defined the programs and reports required and their distribution plan. The increased integration of the client reporting view enabled major customers of the employment services firm to identify the most successful locations and their practices, the least successful locations and their practices, and to transfer best practices accordingly. Weekly and monthly tracking of key indicators was automated and supported by performance incentives.

Summary

On implementing an ERP packaged system, the implementation model is provided by the vendor, so what is most needed from the standpoint of the company installing the package are the requirements for configuring and integrating the package system. When integration models were applied to the companies represented by this case study, they provided the glue between the business area representative's views and the technical team. The resulting solution models were used to orient the staff resources that were brought in by the package vendor. They were also used to carve out the implementation project and orient the internal teams who would carry out the project.

Upon the nationwide rollout of the new system, the company realized the following benefits:

- Branch managers around the country improved customer satisfaction dramatically using integrated customer information.
- Branches increased their gross income because they were now better able to supply customers with the right people with the right skills at the right time and place.
- Efficiencies gained through integration reduced operating margins significantly.

13

Using Integration Models to Synthesize Industry Models

SYNTHESIZING INDUSTRY MODELS means looking outside your company to review the state of the art of approaches to your requirements. How do others view this situation? How do others solve similar problems? What's the benchmark for this technology in the industry today? Can models in other industries be adapted to your needs? What are the best practices in use in companies similar to yours? To answer these questions involves scanning the literature, advertising, and other sources of information about your industry to identify the patterns and best practices currently being applied. This scanning teaches you about the current issues in an industry, and surfaces the latest solutions to those issues. It gets you acquainted with the ins and outs of an industry and puts you in a position to recognize and generate new ideas for solving industry-wide problems.

According to the definition of creativity put forward by Mihaly Csikszentimihalyi, a leading expert on the psychology of discovery and invention, to be creative in the terms of an industry means to introduce something new into the field of play of that industry. "Creativity occurs when a person, using the symbols of a given domain such as music, engineering, business, or mathematics, has a new idea or sees a new pattern, and when this novelty is selected by the appropriate field for inclusion into the relevant domain" [13.1]. Synthesizing industry models is a method of accessing the current state of a domain, and extending that state by introducing something new.

Synthesizing means pulling together the pieces from many different sources and perspectives, and combining them to make a generic model. It helps you not only understand the industry in which your business operates, but get ideas for addressing the current problems and requirements your business faces. It also suggests requirements that you might not otherwise have thought of, but might actually need. It gives you both a broader perspective to work from and access to the ideas of many others operating in the same field of play.

Synthesizing industry models helps you understand the field of play for your endeavor. Especially when you have spent years in one company within an industry, you need mechanisms for grasping the current trends, identifying the ones that can be applied successfully to your company, and turning them to your advantage. The models that appear and are developed within an industry embody best practices. Business models, process models, and information models are all utilized to portray the methods by which companies conduct business.

The Goal of Synthesizing Industry Models

Synthesizing the models of an industry helps you understand the possible ways of doing business within the industry and extract the best practices into a working repository. The goal is to avoid reinventing the wheel by understanding what is already known within the industry and capitalizing on that knowledge. Modeling the information is a way of abstracting the principles and clarifying how they work together to provide new solutions to industry issues. As you develop such a model, the categories and types of solutions emerge, and often ways of going beyond the current models also become apparent.

What Are Industry Models?

Industry models are the modes of operation or practices that evolve within an industry. They embody ways of thinking, ways of relating to customers, and ways of providing products and services. They capture the essence of preferred practices, and they represent the concerns shared by participants in an industry and the common solutions to those concerns. Industry models formulate some successful responses to common problems encountered by industry participants.

When many companies within an industry encounter similar problems, they engage in a search for answers, sometimes collectively and sometimes individually. As an idea for a solution emerges, resources begin to group around it. Industry leaders recognize it as a good solution and they begin to talk about it, the industry press picks it up as a story, and vendors begin to target the market that emerges. Figure 13.1 shows the cycle of innovation that ensues.

Cycle of Innovation

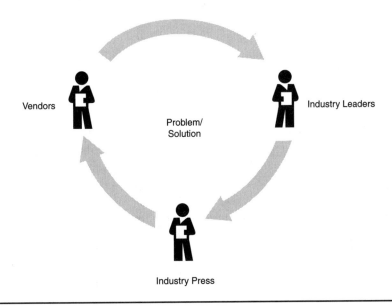

Figure 13.1   Innovation occurs in an industry around three key resources.

Any of the three key resources (industry leaders, industry press, and vendors) can initiate the cycle and contribute to the solutions identified. Innovation is an ongoing process which peaks at times of greatest need and when the industry achieves new discoveries that are then incorporated into all the surviving participants. For instance, the cable TV and telecommunications industries are now racing to incorporate advanced technology to provide increased consumer bandwidth and the services it promises, such as video-on-demand and interactive applications for the retail consumer.

The Migration of Industry Innovations

A similar process occurs across industries, as innovations in one industry are discovered and picked up by another. Revenue management is an example of an innovation in the airline industry that has been replicated for use in the hospitality and other industries. An idea that evolved out of the practice of yield management in the airlines, revenue management has taken on a life of its own and migrated to other industries where it has proved its value. In cases such as this, the model itself (revenue management) becomes more significant than its origins, and moves across industries as an idea. With business now operating on Internet time, we see ideas spreading much like a virus, jumping from one business to another, and from one industry to another.

Because of the influence of technology and the timing of de-regulations, many industries are getting somewhat redefined, and what's good for one industry may be even better or at least as good, for another. With the facilitation provided by Internet communications, these evolving business models are shaping the nature and direction of business so fast that even the companies picking up the trends rarely see the big picture until they're played out.

The goal of this chapter is to formalize this organic cycle of innovation that occurs continually in the business world, and help companies pursue innovation and the evolution of business models across industries more consciously. My intent is to facilitate the process of industry modeling by defining the process and advocating in favor of it.

Examples of Industry Models

Industry models capture and express the existent and emerging solutions to industry-wide issues. They are often conceptual in nature, as many business models are, and might not have ever been rendered in graphical models. For example, in software operations management, *lights out processing* refers to the ability to manage computer operations remotely, in a highly automated fashion, and with minimal operator involvement. Another operations target is the 24/7 model, which applies to any activity functioning continuously for 24 hours a day, 7 days a week.

In telecommunications, *zero-touch provisioning* refers to the quick and easy setup of Digital Subscriber Line (DSL) services for subscribers. "The Holy Grail is zero-touch provisioning," says Abhijit Ingle, senior product manager of OSS/broadband services at Covad Communications Company (Santa Clara, California). "You want to make DSL mind-numbingly simple to buy" [13.2].

Across industries, models such as customer relationship management (CRM), enterprise resource planning (ERP), and business to business (B2B) describe current approaches and types of solutions to common issues.

In banking, various models for database marketing and customer relationship and retention have been important in recent years. Profitability-based customer segmentation provides an example, with its strategies of defining A, B, and C customer profiles and making marketing decisions based on the perceived value of the customer relationship. Current trends see this model giving way before the concept of customer-needs–driven marketing and the customer-managed relationship, where "the customer, not the financial institution, dictates the nature of the relationship with a financial services institution" [13.3].

In the airline industry, revenue management and strategic measures are current concerns around which industry models revolve. Revenue management is an example of an industry model that originated in one industry and proved useful for others, migrating to the hospitality and lodging industries, as well as theatre, rental cars, cruise lines, and television broadcasting.

Current Internet developments are rapidly spawning all kinds of new business models, while technology developments also spur innovation in offline technologies or converging technologies for telephony, networking, and communications.

Industry models emerge as conceptual models, and their methods of solving industry issues can be captured through the use of integration modeling to inform the desired implementation solutions.

Reasons to Synthesize Industry Models

Many reasons exist for corporations to seek to understand and synthesize the existing and new models within an industry. A corporation can be conducting a business-reengineering project, and need to establish new targets which raise the bar for business processes. Another company can be seeking to enter new markets with new products or acquisitions and want to scan the competition to understand the business arena they're entering. Another reason to synthesize industry models is to gain a competitive advantage by moving into a market space by evolving the existing models to move beyond the competition.

A consulting firm or software vendor, on the other hand, often targets an industry or vertical market and needs to keep current with practices within the market, periodically scanning it for new developments. Or, if that consulting firm wants to enter new markets by providing services that cross industries, it can quickly develop a picture of the industry and become conversant with its norms, business models, and terminology.

Synthesizing involves gathering information from many different sources to gain an in-depth understanding of a subject. When you read an article about a new topic, you get one person's viewpoint and ideas. It gives you the limited view of one person's knowledge, with no way of evaluating the information—nothing to compare it to. When you read another source, you can make comparisons between the two and begin to identify subjects and issues in common between the two sources. As you gain more and more views about the topic, you learn your way around the subject area and develop an intricate knowledge of what the issues, specifics, and landscape are for that particular subject area.

Synthesizing also involves distilling the information you have gathered into the essence of the subject area. Gathering expands your knowledge of the subject, whereas distillation consolidates it into the principles of that subject. To help catalyze the distillation process, integration modeling is used to clarify the dynamics of the information and organize it in new ways around those dynamics. The result is a condensed version of the information, honed to precision by the modeling process.

Knowledge tends to evolve in a synthesizing way naturally, in the practice of a discipline and in its community at large. The goal of this chapter is to surface this type of evolution and formalize it so that it becomes available as a tool of learning about any industry or practice that might be applicable to your company's current requirements.

How to Synthesize—What Does It Require?

Synthesizing requires that you create a space to gather information into, in other words, a repository. Your repository might be as simple as a file folder, or as complex as a highly structured database. The important point is to have a place to put the information you gather. As you gather data and learn about the industry or subject area, you will find out the categories of information, and you can allow the structure of the repository to emerge. Working with the structuring and restructuring of the information will bring you a clarity and depth of understanding of the material.

This type of synthesizing requires scanning the literature and information sources. The following are a few of the types of sources that can be scanned:

- Internet sites
- Internet databases
- Industry journals
- Industry associations

Integration models provide a way of organizing the repository. They reflect the dynamics of the problems and solutions under consideration, and help to formalize the innovations of the industry.

Method for Synthesizing Industry Models

Figure 13.2 illustrates the process model for synthesizing industry models.

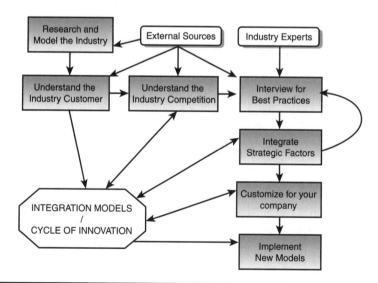

Figure 13.2   Synthesizing industry models is a process of discovery and innovation.

The model shows the high-level steps involved in synthesizing industry models. The first five steps are usually performed concurrently as a process of discovery. The last two steps of customization and implementation ensure that the models reflect the norms and style of your company before deploying them into the field. These steps are described in the remaining sections of this chapter.

Research and Model the Industry

The first step is to conduct in-depth research on the industry that is of interest. In this step you will gather information about the subjects pertinent to your project and begin to distill that information by selecting integration models and building a first draft of industry models. Subsequent steps will add more specific information to the models, test and verify them against subject matter experts and customers, and prepare them for implementation in your company. The sub-processes for this step include the following:

- Classify the industry
- Conduct general research on the industry
- Identify industry success stories
- Select relevant IM templates
- Distill industry models

Classify the Industry

Determine the standard industrial classification of the industry your company belongs to, how it fits with closely related industries, and where the dividing line between industries is drawn. This will enable you to seek information sources within that classification.

Standard Industrial Classification (SIC) codes are being replaced by the North American Industry Classification System for classifying industries. Because this replacement is still underway, it can be necessary to use either or both SIC and NAICS codes, depending on the information source you want to use. You can look up the classification for your industry at the U.S. Census Bureau's NAICS site online at `http://www.census.gov/pub/epcd/www/naics.html`. NAICS information is also available in the official U.S. NAICS Manual, *North American Industry Classification System: United States* [13.4], which includes definitions for each industry, tables showing correspondence between NAICS and SIC codes, and a comprehensive index. You can then use the NAICS code to perform the next step, conducting general research on the industry.

Conduct General Research on the Industry

You can look up the industry in the *Statistical Abstract of the U.S.* [13.5]. This work provides a collection of statistics on social and economic conditions in the United States, some international data, and a guide to sources of other data from the Census Bureau, other federal agencies, and private organizations. The *U.S. Industry and Trade Outlook 2000* [13.6] also provides a good overview by industry of the U.S. economy. It is produced by the Office of Trade and Economic Analysis, and can be accessed at `http://www.ita.doc.gov/td/industry/otea/`.

You can also identify trade organizations, publications, and trade shows to help you understand the issues of an industry. See the source book *National Trade and Professional Associations of the United States* [13.7] for detailed information about industry associations. Online databases of associations also can be used to identify trade associations. These include the following:

- `AssociationCentral.com`, which provides information on services and products offered by trade associations and professional societies.
- ASAENET Gateway to Associations at `http://info.asaenet.org/gateway/OnlineAssocSlist.html`.

Another good source of industry information is annual corporate reports from companies in the industry. You can obtain these by contacting companies directly or through services that provide annual reports, such as the Wall Street Journal's service. You can use annual reports and any other issues identified from scanning the literature to profile an industry and develop a list of the industry's current concerns.

After you have researched the current literature of the industry, you can seek specific models to address the concerns of your business or project.

Identify Industry Success Stories

Success stories include industry problems and their solutions, and embody the collective wisdom of practitioners within an industry. They can be found by searching news and article sites with the industry issues identified previously. These resources contain the current industry models, which you can extract and formalize through modeling techniques. Use them to analyze what worked for other companies in circumstances similar to yours, and to apply their learning to your own situation. Success stories can describe solutions in a particular company or a generic situation applying to several companies. Sometimes vendors and service providers offer summaries of industry successes in white papers.

Your goal is to extract the essence of such stories from several different sources and use that information as base material for compiling your own approach. Your approach will be defined with the application of relevant integration models.

For example, the ideal environment for the customer-managed relationship in banking is the highly interactive medium of the Internet, which would be depicted with the Web template. It enables you to model a networked solution with multiple connections or access paths for the customer to connect to the financial institution.

Other good sources of success stories are case studies, which are utilized in journals, academic writings, and other resources to document industry successes. Some useful sources of case studies are listed below:

- The Harvard Business School Case Studies Index, located at `http://www.hbsp.harvard.edu/products/cases/collections.html`.

- The European Case Clearinghouse provides access to case studies from several different databases, including HBR and California Management Review reprints. It is located at `http://www.ecch.cranfield.ac.uk/`.

- The Darden Case Collection contains over 1600 cases, case series, and technical notes that have been successfully used at The Darden School. Located at `http://www.darden.virginia.edu/research/index.htm`.

Select Relevant IM Templates

Integration models are selected based on the functioning of the industry models you want to distill. This means taking a look at the industry models from the viewpoint of their dynamics.

How the industry models function will determine the choice of integration models. For example, lights-out processing requires that we understand all the layers involved in computer processing and have automated or remote access to manage each of those layers. The Wave template is useful in depicting those layers and helping determine the assignment of resources for managing them.

In telecommunications, the essential dynamic of the underlying technology is one of flow, which makes the Flow template an obvious fit. The zero-touch provisioning model for telecommunications lends itself to the Flow template, which can help depict the many steps of the process through which provisioning information must proceed to speed up that flow-through.

Distill Industry Models

Understanding the essence of a solution to a current industry problem, you can build that solution into an integration model that will illustrate the following:

- **Dynamics**—Determines how the solution functions. It can be cyclical and repetitive as in the Cycle template, or a process with linear steps as in the Flow template. If it employs networked connections, the Web or the Ring template can be used. A solution that is achieved through branching diversification of resources would be embodied by the Tree structure. Discrete packages of information would suggest the Cell template.

- **Requirements**—Modeling a solution to a business problem is the first step to defining the technology requirements for supporting the solution. Integration models indicate how a solution is characterized and suggest what issues to be aware of as you select technology implementations.

- **Usefulness and ways it can be utilized**—The model shows how the solution is used, by whom, and under what circumstances. It does this by placing the core of the solution in the context of the business to which it's applied. For instance, the Web template shows the interconnections that are required and emphasizes the parties that must be connected.

- **Technical direction**—Integration models suggest certain technical directions, such as the Web template, which suggests networked implementations, or the Flow template, which suggests a sequential processing model. Cell models tend to be facilitated best by non-sequential or set processing such as that used in accessing relational database management systems.

After integration models have been selected and utilized to distill industry models, they will be evaluated and modified against the understanding of customer, competition, and best practices, and then validated against the strategic factors at work in your situation.

Understand the Industry Customer

A good way to better understand an industry is to study its target markets and individual customers. If you want to market new products and services in an industry, you need to be able to document expected interactions between your customer and your products and services. These customer scenarios will help you become clear about what's important to customers and the prioritization of their values for your offerings. After you develop your customer scenarios, you'll need to validate them by talking to potential and actual customers and getting their response to your formalization of their needs. The following activities are required to understand the industry customer:

- Research customer information
- Develop customer scenarios
- Validate customer scenarios

Research Customer Information

The goal of customer research is to develop an understanding of the market and to develop profiles of expected types of customers. Articles describing customer views, demographics, and attitudes can be located by searching for keywords on the Internet, and also by accessing targeted resources such as:

- *MarketingClick*, which provides industry news, in-depth feature articles, and other information about Internet marketing, direct marketing, public relations, promotions, advertising and other industry segments. It is located at `http://www.marketingclick.com/`.

- Census information is provided on "Uncle Sam's Reference Shelf" in the *County and City Data Book* [13.8]. Parts of this are available on the Web at `http://www.census.gov/statab/www/ccdb.html`.

- *American Demographics* magazine provides applied demographics and is located online at `http://www.demographics.com/`.

- *Direct* magazine provides news and articles about direct mail and list services marketing, at `http://www.directmag.com/`.

It can also be helpful to identify consumer magazines for the target industry, using the approaches discussed previously to locate trade organizations and publications.

Develop Customer Scenarios

Customer scenarios describe the ways in which customers interact with your company's products and services, whether offline through sales and service interactions or online through a company Web site. Scenarios can be narrative descriptions, scripts with customer actions spelled out, or captured in models such as UML use case and collaboration diagrams. In Web development, customer scenarios can be used to help visitors understand how a Web site is intended to work and what will be required of the customer in a given activity, such as signing up for membership. An excellent example of a site that successfully utilizes customer scenarios to educate site visitors can be viewed online at `http://www000212.webvan.com/default.asp` by clicking on any city area, and then on "Getting Started." Here the customer scenario has been converted into a guide for the customer thinking of signing up for Webvan's grocery delivery service. It offers a clear step-by-step process for shopping at Webvan, with screen prints and helpful information about how each step works.

The rules for developing customer scenarios are the same as those detailed in Chapter 2, "Introduction to Integration Models," for developing scenarios. They are listed below:

- Capture one viewpoint at a time
- Keep the scenario loose and informal
- Keep it focused
- Keep it short
- Feed it back

Following these rules, develop as many scenarios as needed to capture the viewpoints of various customer types or segments.

Validate Customer Scenarios

Depending on your medium, the Internet can be a good source of feedback on proposed customer scenarios. News groups, email list groups, and specially set up Web sites can be a good way to seek feedback and generate interest simultaneously. These mechanisms are set up to facilitate interactions between all kinds of participants in a field, from students to experts, and often attract potential customers for goods and services in the field. They support open discussions about the requirements for products and services and allow participants to learn about current needs and issues in the industry. Some sites that organize such lists and manage directories to them include the following:

- Egroups, which facilitates the setup and maintenance of email lists. It is located at http://www.egroups.com/.
- Topica, a free Internet service that allows you to easily find, manage, and participate in email lists. It is located at http://www.topica.com/.
- Liszt, the mailing-list directory (recently acquired by Topica, but still operating separately), and located at http://www.liszt.com/.

More traditional, and sometimes more appropriate, avenues include interviewing and focus groups with current customers and prospective customers belonging to your target markets. The goal of interviews and focus groups is to present your scenarios as conversation starters, with an invitation to customers to correct and expand on the scenarios as they see fit. In the process, you can collect valuable information about your target markets, customers, or users of your products and services, which will be integrated into the models depicting solutions for your industry.

Understand the Industry Competition

One of the best sources of strategic information is the study of the competition within your field. Annual reports give a lot of strategic information, under the heading of market outlook and business plans. These can be obtained by asking the companies in your industry, or through the sources previously designated on researching an industry.

Competitors' analysis is utilized to define a demonstrable competitive advantage that can help you protect or build each product or business. Figure 13.3 presents an example developed for an employment service company, showing a method of organizing competitor information as it is collected.

Competitor Information

	'92 Annual Sales ($ millions)	'92 Net Income ($ millions)	'93 Annual Sales ($ millions)	'93 Net Income ($ millions)	# of Employees	Year Founded	# of Field Offices	# of Customers	
Adia Services, Inc.	2,191	(149.5)	2,097	(85.7)	430,478	1957	1100	?	
Kelly Services	1,723	39	1,954	45	634,300	1946	1000 +	185,000	
MacTemp	?	?	42	?	5,927	1986	23	?	
Manpower	3,187	(47)	3,180	(49)	750,000	1948	2,069	?	
Olsten	987	21	2,158	(12)	443,000	1950	1,200	90,000+	

Figure 13.3   The matrix of competitor information shows a method of organizing competitor information as it is collected.

On a number of competitors, annual sales and net income were collected for two years and combined with information about the number of employees, the year the competitor company was founded, number of field offices, and the number of customers. The chart helps place the employment services company in the field of its competitors and is used to help answer the question, "How do we measure up to our competitors?"

Gathering competitor information involves the following activities:

- Identify similar companies
- Understand the type of competition
- Identify future directions

Identify Similar Companies

Several tools are available to help you identify similar companies within an industry. They include the following sources:

- *Transportation and Public Utilities USA, Finance, Insurance and Real Estate USA, Manufacturing USA, Service Industries USA*, and *Wholesale and Retail Trade USA* [13.9]. These publications, from the GALE Group, deliver industry analyses, statistics, and leading companies for the indicated industries.

- Using the look-up service on sites such as Quote.Com on the Web can help identify stock symbols for publicly traded companies.
- The Thomas Register is a well-known reference that provides company listings for product manufacturers. Listings include company address and annual sales estimates. The register is available online at www.thomasregister.com.
- Hoovers Online provides multiple resources for company research, profiles and information at http://www.hoovers.com/.
- SEC (Security Exchange Commission) filings for many companies are available on the Web at the Edgar Database of Corporate Information at http://www.sec.gov/edgarhp.htm.
- Sites such as PR NEWSWIRE provide recent and archived company press releases.

Understand the Type of Competition

You need to understand in which segment of the market the competitor being studied operates, based on strategies and competencies as identified in your research.

Figure 13.4 shows how competitor information is organized upon being collected, for an employment services company.

Business Categories
Strategy + Competencies = Competitive Initiatives

STRATEGIES / COMPETENCIES	Powerful Clients	Specialized Payroll Operations	Large Client Base	Elaborate Training Programs	Experience in Training	Secondary Market	Experienced in Specialized Recruiting	Ability to Tap New Technologies
Cost Leadership		Payroll Service for Client's Employees		Outsourcing Service for Aide Agencies		Referral-based Financial Staffing		Collection Services
Niche Marketing	Synergy-based Joint Venture				Speaking and Training	Temps-computer Specialists	Recruiting for Client-Financial Aide	
Market Dominance			Service Expansion to National Accounts			De facto Partnering Clients		
Increase Share of Wallet								Multi-Media Service Center
Move up the Spectrum of Services								

Figure 13.4   The Business Categories model maps strategies against competencies to evaluate competitive initiatives.

The Business Categories model helps surface the areas of opportunity where no initiatives are under way. It can be applied within a company, as shown, or to a segment within an industry, with competitors' initiatives filled in the cells, and will help quantify the windows of opportunity within the industry.

Identify Future Directions

To understand where your company stands in the industry, it is important to identify the future directions of the competitive landscape and the lines of business and product or service decisions that will differentiate your company. Figure 13.5 shows a matrix comparing competitor companies to lines of business in which they operate.

Business Categories
Competitors vs. Lines of Business

Lines of Business

	Administrative	Light Industrial	Teleservices	Accounting	Technical	Home Health Aid	Site Services	Financial	Executive Speakers
Adia Services, Inc.	✓			✓		✓		✓	
Kelly Services	✓				✓	✓			
MacTemp			✓		✓				
Manpower	✓	✓				✓			
Olsten	✓			✓		✓			

Figure 13.5 The Business Categories model shows which lines of business the primary competitors are engaged in for an employment service business.

Future directions for your industry model will be important in making decisions about timing, investment options, and market strategy. This understanding will be encoded in the integration models as they are updated, based on feedback from this step.

Interview for Best Practices, Benchmarking, and Collaboration

Some companies choose to participate in information exchange in their industry through industry associations, benchmarking, collaborations, and other forums. Others choose not to share information, considering it counter-productive to their competitive position. None will share critical strategic information, but many find collaboration helpful. Your goal is to locate the companies that are open to exchange, and set up information exchanges that make sense for your project.

Working from your earlier research on companies in your industry, make arrangements through media relations departments, contacts from association meetings, and existing forums and exchanges, many of which are facilitated through academic sources. Interviews should be open-ended to allow for discovery during the process, though it is helpful to provide a short list of discussion points when you schedule the meeting, so that participants can come prepared. The steps to carry out include the following:

- Quantify the knowledge of internal experts
- Consult external industry experts
- Purchase information from industry providers as needed

Quantify the Knowledge of Internal Experts

Determine what you already know about the subject area and what you currently do well. What are your strengths and weaknesses and those of your internal experts? Also, seek to quantify the skills you need to develop and the information you need to seek out. Develop a set of criteria that delineates the areas that you need help with, and a listing of issues of concern. This would be a good time to seek input from an experienced consultant in your field who knows the general landscape and can help you evaluate what's needed. Whether you do this on your own or with consulting help, the focus of this step is on your company and its current knowledge and expertise.

Consult External Industry Experts

Using the criteria and issues you formulated in the previous step and your research on the industry, search for industry experts. After you know what issues you're most concerned about, determine who's doing a good job with them. Is another company in your industry doing something better than your company is, or do you need to look beyond your industry and seek models in other areas? Industry success stories and case studies often include names and contacts that you can approach for their expertise.

Purchase Information from Industry Providers as Needed

You might also need to consider incorporating purchased information from industry providers to fill in the gaps in your current knowledge. Some commonly used service providers are listed below:

- Lexis-Nexis provides legal and government, business, and high-tech information products and services at `http://www.lexis-nexis.com/lncc/`.

- Hoover's Online is one of the oldest providers of company and industry information online at `http://www.hoovers.com/`.

- The Dialog Corporation provides Internet-based information and technology solutions to the corporate market at `http://www.dialog.com/`.

- Dow Jones Interactive is a customizable, enterprisewide business news and research solution. It integrates content from top national newspapers, Dow Jones and Reuters newswires, business journals, market research reports, analyst reports, and Web sites at `http://bis.dowjones.com/`.

Integrate Strategic Factors

As you narrow the subject area that your industry models cover, you will begin to incorporate the strategic factors bearing on your particular situation. These must be identified and integrated into the overall picture represented by the models. Areas to consider include the following:

- Economic influences
- Legal and regulatory climate
- Market conditions
- Geography
- Social and demographic influences
- Evolving technology

Economic Influences

Research and understand the economic ratios, industry norms, and key business ratios applicable to your project, your company, and your industry. Study annual reports, statements on the industry, and other reference works providing indicators in your industry.

Legal and Regulatory Climate

You must also understand the legal issues that are of consequence to your industry, many of which are discussed in annual corporate reports. Legal resources for current case information include the following:

- U.S. Supreme Court Web site at `www.supremecourtus.gov`.

- The law library at Emory University provides federal court decisions and cases at `http://www.law.emory.edu/FEDCTS/`.

- Public access to Court Electronic Records Directory is available at `http://pacer.psc.uscourts.gov/pubaccess.html`.

Regulatory issues of the industry can also play a major role in the development of industry models. Industries such as utilities, food and drug, transportation, firearms, and medical devices are typically highly regulated. If and when industries such as these are deregulated, as has occurred with banking and telecommunications, major changes will occur as new competition unfolds and industry consolidation takes place. Regulatory reports from companies in regulated industries are often available as part of the public record, and industry bodies that regulate the industry can provide publicly available information. Some places to look are the following:

- Government regulations for many industries are provided online by the Library of Congress at the Thomas site `http://rs9.loc.gov/home/thomas.html`.
- The Code of Federal Regulations (CFR) is a codification of the general and permanent rules published in the *Federal Register* by the executive departments and agencies of the federal government at `http://www.access.gpo.gov/nara/cfr/cfr-table-search.html`.
- U.S. Department of Labor, Occupational Safety and Health Administration, provides regulatory information at `http://www.osha.gov/`.

Market Conditions

Saturation and penetration by competitors of the desired target market affects the timing and extent of your company's expansion into new market areas. Cost of entry is another factor that must be considered. Market readiness through awareness campaigns and competitive action must be assessed. All these factors contribute to the market conditions and should be integrated into the industry models.

Geography

Determine whether the industry or innovation under consideration is locally, regionally, nationally, or internationally based. Where major competitors are located or clustered is important. The geographical distribution of suppliers and customers must be understood, along with predicted changes in the near versus long term status.

Social and Demographic Influences

Determine which social and demographic influences might affect your industry models. Telecommuting is both a social trend and a technological advance. It affects companies in the telecommunications industry that often have very progressive policies for employees to telecommute, because such policies are in alignment with their product strategies. Other social trends include the increasing use of the Internet and the increasing need for leave of absence to care for aging parents or for children. Market demographics affect the potentials of certain industry models, and should be incorporated as well.

Evolving Technology

In the technical arena, new developments turn over about every 3 to 6 months. Industry resources such as Gartner and Meta-Group, monitor and report on technology trends, but given that they tend to run approximately 6 months behind the curve, avoid making them your only source of information. They can provide breadth and depth on surviving technologies and trends, but you should seek other sources for the newest and latest happenings. Keeping a finger on the pulse of technological developments is the point here. As technology evolves, new capabilities emerge, and that causes your business models to evolve. The relationship between business and technology is a cooperative one with mutual influence exchanged.

You need to understand the advances in technology for the models you are synthesizing. There's no way to read everything that comes across your desk in today's information-rich climate, so your job is to scan the available literature and note variances. One CIO told me he likes to take the industry magazines and scan the advertisements to get a sense of what's going on. Monitor news and other sources for developments. The following are some places to look:

- **Industry magazines**

  Information Week

  Application Development Trends

  Harvard Business Review

  Sloan Management Review

  America's Network

  Enterprise Development

  Electronic Commerce World

  E-business Advisor

  eAI Journal

- **Online technology reviews**

  Cnet at `http://news.cnet.com/`

  TechRepublic at `http://www.techrepublic.com/`

  `ITKnowledge.com`

- **New books**—Identify the area of interest and search online bookstores for new titles, using the subject area as a keyword.

  `amazon.com`

  `barnesandnoble.com`

- **Technology industry trends, services, and industry conferences**

  Gartner Interactive at `http://gartner6.gartnerweb.com/public/static/home/home.html`

  Meta-group at `http://www.metagroup.com/`

IDC at `http://www.idc.com/`

Jupiter Communications at `http://www.jup.com/home.jsp`

Technology Vendor Overviews

Software and services vendors in the technology arena frequently offer half-day to whole-day overviews of the technology their products and services support. Geared to the executive and management level, these meetings are a great way to keep abreast of developments in a field without investing the time and money required by specific training. These overviews are not open to the public, but are usually free to qualifying participants. To find out about such opportunities, join mailing lists by subscribing to industry journals, or in many cases by visiting the Web sites of vendors of interest. Many vendors have online information and registration for overview opportunities.

Customize the Industry Models for Your Company

Industry analysis extracts the best practices and current models of an industry. It represents generic information, synthesized from the industry at large. To adapt these synthesized models to your company requires aligning them with your corporate identity and strategy: the policies, images, values, and operating models that set your company apart. Then the new models are elaborated in the preferred style and language of your company so that their implementation is consistent with existing norms. Practices that are inconsistent with policies or operating models are weeded out and only those that fit your company are incorporated into the new models. This step involves the following activities:

- Select useful industry models based on project goals
- Modify these for your corporate identity and strategy
- Elaborate and expand the new models according to company norms

Select Useful Industry Models Based on Project Goals

In carrying out the research and modeling steps for your industry, you might have found a need to include certain models to gain a sense of understanding and perspective on the area of interest. Although such models can be very useful in helping different factions to communicate and succeed on a project, they are not to be carried forward necessarily, and will be deselected at the time of implementation.

A subset of the industry models will be selected, which emphasizes the goals of the project, and will be used for implementation.

Modify for Your Corporate Identity and Strategy

As models are identified and signed off as ready for inclusion in the corporate lexicon, they will be modified to be sure they reflect your corporate identity and strategy. All companies have various symbols that encode their identity, their beliefs, and their values, and that convey these to employees and external parties such as customers, suppliers, and advertisers. The symbols that have bearing on technology and automation should be identified and in some way included in the models. This can take the form of using a company logo on each slide of a presentation, or using the company font, advertising symbols, or slogans in creative ways. The goal is to make the models look like they belong with your company, while introducing new methods and technologies through them.

Elaborate and Expand the New Models According to Company Norms

Having identified the desired symbols and norms in use in your company, your industry models will be modified as necessary. Depending on your standards and requirements, expand and elaborate by developing the required documents to carry out a project of this nature in your company. Some companies require a set collection of documents for every step in a technology project's process. Others are less structured, but have certain requirements to meet quality assurance standards. Some models will be translated into business action plans, whereas others are translated into more detailed technical implementation models. As you carry the integration models forward into implementation efforts, be sure to allow them to conform to company norms and standards, even though the ideas can be innovative. This will provide a sense of continuity to help manage the impact of change that can be brought about by any significant integration project.

Implement the New Models

Put the new models into practice, planning and scheduling the necessary projects to make the new vision a reality. Integration projects require implementation strategies that are managed by objectives, with frequent mid-course corrections. It's important to identify early successes, which can be used to stimulate momentum and buy-in from project constituents. These constituents, or project sponsors, must be cultivated and positioned to author the success of the project, starting with pilot projects they own and nurture.

Define Required Projects

Identify the projects needed to carry out your initiatives and changes. You can have a combination of business initiatives and technology projects that must be completed to deliver what is specified in the new models.

Develop a Flexible Implementation Plan

Your implementation plan should be flexible and oriented along the lines of an integration project for best results. For example, at an employment services firm, the implementation plan calls for business area sponsors to run pilot projects in their area, and then provide feedback to the integrators. This is incorporated into the rollout strategy for the entire project. The implementation plan will specify the activities required to carry out the implementation, with information such as target dates, hours required, deliverables, and so forth. Typical implementation plans are developed in project-management tools such as MS Project, PlanView, or Primavera tools, and serve to coordinate the efforts of participants, including some or all of the following:

- Developers
- Database designers and administrators
- Business area contributors
- Production support
- Quality assurance
- Network engineers
- Systems analysts
- Data managers
- Software product vendors
- Data providers

Conduct Projects

You will need to monitor and manage an integration project with a higher level of leadership involvement for mid-course corrections, as compared to a typical software development project. The breadth of scope and high profile and priority of many integration projects also demand a higher level of leadership involvement. Regular status meetings and reporting, with meaningful milestones for signoff and approval, are also recommended.

Conclusion

Synthesizing industry models upgrades the skills and knowledge available in your company by referencing models being utilized in the industry at large. It enables you to gather information and synthesize it into an abstracted form for studying, improving, and replicating the best practices. When such synthesized information is tailored to reflect the identity and norms of your company, it can be delivered through specially designed implementation projects, which carry the new methods, technologies, and solutions to all areas of your business. Whether working on a small, localized project, or an enterprisewide integration project, synthesizing the industry models can help you locate and deliver solutions that raise the bar for your company and your industry.

14

Data Strategy, Warehousing, and Architecture with Integration Models

FROM THE INITIAL CUSTOMER CONTACT to the acceptance of customer payment, at the heart of every business transaction is the creation, capture, or exchange of information. Managing such information is the focus of data strategy, warehousing, and architecture efforts. The data that business events revolve around is the currency of information systems. Ensuring that it is current, well-integrated, and sharable between business applications is the job of data management.

To understand a process to automate it, we track the steps of the process, the flow of information exchange, and the business events that occur to pull them together. Data management focuses on dealing with the information exchange, making sure that data retrieval is efficient and stored information is accurate, for use in a variety of business applications.

Data Management

Data management encompasses the activities required to see that data is captured accurately, stored properly, and made available for sharing and retrieval efficiently. It includes the management of corporate information as an asset, using the techniques of data modeling and analysis, object modeling, and design. It also includes data architecture design and setting data strategy for enterprisewide information sharing.

One common structure that data management sets up is the corporate information control group or data services type group. In large companies, localized data occurs in the departmental application systems of different business areas. This type of information can be seen as a vertical slice—for instance, all the information belonging to the loan department of a bank, or all the data belonging to checking account processing. Many vertical slices exist in the application systems of any corporation, and they are managed locally, sometimes with local architectures that are quite significant.

The other type of information required is the horizontal slice, which is data occurring and collected across the vertical components. This data is sometimes captured at the very lowest level of detail, for statistical and performance reporting. For example, wireless services companies collect statistics on cellular phone calls, such as calls completed, calls dropped, calls incomplete, and so forth, for performance reporting purposes. Another example is the employment services provider that collects information on services rendered, jobs filled, and resources required and reports it to customers. This type of self-monitoring and sharing results with the customer is often required by contract for large customers in employment services.

Horizontal data is sometimes captured at the highest level of summarization and aggregation for management information, marketing uses, and decision support.

For instance, in a financial services company, different products (checking accounts, savings accounts, and loans) belong to different vertical components. The daily processing of a checking account occurs within the architecture designed to support different types of demand deposit accounts. A loan product is processed by different systems with different architecture, as are savings accounts, and so forth. For the bank to approve and issue loans, and manage checking and savings accounts, this vertical slice of information is sufficient. But for the marketing department to analyze product pricing and performance, high-level information is required from each of the vertical components (checking accounts, savings accounts and loans). This horizontal slice consists of information summarized by product, showing how products are performing in the marketplace, and whether their pricing makes them profitable to sell and service.

Data management's agenda is to create a structured environment, in which all this data can be captured, stored, and retrieved in all the different ways the business needs to retrieve it. Any data services group will have the goal of building a long-term infrastructure to control and manage the collection and dissemination of information with the help of relevant technology.

The Goal

The goal for information systems in today's technical environment is to manage data as an asset. Platform standardization and data architecture reduce the required investment over time, allowing application development to become the primary activity. In Figure 14.1 the Seed template illustrates the desired outcome of data management.

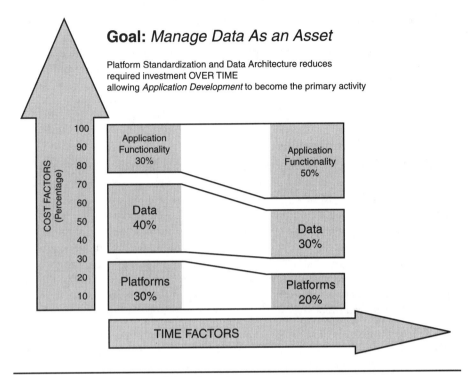

Figure 14.1 The goal for information systems is to manage data as an asset.

Managing data as an asset means treating information as a corporate investment and committing resources to secure, update, and maintain it. These resources take the form of data architecture, data models, model management, databases, and data storage techniques and technology. They are employed to take a systematic approach to managing data.

Defining the Terms Used in Data Management

Many terms are used in the business of data management, often carrying different meanings to different people. The following are definitions of the terms as I'll be using them in this chapter:

- **Data strategy**—The process of developing a plan for managing your company's data as an asset. It addresses the required architectures, models, designs, and plans for data management.

- **Data architecture**—The infrastructure framework for housing data across the corporation. Data architecture is the "city plan" which designates how business subject areas are defined, and how the data within subject areas is structured and stored.

- **Data warehousing**—One component of an architecture. It is the practice of making copies of production data and storing it separately for reporting, extracts, and analytical access. To avoid degrading the processing of day-to-day operations in a business, data warehousing removes the information access from the critical path of information processing. It is the most encompassing component, because it can involve or force a cleanup of all data architecture components.

Cycle of Data Management

A day in the life of a piece of corporate data will see that data move through many different perspectives of use and handling. First it is captured, and then checked for errors in entry, format, and other attributes according to its validation rules. Next it travels to the systems that utilize the data for primary business contacts, processing transactions, and supporting primary business functions such as sales, order-fulfillment, and services. After being cleaned up for corporate standards, the data moves on to be shared with other systems that need it to complete their picture of the company's business, and is manipulated and stored in decision-support holding areas. Finally, the data is distributed for selective viewing of both company insiders and external users such as customers and suppliers.

Data management needs to recognize the cycle around which data stewardship revolves. At each step of the process, different priorities will surface. They will require different technical design and development approaches employing defined terms and agreed-upon structures. Figure 14.2 shows the steps of the cycle and some of the supporting technical structures. It adopts a starting point where customer and supplier interactions initiate business transactions that must be processed. Keep in mind that although it's a common starting point, it is a little arbitrary because activities in any step of this model can act as a starting point.

The following are the steps of the Cycle of Data Management:

1. Process business transactions
2. Transform data for sharing
3. Support business decisions
4. Create internal portals
5. Create external portals
6. Interact with customers and suppliers

Process Business Transactions

Business events, such as a customer contact resulting in a sales order being placed, or a customer request that is filled by customer service personnel, produce data which must be managed. They involve relatively small amounts of data that must be maintained with a high level of accuracy at the time of the transaction and access of the data.

Business transactions are typically simple transactions involving very detailed data. For example, a customer order includes specific mailing address, product information and pricing details.

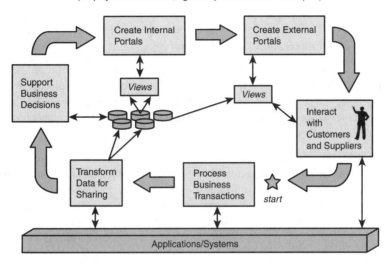

Cycle of Data Management
(Employs defined terms, agreed-upon structured techniques)

Figure 14.2   The Cycle of Data Management depicts
how data is utilized at each step of the process.

The systems that support such business transactions must handle many simultaneous updates, reads, and insertions of data. They must often be available for processing on a continual basis, 24 hours a day, 7 days a week. They have low requirements for storage of historical information, usually needing only that information required for supporting the flow of work.

The data model for supporting business transactions is usually highly normalized, which means that data components are structured so that they are stored only once for convenient control of updates. The data model also attempts to achieve a balance between design for state modification (insert, update, delete) and speed of retrieval or data access. Because the data usage is predictable, the data model can be optimized for these performance concerns.

Data management in business transactions usually prioritizes data persistency and state management. It will be utilized by down-stream systems (subscribers to the information) which are usually unrelated to the systems producing the data.

Transform Data for Sharing

The data produced in business transactions must often be transformed before being shared with other applications. Sometimes sensitive or irrelevant information must be removed before sharing. At other times information must be made generic so that it matches the definitions of other application views. Some data will be summarized and used to support analytical processing or decision support. Other information will be used internally by other departments such as operations or financial reporting, whereas some data is selected for sharing with customers and suppliers, depending on the requirements of their interactions with the company.

Data extraction, transformation, and middleware tools are all means of transforming data to make it suitable for sharing. Extraction and transformation tools usually help to convert, cleanse, and standardize data. Middleware and messaging technologies facilitate the physical aspects of sharing data, through the use of data delivery mechanisms and subscription maintenance machinery.

The priorities at this stage are for credible data, verified, cleansed, and transformed in a streamlined process. Speed of data availability for sharing with mission-critical applications is also an important factor. In some cases, speed of data availability is considered more important than one hundred percent accuracy of the data. For example, data that is summarized and used for forecasting might be accurate to within a 5% margin of error, a margin that would not be acceptable for the processing of business transactions.

Support Business Decisions

The data that is delivered to decision-support applications is used to help companies measure performance, manipulate revenue and yield ratios, make market decisions, and monitor operational statistics. It is earmarked for business management and strategic functions, and used in determining competitive advantage. It can be used to identify opportunities for improvement and growth of the company.

Decision-support data is often derived through summarization and calculations applied to detailed data taken from transaction processing systems. It often involves large volumes of data, with significant amounts of historical data used for trend analysis and reporting of regulatory and markets information. Analytical processing usually involves complex transactions or queries against the data, utilized in unpredictable ways by processes characterized by discovery. A fairly small user community (managers, executives, and analysts) needs actual access to the data.

Data models for analytical processing are optimized for rapid access through non-repetitive queries, producing unpredictable workloads. The priority is on efficient data retrieval, which requires that data be heavily indexed and de-normalized (more than one copy of a data component stored) for convenient access rather than normalized for convenient update. Integrity constraints such as those utilized for transaction processing (primary keys, foreign keys, and column constraints) are generally relaxed in decision-support systems because the source systems can be expected to enforce the referential integrity that is required.

Create Internal Portals

Internal portals allow parties within a company to access data according to the needs of their particular business or application viewpoint. Data warehouses spawn data marts, which house application-specific views of data replicated from the central repository. Intranet portals provide windows on data that can be needed by operational personnel or marketing analysts.

Internal portals represent multiple views against the company's information and are generally accessed with low security requirements, within the confines of a company firewall.

Create External Portals

External portals provide access to customers and suppliers for carefully selected portions of a company's information. Portions of the business process in which customers or suppliers participate can be detailed on public Web sites. Financial performance can be provided in annual reports online or investor information packets. Product and service specifications and pricing can also be made available through an external portal on company information.

Characterized by selective viewing, external portals usually reside outside a company's firewall, providing a highly secured environment for customer and supplier interactions.

Interact with Customers and Suppliers

Interactions with customers and suppliers can occur through the window of an external portal, or they can be facilitated by business transaction processing systems. Sometimes they occur with replicated versions of company data carried by a sales or marketing representative in a remote device, such as a laptop computer configured to provide price quotes and service specifications.

Distribution of data becomes important in the interaction step, with an emphasis on convenient access and accuracy to certain limits established within a window of time. Partitioning and data replication are schemes that provide the desired distributed deployment of components of data.

How IM Supports Data Management

Data management is essentially an integration effort. As such it requires the same kinds of supports as any integration project. It needs to deal with issues of enterprise-wide scope, higher levels of chaos in its definition or charter, data sharing, and integration, and the need for a broader repertoire of models. Data management deals with many unknowns because of the evolving nature of both information and business process, and it requires different thought paradigms. Data management must be organized by some principle without being limited by that principle, and it must be unified across diverse business activities and systems. It must also involve non-technical people at certain stages, because they are the owners and true experts in much of the information a business must manage.

IM Excels in Handling the Multiple Perspectives of Data

Throughout the life cycle of data management, there is a need to view data not as it travels from one step to another in the cycle, but to view it across applications and according to the dictates of the various disciplines that cooperate to manage corporate information. These disciplines represent several different perspectives against which data must be understood and managed. Integration modeling has mechanisms that are designed to handle multiple views and the complexity they introduce. Integration models provide a basis for understanding how data is managed from the following perspectives:

- Business view
- Application view
- Logical view
- Physical view
- Distribution view

Business View

The business view describes how the actual business area that generates or uses a piece of information sees it. It is the highest level of the views and yet is informed by the hands-on knowledge of the business expert using the data, which is often a very detailed knowledge. The business entity model and various types of narrative descriptions, definitions, and dictionaries of terms represent the business view.

Business areas of information are called subject areas and are analyzed according to the dynamics of the data and the organizing principle around which the data occurs. Subject areas can be static, in that their contents describe constant data requirements. Customer, employee, and price are examples of static subject areas. Subject areas can also be dynamic, expressing the relationship between other subject areas. For example, revenue expresses the relationship between customer and price. Figure 14.3 shows an example of an integration model that supports subject-area analysis, using the Cell template.

Extended Subject Areas
Customer

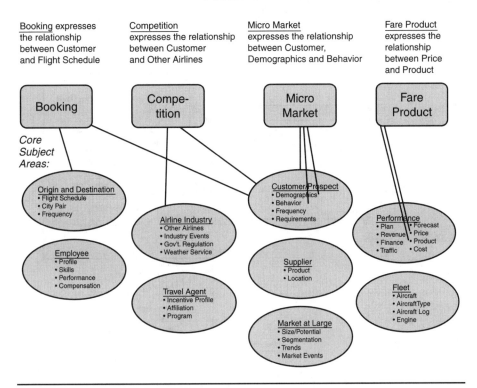

Booking expresses the relationship between Customer and Flight Schedule

Competition expresses the relationship between Customer and Other Airlines

Micro Market expresses the relationship between Customer, Demographics and Behavior

Fare Product expresses the relationship between Price and Product

Figure 14.3 The model uses the Cell template for subject area analysis in an airline setting.

Developed for the customer applications in the airline industry, the model describes core subject areas (static) and extended subject areas (dynamic) which are used as a basis for a publish and subscribe strategy of data management. This is only one of the types of models that is used to represent the business view of data.

Data is mapped into subject areas by logical and physical data models or entity relationship diagrams (ERDs). The data architecture creates a "city plan" for the subject areas, which is then subdivided with the use of the logical data model. The physical data model is used as a map to manage the integrity of data subscriptions, or end users of the data in question.

Application View

Viewpoint analysis models and scenarios are most useful in depicting the application viewpoint on data. They describe the concerns and definitions of the business area owning the application, and help clarify how users in that business area need to interact with the data. Figure 14.4 shows how a wireless services company can collect network data from a cellular switch.

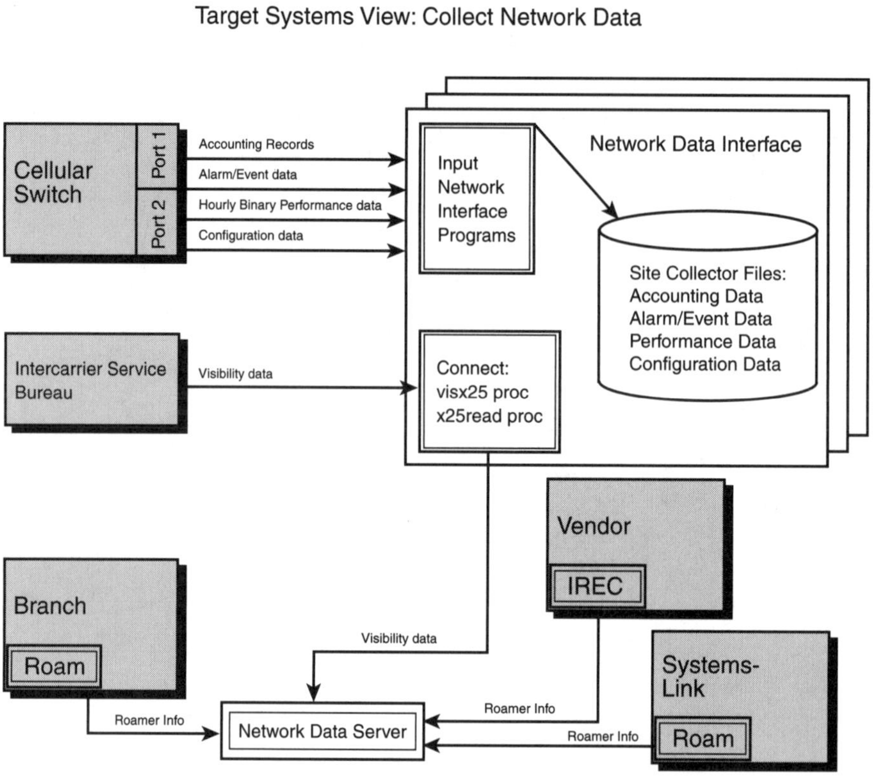

Target Systems View: Collect Network Data

Figure 14.4   The Target Systems View: Collect Network Data
model shows an application view of the data collection process.

Representing the viewpoint of the applications that will utilize the network data collected from the switch, the model shows what kind of information is collected. Accounting, alarm and event, performance, and configuration data is collected at a detailed level, for support of fraud detection software applied to protect the accounts of roaming customers. Other models and narratives will fill out the understanding of how the data is used for business purposes.

Logical View

The logical view describes how the data can be broken up and structured, without regard for its physical implementation. Where or how data is stored is not the focus.

The categories of data and their interrelations are most significant. These are modeled with entity relationship diagrams, which can pick up the patterns utilized in previous views and carry them forward to organize the logical model and bring continuity between the levels. For example, in many decision-support design efforts, the Seed structure depicts a centralized data repository. Subsequent logical view models can be organized around a Seed structure (sometimes called the star schema), providing a unifying structure that carries through into the physical models.

Physical View

The physical view describes how data is organized for physical storage, sharing, and retrieval. It disregards the logical divisions and seeks to establish physical structure and segmentation of databases for the best performance for business uses. Integration models that are used to support this view include the Wave template for layered analysis, the Seed template for a core repository or hub, and the Cell template for categorization and specialization.

Distribution View

Data distribution is achieved through networking, middleware, and messaging, and various protocols allowing data to be passed, replicated, and shared. The distribution view employs Web structures to depict the requirements for networking, illustrating nodes and connectors, and ring structures for design of connectivity through area networks. Data distribution through replication can also be supported using the Cell template.

Organizing the Data Architecture

Data architecture provides the "city plan" for capture, storage, and retrieval of corporate information. It is expressed through architecture views, which delineate the major components of data or business entities that must be managed. It also requires an understanding of how data will be mapped and managed through architecture planning, and how models themselves will be managed. Data architecture includes the understanding of what the data environment itself looks like, both logically and physically or in terms of platform.

Enterprise Domain

The enterprise domain model represents data as it is exchanged at the highest level, describing the major components of information that are important to a business. Domain models can be drawn in very broad terms, or they can be carried to significant levels of detail, depending on a company's need and timeframes. Figure 14.5 shows a high-level domain model for the employment services industry. Its structure is taken from the Seed template.

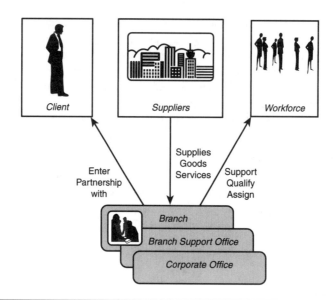

Figure 14.5   The Seed template offers a structure for the business
entities of importance in the employment services industry.

The enterprise domain model is accompanied by narrative business definitions such as
the following:

- **Business Entities**—Depict, at the Enterprise Level, the most significant information involved in delivering the business goals of a company. The four broad groupings of information at this level are client, workforce, supplier, and the company itself.

- **Client**—Receives service and pays for delivered service. Based on existing business relationship, a national account client or a local client with a single handshake agreement with the company, are all valued customers. It is important to introduce a capability to recognize and track relationships between accounts. Two local accounts in two different locations can in fact represent the same client. This composite client, that is, a client with multiple accounts, fits the definition of the client-oriented business.

  Sometimes an intermediate agency plays the role of the client. Such an agency can have an exclusive contract with the receiver of services or be one of the selected providers to fill orders and can use the company's workforce.

- **Workforce**—Consists of human resources personnel who are either associates directly engaged in delivering work for the company's clients, or candidates for full-time staffing brought in through company recruiting services to become full-time employees of the company's clients.

- **Supplier**—Provides goods and services as needed by the company and its affiliates, entering partnership arrangements as defined by the company's policy and contract agreements. Human resource supplier (other employment services company) supports the company's process by providing, respectively, opportunities for growth by acquisition and ongoing supply of candidates and associates.

- **Branch**—A full-service company-owned field office that provides order fulfillment, marketing and sales activities, coordination of services, and recruiting and leadership of the workforce.

  Branches are located in proximity to existing and potential clients and serve to maintain a local presence to strengthen and expand relationships with clients as well as to acquire new clients.

  Branches can have satellites, such as additional recruiting offices that provide local presence in areas that are distant from the full-service branch serving them.

- **Branch Support Office**—Provides local branch offices with necessary support in some of the following functions:

  - Back-office functions, such as payroll, billing, and accounts receivable.
  - Headquarters functions such as just-in-time training, recruiting, technology, financial planning, forecasting, reporting, marketing, and sales support.

  Headquarters of merged or acquired companies, and regional offices are examples of branch support offices. The scope of services offered to branches varies from one support office to another. Sometimes a branch serves as a branch support office for another branch.

- **Corporate Office**—Provides the infrastructure for service delivery in such areas as technology, finance, legal, sales and marketing, and training, and performs centralized functions such as strategic planning and acquisition planning.

Architecture Template

Data architecture includes the visualization of the environment in which technical solutions are deployed. It describes the structure and layers of technology required for supporting corporate requirements for data capture, storage, retrieval, and distribution. Figure 14.6 shows an Architecture template that depicts one way of organizing a company's information environment.

This example takes a common architecture for corporate information systems (the applications, transformation, and warehouse model popularized by William Inmon [14.1]) and turns it on end so that it can depict the layers required for a publish and subscribe implementation.

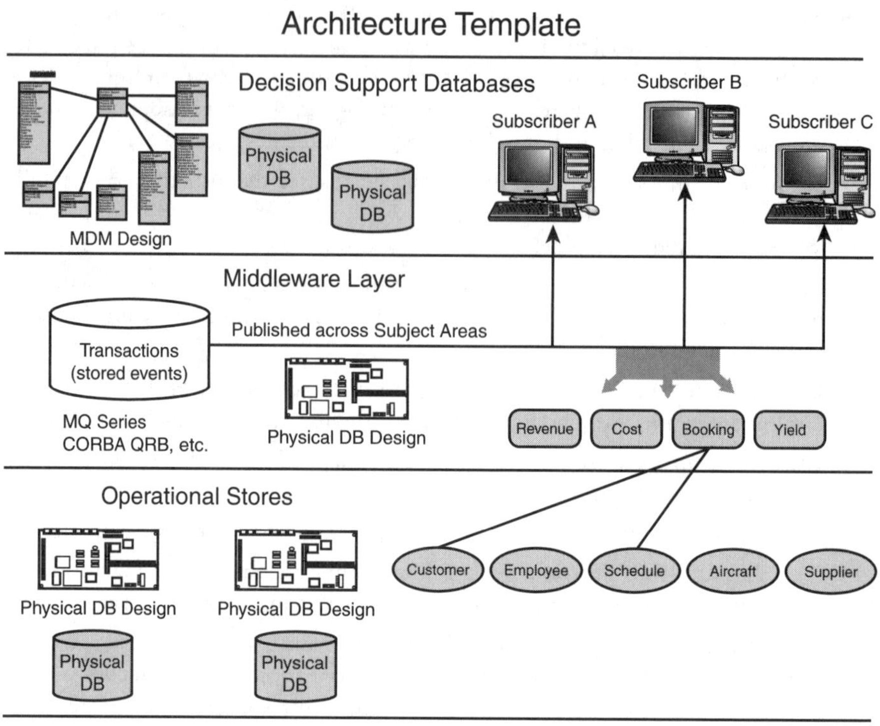

Architecture Template

Figure 14.6 The Architecture template shows how the Wave template supports the analysis of layers of data architecture.

Shared Data Architecture

Architecture for shared data focuses on a different view of the data environment. Addressing the various technology components required for data sharing, it depicts how these components fit together to support the objectives of a data strategy. Figure 14.7 shows the shared data architecture developed for the Department of Defense data services. It is a good example of the use of layering (Wave template) and cells (Cell template) to manage the complexity of the data environment.

The SHADE Architecture model incorporates the layers of applications that must share data, metadata management, and shared data access. It also includes data management and database segmentation and supporting disciplines, repositories, and tools.

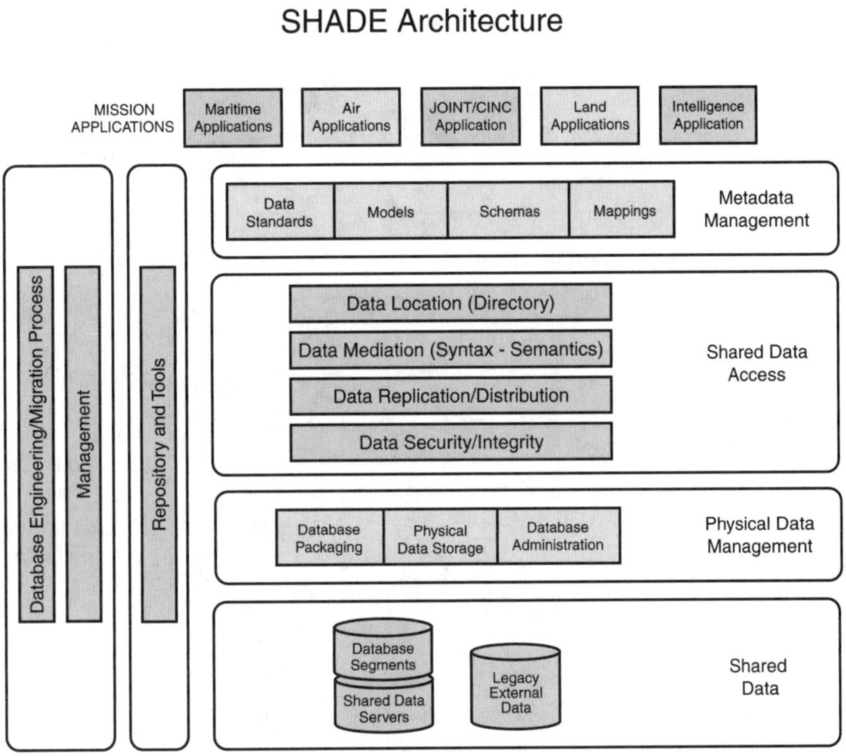

SHADE Architecture

Figure 14.7 The SHADE Architecture model shows how layers and cells are used to depict the complexity of the data environment.

Database Segmentation

Database segmentation schemes describe how data storage devices will be utilized to house predefined segments of data for the purposes of sharing. They present plans for server allocation for database storage and access, determined by the type of data being stored. Shared data resides on shareable platforms whereas non-shared or application-unique data can reside on a platform that is closed or proprietary to the application. Figure 14.8 shows the database segment types used by the Department of Defense data sharing strategy. It is a good example of the shared repository (Seed template) combined with layering (Wave) of types of data.

The scheme depicts the mechanisms that will be employed to manipulate and control data access and distribution, such as database views, replication, and security privileges.

Database Segment Types

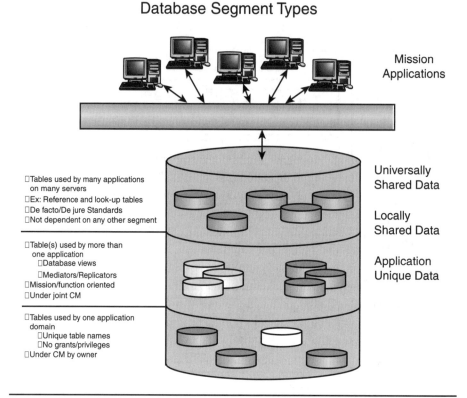

Tables used by many applications on many servers
- Ex: Reference and look-up tables
- De facto/De jure Standards
- Not dependent on any other segment

Table(s) used by more than one application
- Database views
- Mediators/Replicators
- Mission/function oriented
- Under joint CM

Tables used by one application domain
- Unique table names
- No grants/privileges
- Under CM by owner

Mission Applications

Universally Shared Data

Locally Shared Data

Application Unique Data

Figure 14.8   The Database Segment Types model combines the Seed template for a repository and the Wave template for the layers of data types.

Elements of a Successful Data Warehouse

Successful data warehousing requires a data strategy that reflects both understanding the business needs and supporting their delivery with application and technology platforms. This strategy must be flexible enough to provide for the inevitable, inherent changes the data warehousing environment will require as it matures within a company. Integration modeling supports the elements of a successful data warehouse implementation.

Use a Defined, Repeatable Process

The model in Figure 14.9 defines a methodology for building a data warehouse. As the model shows, it is a very iterative process, where the idea is to get all the way through the process (or a sub-process) with a component of data, and then add another component and get it all the way through the process again. It is the model that most of the data warehousing industry now follows, developed because the warehousing process is essentially a process of discovery. The iterative approach allows you to build in new knowledge gained during data research, data design, build and testing, and application deployment, as you move ahead in the overall project. As the project proceeds, the team's knowledge keeps growing, expanding on correct information and replacing early guesses that can be made more exact with the addition of new findings. Iterative approaches provide a model for ongoing learning and the constant incorporation of new information.

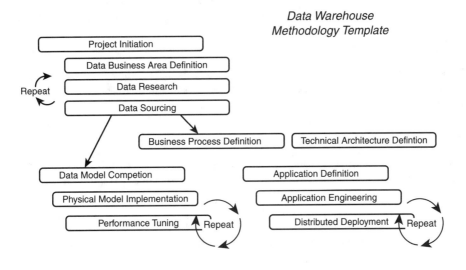

Figure 14.9   The Data Warehouse Methodology template defines
a methodology for building a data warehouse.

The Data Warehouse Methodology template incorporates elements of both the Flow and Cycle templates. The next sections define the following steps of the data warehousing process:

- Project initiation
- Data business area definition
- Data research
- Data sourcing
- Data model completion
- Physical model implementation
- Performance tuning
- Business process definition
- Technical architecture definition

- Application definition
- Application engineering
- Distributed deployment

As the model in Figure 14.9 shows, the first four steps are sequential, with steps two through four repeated as necessary. The remaining steps divide into two branches, one for the data modeling, implementation, and performance tuning, and the other for the definition of the business process and its automation through application architecture and components. Each of these branches also incorporates an iterative development approach.

Project Initiation

Define the business case, project scope and feasibility. Seek ongoing sponsorship and executive buy-in. Identify allies early, establish their goals, and include them in the scope.

Data Business Area Definition

Keep the scope focused and manageable by determining the areas of the business most important to the organization at this time. Their priority depends on questions such as the following:

- How much information is available through automation already?
- What are the industry trends and competition?
- What are the events driving the business at this time?
- How much is known and understood about this area of the business?

As these factors are clarified, an understanding of the following points will emerge:

- Certain areas can be researched and mined for data immediately. These constitute the "low-hanging fruit," which can deliver early returns for use in promoting the project.
- Some areas are well-understood and the amount of research can be estimated and started immediately. These areas will define the near-term deliverables.
- Other areas are little understood and need further research before they can even be estimated. These are the more long-term areas of interest.

Conducting this type of analysis early and often will keep a data warehouse project focused on the real goals of the business and will assure that the research and data sourcing that is undertaken is feasible, meaningful, and realistic.

Data Research

Determine how the relevant business process will use the data. Inventory, question, and define business rules for sending (source) applications. Expect that the receiving business process will undergo a transformation as the result of new awareness and new understanding because of having more information than ever before. Expect the requirements to change quickly because the access to information represented by an effective data warehouse will cause rapid growth and change in the functions using the information. Research data availability and value. Continually evaluate priority and benefit of desired data versus cost and time involved acquiring it.

Data Sourcing

Identify systems, suppliers, and vendors that will provide data. Prioritize the data needs based on revenue implications and strategic and competitive concerns as well as usage and actual availability. Gather valuable information from sourcing to be returned to the next iteration of business area definition and data research as data discovery results. Equip and train teams performing sourcing to collect information to be returned to researchers.

Data Model Completion

Select a portion of the Enterprise model to implement through the analysis of the business area. Define data relationships and resolve anomalies such as many-to-many relationships.

Define schemas for data constructs, which will provide greater flexibility and understandable data structures for the business user. Define facts that will be stored, dimensions to report, and hierarchies to be supported, and determine limits of data sparsity. Define and model common business dimensions such as time, scenarios, geography, product, and customer-using, multidimensional modeling techniques such as summarization and star diagrams.

Physical Model Implementation

Depending on the performance requirements and other architecture considerations of the system, choose one of the following:

- Relational DBMSs such as Sybase, SQL Server, Oracle, Informix/RS6000, DB2, and so forth
- Multidimensional Databases such as PaBLO, PowerPlay/Cognos, Mercury, ESSBase/Arbor, Lightship Server, Acumate ES/Kenan, Express/Oracle, Gentium, or Holos
- Relational OLAP (or OLAP-on-Relational) tools such as Metaphor, Information Advantage's AXSYS, Prodea's Beacon, Redbrick Data Warehouse, Alpha Warehouse (ISI & Digital), or Decision Warehouse from Sun Systems

Performance Tuning

Determine the workload the database will need to support. Bitmap and other indexing schemes are employed to significantly improve response time over traditional indexing methods by greatly reducing the number of read operations to the data. These schemes also enable more users to access the warehouse simultaneously, making it easier for users to pose a series of queries to analyze the data. Such schemes achieve an acceptable level of responsiveness with lower hardware expenditure than with traditional indexes.

Business Process Definition

Define and validate the process to be automated through accessing the data warehouse. Utilize business modeling to clarify and redesign if necessary. Highlight decision-support requirements for analysis.

Technical Architecture Definition

Define the hardware and technical constructs to be applied in providing the business solution. Select core technologies (platform, networking, RDBMS, and so forth). Address structural issues. Data warehousing architecture includes the following:

- Sourcing of data from legacy systems and other applications (data collection, editing, and preparation).
- Transformation and data integration, with storage issues resolved and atomic versus composite levels of granularity defined.
- Distribution of data to actual warehouse tables (further distribution to subject area databases or data marts is sometimes in order).

Give consideration to the nature of the data, answering the primary question of whether it serves the informational or the operational community.

Application Definition

Define the processes that will access and manipulate the data. Consider incorporating an Application Server, removing the business logic to a three-tiered architecture which addresses performance, reliability, and resource management by moving complex application logic to an application server independent of server databases and client PCs. The following are the three tiers:

- Application server provides efficient data access, accelerated response, and scheduled background processing and serving of pre-processed reports.
- Client is dedicated to presentation logic and services, and has an API for invoking the applications in the middle layer.
- Database server is dedicated to data services and file services.

Application Engineering

Develop the physical design, test plans and scripts with definitions of expected results, and build the plan. Application definition, engineering, and deployment are iterative, with successive prototypes developed, providing early requirements gathering to third-level systems that will graduate to production.

Always put test data in test tables; never load it to production. Early prototyping efforts in data warehousing often deliver data that is below performance thresholds for accuracy. Performance thresholds should be defined early in the process and signed off as part of the data research phase. Warehoused data is sometimes not required to be 100% accurate. Certain marketing applications, for instance, can tolerate a margin of error up to 5%. Expectations must be documented and adhered to, but test data that falls below standards should not be loaded to production databases.

Distributed Deployment

Deploy architecture, including such components as server, client, and application. Consolidate metadata (data about the data) for publication. Data credibility hinges on managed expectations and consensus in the definition stage.

Adopt an Iterative Approach

The single most important development in warehousing today is probably the iterative approach, as represented by the Cycle structure on the Data Warehouse Methodology template. Data warehouse projects risk getting bogged down in traditional waterfall approaches, where phases are not allowed to overlap and project "scope-creep" causes the collection phase to expand, never becoming complete enough to move on to the data delivery phase.

Frequently this phenomenon is caused by the fact that the corporation's information needs are little understood in key areas. Required data has not been available in the past, so business users literally don't know what's needed, what will be of use, and what will not. Of course, some needs are obvious, but the more subtle requirements only surface after iterative exploration of what's available versus what's meaningful.

These problems have led to the industry's adoption of the iterative model of data research and discovery, leading to the iterative model for development of databases and applications to access the data. Until the availability question is settled, presentation will tend to shift and grow.

Deliver Manageable Components of Data

It is better to deliver 70% of the required information in a given business area than to deliver 5% in 10 different areas, because the data becomes meaningful (that is, becomes intelligence) when it can be placed in context. Of course, 100% would be ideal, but the timeframes required to deliver 100% accuracy and completeness of data are never acceptable to the business. And with the shrinking shelf life of the value of data over time, 70% now can be much more valuable than 90% two months from now.

All information is not equally valuable, but requires the prioritization process to find out what's most critical and focus acquisition efforts there first. As the business picture shifts and changes with competition and trends, the priority of data delivery will change to reflect that activity.

When data can be isolated into manageable components, and delivered rapidly, more business needs get met, and the sponsors are much more likely to sign on for another parcel of information to be delivered in a reasonable time frame, just like the first.

Integration Is the Key

In data warehousing as in data management, finding successful methods of managing integration is the key. Integration modeling helps the modeler and data manager understand the viewpoints of the many business areas which must work together to define and support the development of a corporate data warehouse. It helps clarify the dynamics of data in the data management cycle, which must also be considered in planning a data warehouse. Knowing where you are in that cycle places any effort at warehousing in the context of the larger business picture. Integration modeling also helps you define the architecture views, templates, and data sharing and segmentation schemes required for making the data warehouse environment efficient.

Data warehousing converges with business process re-engineering and Internet disciplines to complete the corporate data architecture for an enterprisewide data strategy. The successful data warehouse often drives the reengineering of business data and processes by surfacing the contradictions and confusion in current application systems. Internet technologies are utilized both internally and externally to provide increasingly important portals, which act as windows on the world of business information.

Case Study: Integration in Telecommunications

"THESE GUYS ARE FROM DIFFERENT PLANETS," the consultant said knowingly. "Are you sure you'll be able to get them all into the same meeting when you have to?" Although I was sure of my meeting-calling skills, I knew they would not be the main tool I used to get "these guys" to come to some kind of working agreement. I knew that the many consultants who came before me had gotten mediocre results. There had been no meeting of the minds among the database designers, network engineers, and service personnel involved in the project. What they were missing, I was convinced, was the conviction that the "guys" in question weren't just being silly. They had different worldviews and a sense of protectiveness about the wisdom of their own point of view. If I didn't try to take that away from them, I knew I'd be miles ahead of the last consultant they'd seen from this consulting arm of a large systems integrator. With the tools of integration modeling, I could capture the nuances of what was really important in their viewpoint and make sure it stayed out front.

This chapter shows how leaving different worlds intact can bring them together faster.

Background

The systems integrator has been brought in to help out with a large project being carried out by two telecommunications companies, in a joint effort. Their test management platform is suffering from fragmentation in the information that flows through the business processes, and the companies are having trouble achieving the desired integration of platforms. One cornerstone of their process is a very large equipment inventory database, which stores equipment information down to the level of the IP address and provides equipment address information to the systems that support test management. These systems need to know where a piece of test equipment is located in the network relative to other pieces of equipment, so that when a report of trouble is on the line, test engineers can track it down and repair it automatically.

The systems integrator's role is to make the large database talk more effectively to the test management system, providing data as needed. The method of providing data is through an information broker, which acts as a front end for the Inventory database and handles information requests from client applications down the line. The client applications can be set up to receive scheduled deliveries of data on a regular basis.

One problem the integrator encountered is that the team designing the inventory database has a very different worldview from the engineers they must solicit requirements from. The database team sees everything in structured terms, and is trying to modify a very structured database. The engineers see the world as basically flat. All their drawings are linear and all their concepts are executed in two dimensions. For network engineers, the world is made up of nodes and connectors, not hierarchical or relational (that is, database-style) structures. Additionally, the teams need information from the provisioning services department, where there is a different worldview still. From the provisioning view, the world is populated with facilities for assignments and systems for creating assignments. The primary concern is getting a customer order to flow through the system, without getting stopped at any of the obstacles along the way.

One of the drivers of this project is that the company is patching in new test equipment, which requires the following:

- Adding the new equipment to the inventory database and creating a new slot to put it in
- Changing the test management system to handle the newly added pieces of information
- Modifying other applications to accept the newly added pieces of information
- Changing the database feed from a push to a pull architecture to handle timing considerations
- Modifying the information broker to carry the newly defined information

The prime directive is that there must be only one integrated test platform. That means one terminal, like a cockpit, from which all products and services can be tested and repaired. This operating model is another "Holy Grail" of advanced telecommunications technology.

The issues include the following:

- Fragmented information
- Differing worldviews between project participants
- Technical disparities between internationally distributed systems
- Timing—You need it yesterday
- Multiple non-unified interfaces to test and monitor equipment
- The Inventory database is designed in such a way that it's hard to read (so we need an information broker).

Sources of Fragmentation

Many sources of fragmentation are in information systems. All you have to do is not pay attention to integration, build a few systems, and you can create fragmentation. And that's what many companies have done. Without an overall plan, updated on a regular basis for new requirements and priorities, any systems environment will rapidly deteriorate into a fragmented puzzle.

In the case of this telecommunications provider, the sources of fragmentation include merged operations, rapid growth without architecture, and new product introduction.

Merged Operations

Attempting to merge the operations of one or more acquired companies is a common source of fragmentation in today's acquisition and merger environment. Mergers originate on the business side of the house, but are carried out for synergies between companies in the back office where systems must be made to work together. Some companies avoid integration issues by standardizing on one platform and one view of systems-related data, but many companies don't have that luxury for many reasons. It is costly to standardize, because it can require replacing large systems already in place, upgrading platform, language, data, and processes. And some companies don't want to compromise innovations and creativity in the field by stifling them with imposed constraints.

Consequently, mergers can result in systems that need help talking to each other, and their integration must often be accomplished under tight deadlines or regulated closures and consolidation of assets.

Rapid Growth Without Architecture

Ordinary systems development without architecture is bad enough, but when a business grows rapidly, and does so without the benefit of infrastructure supports such as architectural planning, things can really get out of hand. Rapid growth intensifies the need for architecture, because size requires structure to support it. Integration models can help provide flexible, reliable structures that accommodate rapid change.

In this case, the industry has seen deregulation, leading to increased competition as companies race to bring new products into an emerging marketplace. As the customer base expands and shifts, competition raises the bar for customer service expectations. Both new products and new customers represent growth of the business and heightened demands on customer service. To meet these demands requires integrated systems that speed up problem solving for customer complaints, reducing the time that customers lose service for any reason.

New Product Introduction

Introducing new products often causes a problem of too much success. In this case, you see the rapid introduction of products that have not been integrated into the overall portfolio at the technical level. This type of non-coordinated product introduction can lead to trouble when it comes to supporting all those products, particularly trouble-shooting the problems that arise at customer sites. When customers who can have any of 15 different products and services call in with a complaint, they all call the same number. The operator takes a trouble report and forwards it to technicians, or handles it him or herself. Typically what happens is that new products are introduced without back-end integration, and then supported by an additional terminal at the trouble-tracking level. The result is that the engineers who perform trouble-tracking duties must learn several different systems for tracking down the problem (several layers) and must patch fixes into multiple systems before the problem is resolved.

Applying Integration Modeling

When integration modeling techniques are applied to this platform integration puzzle, they fill the gap by reconciling the world-views of project participants through collecting information and consolidating it into models that can be taken in at a glance. The models are used to keep the priorities visible and enable the team to bring in outside help from vendors for rapid integration. Integration models are used to analyze requirements for a unified interface and to orient the technical teams modifying the databases and the information broker and administering the test equipment itself.

Reconciling World Views

The network engineers need to communicate requirements to their database analysts, but a number of differences exist in understanding. An example is the confusion over logical and physical in the systems design. In data design, plans are drawn first at the logical level, and then translated into physical database implementation. In descending order, the levels go from business to logical and then to physical. In telecommunications, a similar concept is in the provision of services through circuits. Service is a logical concept. A customer receives services by being allocated a certain bandwidth, such as 56K. To deliver that 56K, the logical (service) is allocated to the physical (circuits). A circuit can be subdivided into channels, which is considered a logical subdivision. Therefore, in telecommunications lingo, the descending order is from business to logical, and then to physical and back to logical. The Equipment Address model in Figure 15.1 uses a cell structure to help illustrate these concepts and clear up the misconceptions that take place around them.

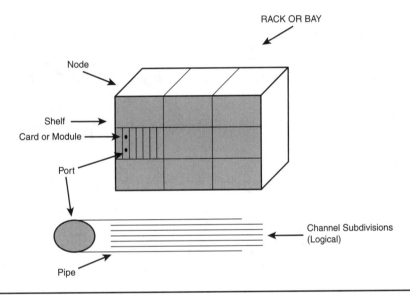

Figure 15.1   The Equipment Address model shows the components of an equipment address and logical subdivision of a physical pipe, or circuit.

The model shows where circuits hook up, through the port on a rack or bay. Ports exist in cards or modules in a shelf within a node on the rack. When a circuit emerges from a port, it is a physical connection, but it can be subdivided at a logical level at that point. To the database designer, uninitiated in these mysteries, the confusion this situation creates is unbelievable. After you understand it, a whole new world opens up. Until you do understand it, you can't really communicate with the engineers who are supposed to be providing requirements.

Keeping the Priorities Visible

Viewpoint analysis models help keep the team aware of the priority of the prime directive, which states that there must be only one integrated platform. Illustrating the problems of having multiple terminals managed by one employee helps to show the contrast between the desired outcome and the current reality. Figure 15.2 shows an Integration View model designed to illustrate the situation from the point of view of customer service for trouble tracking.

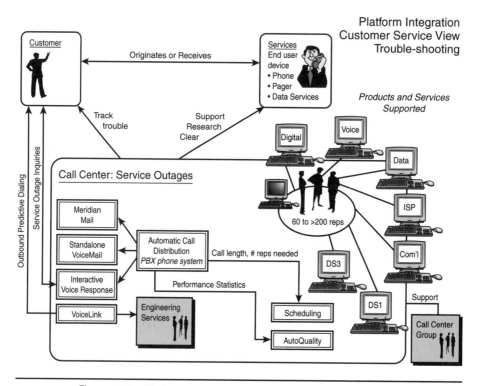

Figure 15.2   Platform Integration Customer Service View illustrates the multiple user interfaces with which the engineer must deal.

The call center that handles service outages receives inquiries from the customer that result in trouble reports. Service representatives field the trouble reports with other call centers and engineering positioned to provide second-and third-tier support. To research a trouble report, the customer service representative must interact with up to seven different systems through different terminals, all of which have their own different user interface standards. Consequently the learning curve for a service representative is over two years, and only senior engineers can solve advanced problems. The resulting pressures for senior engineers to get involved with trouble resolution draws expensive, highly trained resources into day-to-day problem solving at great cost to the company.

Rapid Integration

One of the issues of this project is that the bleeding off of senior resources puts great time pressure on the project schedule. The solution is needed yesterday. This leads to the use of outside vendors to shorten the project schedule timeline. To facilitate the selection process, a Request for Proposal (RFP) is developed, based on view models that illustrate the options for implementation, which vendors are to address. They serve as a requirement document for the vendors, expressing the exact options for which they must prepare. Figure 15.3 shows a sample of the Implementation Options model.

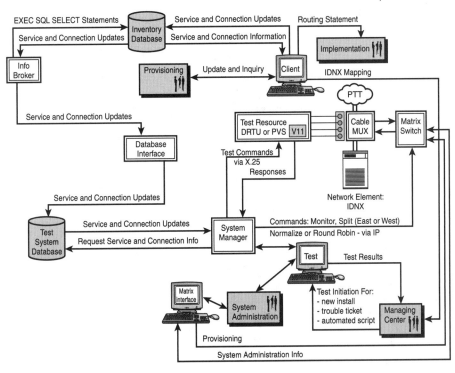

Test Management - Integrated Platform
Phase 1 Implementation

Figure 15.3   The Test Management Integrated Platform model illustrates one of the implementation options for a vendor RFP.

In this option, the system manager supports the test function for the managing center user. The system control server is integrated in the matrix switch and provides an interface between the host PC and the I/O, middle matrix, and diagnostic modules. The network element manager client is utilized to support provisioning and system administration functions. A data build is required for the test function. The integration team must develop a data feed utilizing the information broker, from the inventory database into the testing database through the database interface module.

Other options are also developed and documented for presentation in the RFP. Based on these models, service vendors propose solutions, timelines, and resources needed to deliver the various options, so that the hiring company can develop budget and project proposals to select and accomplish the solution.

Delivering a Unified Interface

The overall goal for this project is to provide one integrated platform for all test management activities. To deliver this goal, certain methods and approaches are employed, which must be introduced to the contributors and subject matter experts involved. Figure 15.4 shows the Platform Integration Introduction that is presented to all participants to help them understand how the project will work.

PLATFORM INTEGRATION
Introduction

GOAL:

Understand the Integrated Platform Process
in order to Support & Enable it through Technology

METHOD:

Serial Interviewing
to build:
Business Requirements Model
• Map of Current Business Functions
• Business Usage of Current Application Systems
• Test Equipment Components and Major Interfaces
• Integration Views

APPROACH:

Iterative & Improvisational for Early Returns
Mix of Formal & Informal As Needed
Pragmatic With Mid-Course Corrections
Planning uses "Management By Objectives" Model

Figure 15.4   The Platform Integration slide introduces the goal, method, and approach that will be used by the project.

The goal of the integration team is to understand the platform integration process to support and enable it through technology.

The team will use serial interviewing as the method to build a Business Requirement model. The model includes the following components:

- Map of current business functions
- Business usage of current application systems
- Test equipment components and major interfaces

- Integration views

  The approach utilizes a management by objectives model, which includes a mix of formal and informal techniques, as needed. It is pragmatic with mid-course corrections, and is iterative and improvisational to provide early returns for making the project's value visible.

Map of Current Business Functions

The integration team utilizes process modeling and view analysis modeling to analyze the core processes that the test platform supports, which include the following:

- Delivery channels
- Support and service functions
- Equipment inventory

Figure 15.5 shows a sample of this type of model, used for mapping the current business functions. It combines the Flow template and the Seed template for a repository-based process.

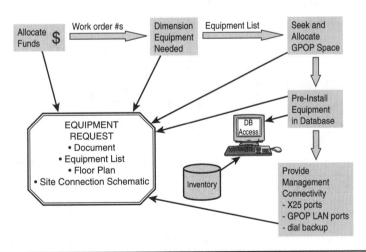

Figure 15.5   The Order Equipment Process model depicts the process for fulfilling an equipment request.

Business Usage of Current Application Systems

View analysis models are employed to show how the current application systems participate in the update of the inventory database, producing components of data that must be managed by the information broker. Requirements are developed for changes to the inventory database to store the identified information components, and any needed changes to current application systems are identified.

Test Equipment Components and Major Interfaces

The Wave template is used to define the components of test equipment and their major interfaces. Figure 15.6 shows the diagram used to depict these facts.

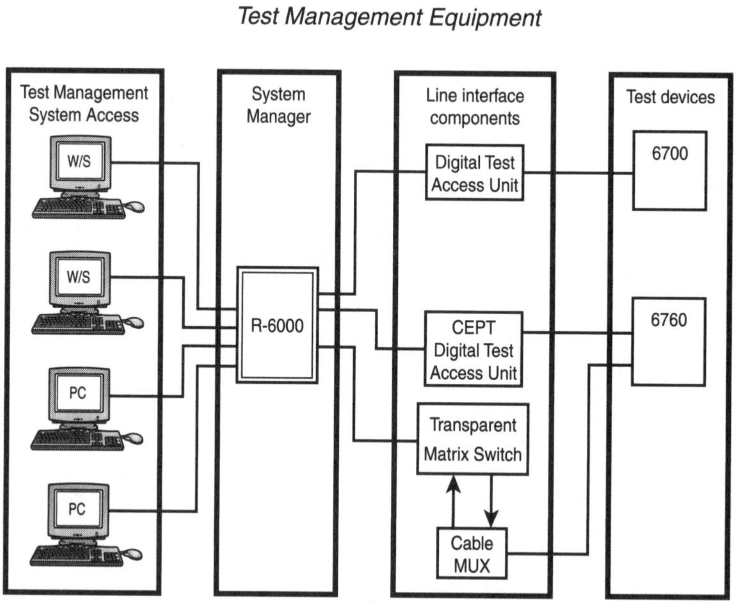

Test Management Equipment

Figure 15.6   The Test Management Equipment model uses the Wave template to illustrate the layers of equipment and how they fit together.

This model helps the integration team determine how test equipment will be plugged in to the existing production equipment architecture. It is based on an Engineering View model and modifies the view by separating it into layers.

Integration Views

Integration models are employed to depict possible future implementations of the integrated platform for other products, including DS3, frame relay, ATM packets, and so forth. Other required views include the Network Engineering and Network Management views for understanding how they interface with the technology solution.

Employ the Management by Objectives Model

Management by objectives means that rather than scheduling all project activities in advance and then managing to that preset project schedule, this project will be planned and scheduled in shorter increments. Attention is given to setting the objectives for the project, and then taking all possible means to meeting those objectives, reporting on a frequent basis the progress against the objectives. It is characterized by the following:

- Planning in 30–60 day increments
- Project champion involved in setting objectives
- Mid-course corrections

The issues in this project make the management by objectives approach useful. Operating with relative unknowns, across application and international boundaries, and under severe deadline pressure all raise the project's risk of failure, and point to a pragmatic approach, which is handled with independence balanced by the occasional hands-on management intervention.

Conclusion

The use of integration modeling helps bring together the many resources required by a platform integration project. To create a unified interface requires that legacy systems be understood and their interfaces clarified. The business processes they support must be modeled and then modified as needed to achieve the end of one test management platform for all products. Then the requirements identified for database, vendor software, and engineering modifications must be understood and translated into technical designs and specifications.

Integration models are used to fill in the gaps, to place requirements in context, and to unify the worldviews of project participants. They are not the only type of models required to accomplish the project, and they are developed on an as-needed basis rather than an across the board one. If the team doesn't find it necessary to complete models and documentation on certain aspects of the project, there's no rule that says it must be done. Integration models are designed to be inclusive, not intrusive, and shouldn't require high overhead and extra resources. They provide a needed tool for integrators when other techniques don't quite cover the terrain.

16

Conclusion

INTEGRATION MODEL TEMPLATES CAN HELP clarify the dynamics of any model, whether in UML, CASE, O-O, or any other notation or language. They are not a notation in themselves, but are more like a background formulation of principles for integration. As such they might make a good set of "snap to grid" formats for tools to adopt. Their influence is subtle, yet pervasive, providing a powerful mechanism for unifying diverse views that must be supported by information technology.

Integration models make the models that are based on them tend to match each other, bringing an organizing principle to all levels in the project repository. They cover a broad spectrum of structures and are applicable at any level. They tell us how the current problem set might work, where it will likely go next, and what its characteristics are. Integration models can also suggest technological options. Some templates translate directly into O-O design patterns (see *Design Patterns* by Gamma, et al. [16.1]).

Clarifying the Dynamics of Any Model

Technical models and business models both seek to employ an organizing principle that makes sense for the objectives of the model. Sometimes modelers mistakenly try to take that organization from the organization chart of the company or the current departmental structure or technology structure. If you're developing a physical model at a very low level, this can be acceptable. But if you're working at higher levels, or at the level of enterprise application integration, it will definitely not work. You need a device that will leverage you out from under the current structures, and point the way to new possibilities.

To find that new way and new organizing principle, it helps tremendously to begin to understand the dynamics of the situation, with the assistance of modeling techniques. Integration models embody certain dynamics by design, and when you apply them to the problem set, they can help you identify the dynamics under which the problem functions, and suggest new directions for solving it.

Understanding the Current Problem Set

When you first approach an issue, whether isolated to your company or endemic to the industry, it can appear larger than life, chaotic, and ill-formed. By modeling the pieces of the problem, you begin to cut it down to size and get your arms around how the problem works. It has been said that formulating the question is 90% of the work of getting to an answer. Integration modeling is a technique for helping to formulate the question based on the encoded information of solutions that have worked in many other situations. It is also true that the simplest way is often the most difficult, whereas in the embracing of complexity there is ease.

As you elaborate the models, you clarify the problem space, delineate its boundaries, and identify issues that fall outside its scope. You also identify the related issues that must be addressed or communicated for a full solution to be possible. As all of this work gets completed, you will find that the problem becomes manageable, understandable, and solvable, and a clear set of guidelines for the answers will emerge.

Mechanisms

Integration models are a mechanism for turning the problem into a solution. They catalyze the process of gathering information and distilling its principles by providing a way of leveraging the dynamics of the problem into a fully expanded view of the solution. They provide a method of gaining consistency across many different types of models and modeling techniques, and a method for depicting the desired interrelations between project components.

As a mechanism, integration models act as a lever to turn gathered information into technical solutions. Many learning approaches utilize the gathering of information, often into predetermined categories and cubbyholes. Where they break down is the point at which the information must be synthesized into something new and innovative. Integration models help make this synthesis by providing a dynamic on which the new models can emerge. It is a dynamic whose properties have been observed and recorded in a catalog for ongoing use so that they can be applied consciously.

Technical Directions

Integration models can indicate the technical directions that a project should take by providing information about the dynamics of how the solution functions. They point the way to technical implementations before the technical implementation has been selected. Technical models don't come into play until the technical direction has been nailed down, and so they don't help with this early stage of the project. Integration models are not tied to technology and so are helpful in the early stages of a project. Because they are not confined to a particular technology, they are also helpful in the detailed levels of modeling, where they help organize and unify design models.

Characteristics

The models help to identify the characteristics of a problem set to model the issues of an industry and their solutions. They provide a visual language for expressing both the requirements and the technical solutions for delivering the requirements. As you work with the templates, you will internalize the characteristics that each represents, learning to select the model that best depicts the most important characteristics of a given situation. The templates will become a set of mental models against which you can test new problems to seek proven solutions, or to determine that something more is required. At that point, new templates will be formulated and added to the lexicon of the modeling catalog.

Integration models represent a problem's characteristics in a visual way that can be taken in at a glance. Using them is intuitive and they are accessible to a wide audience regardless of their background in technical concepts. The Cycle template shows visually that you are dealing with a repetitive, self-reinforcing problem, and thus you know that certain consequences must be considered in applying the Cycle to the situation. The Web template shows that other characteristics will be important, such as connection, navigation, and networking. Understanding the characteristics of the problem set helps identify the characteristics of the solution.

IM as "Snap-to-Grid" Formats

Current modeling tools often employ the grid as a background, which modeling objects can be "snapped to" to facilitate their alignment and organization on the model. For instance, in MS PowerPoint, you can add a series of boxes on a slide, with an option to select all the boxes and align them at the left, right, top, or bottom. The tool accomplishes this through the use of a background grid.

Integration models are similar to this background grid, in that they give you a way to align and organize your models, based on the helpful principles of the IM templates. If a vendor were looking for new, more flexible and useful ways of allowing users to snap objects to a background template, the integration models would be a good template to employ.

Pointing the Way to Implementation Strategies

Early in an integration project, you will be gathering information, distilling its essence into integration models and ensuring those models reflect the requirements, identity, and norms of your project environment. You can produce a series of viewpoint analysis models and narrative scenarios as a basis for the integration models. You can go straight to the strategic models that would indicate business solutions and from there into technical models, depending on the needs of the project.

The nature of the integration models and other models that are developed will indicate some directions in the implementation strategies to be employed. If you have a balance of many different types of models, you're probably conducting an enterprisewide effort, which will require many supports and pragmatic approaches. Early returns, publicized successes, project sponsorship, and project pilots conducted before general implementation will all help to ensure a successful rollout. If you find that most all your models are of one type, for instance Web models, that indicates a high interest in interconnections and networks. These technologies will be emphasized in the project's implementation.

If relatively few integration models exist, the templates can serve more as guide and influence in creating a set of technical models for implementation through traditional means. They will provide an organizing principle and an integrative function, while not dominating the overall implementation.

Translating IM into Technical Implementation Models

One of the difficulties of many modeling techniques is their relative obscurity to the uninitiated. To the average businessperson, they're hard to read, hard to follow, and in many cases not worth the effort of learning the notation. Integration models help bridge this cultural gap by making both business and technical models more accessible to business people. They provide organization and increase visual comprehension by using common templates for common solutions. The visual language of integration models allows the modeler to render technology solutions that the non-technical person can embrace.

As integrators develop models, and the business contributors and other subject matter experts approve them, they are used to orient the technical team and are translated into technical models where appropriate. Some integration models translate directly into O-O Design Patterns, such as the Seed template, which translates naturally into Gamma's Strategy pattern or in some cases, the Facade (see *Design Patterns* by Gamma, et al. [16.1]). Other examples include the Tree, which can be converted into the Composite pattern, the Wave, which will convert to the Abstract Factory pattern for families of products, and the Cell, which can be translated to the Adapter pattern. Other integration models can be translated directly to traditional data models and process models, without going through the rigorous structure of a pattern. These examples are not intended as an exhaustive list by any means. They are meant to suggest places to look and directions to pursue in making integration models a tool that can be leveraged through other patterns already in use. A one-to-one correspondence is not suggested, but a judgement call, which assumes knowledge of the technical options in various implementations of modeling techniques and tools. The recommendation is to work from what you know, using common sense to help identify the connections to technical models.

No attempt at this point is made to create a "round-trip" engineering cycle for transferring knowledge back and forth between early and business-level modeling and technical implementation modeling. If you have an existing repository with "round-trip" functionality, integration models can be judiciously employed to give your repository a higher order of organization. If not, they can be used sparingly and managed manually for the same purpose.

Patterns, Templates, and Other Reusable Components

One way to use the models in this book is to base your own templates on them and build your own library. Another way is to use the models provided in the following sections as a starting point. They are presented in the UML notation as a starting point for building your own template library. The models are included below with their descriptions.

To use them, you need to copy them from the samples to your catalog, and store a version of them as read-only. A project modeler would then make a copy of the template, and modify the object names, adding or deleting model objects as required by the project. These models are intended as a starting point to bring modelers up-to-speed on integration templates quickly. Departures and additions to the basic catalog should be expected and welcomed. However, it would be prudent to expect a justification or rationalization that ensures any new template is needed and well thought out by modelers.

Cycle

The UML version of the Cycle template utilizes sequentially numbered use cases and associations in a use-case diagram. Figure 16.1 shows the model, which presents a directional process model for cyclical processes.

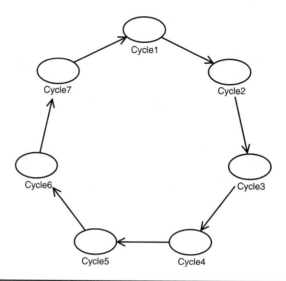

Figure 16.1   The model shows the UML version of the Cycle template, utilizing use-cases and associations in a use-case diagram.

Seed

The Seed template in UML employs an actor class as the core controller and use cases to depict the activities, which are connected by associations. Figure 16.2 shows the model. This template could also be developed in a UML collaboration diagram, depending on the needs of the project.

Web

The Web template in UML uses a component diagram with components as nodes and connections set up as dependencies. It could also be executed as a class diagram or even a use-case diagram, depending on the project needs. Figure 16.3 shows the model.

Flow

The Flow template is illustrated in UML through the use of an activity diagram, which is created as subordinate to a Flow class. It employs activities and state transitions to illustrate a movement through the steps of a process. The Flow template could also be rendered in a use-case diagram or state diagram, depending on project needs. Figure 16.4 shows the model.

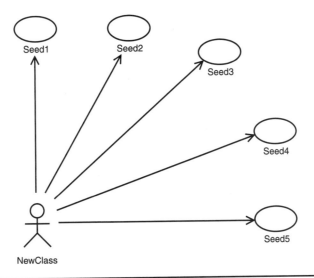

Figure 16.2   The model shows a UML version of the Seed template, employing an actor class, use cases, and associations.

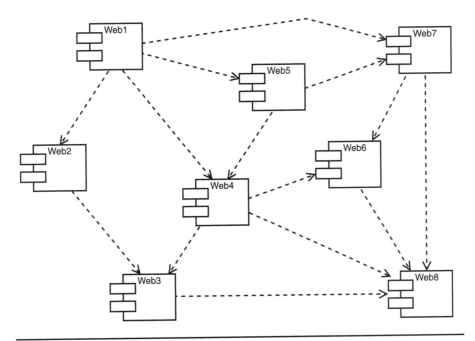

Figure 16.3   The UML version of the Web template employs components and dependencies in a component diagram.

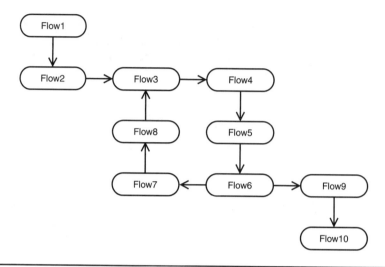

Figure 16.4   The UML version of the Flow template
utilizes the activity diagram with activities and state transitions.

Wave

The Wave template is developed using a component diagram in UML notation.
Columns are captioned by UML notes, and populated with components. Figure 16.5
shows the model.

Ring

The Ring template is rendered in UML notation using actors and associations on a
use-case diagram. It could also be represented with use cases, or in a class or component diagram. The Ring would also be suitable for a deployment diagram in UML.
Figure 16.6 shows the model.

Cell

The Cell template in UML utilizes a class diagram with classes and associations. It
could also be rendered with use cases and associations on a use-case diagram, or components on a component diagram, depending on the project. Figure 16.7 shows the
model.

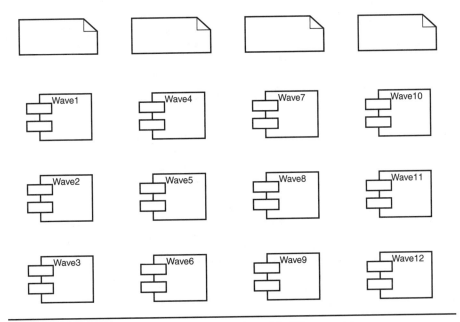

Figure 16.5   The UML version of the Wave template utilizes components and notes in a component diagram.

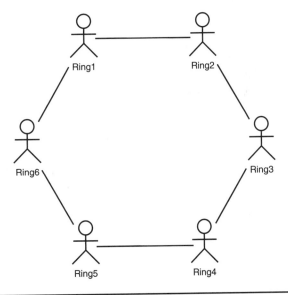

Figure 16.6   The Ring template uses actors and associations in a use-case diagram.

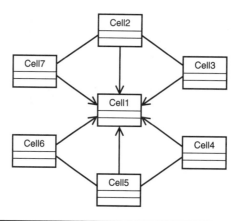

Figure 16.7   The UML version of the Cell template
utilizes classes and associations in a class diagram.

Tree

The Tree template is depicted in UML notation employing use cases and associations on a use-case diagram. It could also be developed in other diagrams such as a class or component diagram. Figure 16.8 shows the model.

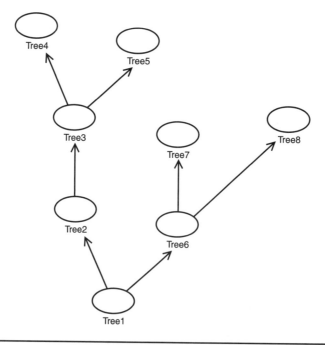

Figure 16.8   The UML Tree template is illustrated
by a use-case diagram with use cases and associations.

Summary

The catalog of IM templates, provided here in UML notation, can help modelers move quickly into applying integration models. If your project or company employs other standard notations, it can be useful to develop your own set of templates in the required standard. Because integration models are flexible and customizable, there is no single "right way" to translate them into templates. The needs of your modeling environment, taken together with the requirements of specific projects, should be allowed to determine how the models are translated. The primary benefit is to develop a working set of guides that can support a broad range of project types and business goals.

IV

Appendices

A
Footnotes

0.1—Gamma, Erich… et al., 1995, *Design Patterns*, Addison Wesley.

0.2—Alexander, Christopher, 1977, *A Pattern Language*, New York, Oxford University Press.

0.3—Bateson, Mary Catherine, 1989, *Composing a Life*, New York, Penguin Group.

0.4—Peters, Tom, 1999, *The Brand You 50*, New York, Alfred A. Knopf.

0.5—Csikszentmihalyi, Mihaly, 1997, *Finding Flow*, New York, BasicBooks.

1.1—Taylor, Frederick W., 1911, *The Principles of Scientific Management*, New York, W. W. Norton.

1.2—Peppers, Don and Rogers, Martha, 1997, *Enterprise One to One: Tools for Competing in the Interactive Age*, New York, Doubleday.

1.3—Newman, David, 1996, *DM Review* magazine, Faulkner and Gray.

2.1—Gamma, Erich… et al., 1995, *Design Patterns*, Addison Wesley.

2.2—Alexander, Christopher; Ishikawa, Sara and Silverstein, Murry, *A Pattern Language: Towns, Buildings, Construction,*
Oxford University Press (Trade), 1977.

2.3—Zachman, John A., 1993-1997, Zachman International, Inc.,
`http://www.ies.aust.com/~visible/papers/zachman3.htm`.

2.4—Senge, Peter M., 1990, *The Fifth Discipline*, New York, Doubleday.

2.5—Hammer, Michael and Champy, James, 1993, *Reengineering the Corporation*, New York, HarperCollins.

2.6—Mr. Erlich was paraphrasing Authur C. Clarke's third law as formulated in the book *Profiles of the Future: An Inquiry into the Limits of the Possible*, 1985, Warner Books.

3.1—Haeckel, Stephan H. and Nolan, Richard L., "Managing by Wire," *Harvard Business Review* article, September 1, 1993.

3.2—Zachman, John A., 1993-1997, Zachman International, Inc., `http://www.ies.aust.com/~visible/papers/zachman3.htm`.

3.3—Hopper, Grace, from *The OCLC Newsletter*, March/April, 1987, No. 167 (Philip Schieber, editor and article author), "The Wit and Wisdom of Grace Hopper," `http://www.cs.yale.edu/~tap/Files/hopper-wit.html`.

3.4—Toffler, Alvin and Heidi, 1990, *Powershift*, pages 181-182, New York, Bantam.

4.1—Carnegie Mellon University, Software Engineering Institute, `http://www.sei.cmu.edu/activities/cmm/`.

6.1—Sun, Q. and Langendörfer, H., "Routing for Supporting Realtime Applications in High-Speed Networks," the research group Distributed Systems and Network Management at the Technical University of Braunschweig, `http://www.ibr.cs.tu-bs.de/projects/mcast/`.

6.2—Modeling of routing algorithms: Network simulation modeling tools by MIL3's OPNET software, `http://www.mil3.com/products/modeler/home.html`.

9.1—U.S. Commerce Reports on IDG—on the Digital Divide, `http://www.idg.net/crd_divide_77972.html`.

9.2—Shared Data Environment (SHADE) CAPSTONE Document, `http://dii-sw.ncr.disa.mil/coe/docs/shade-capstone/v-1/html/index.shtml#toc`.

13.1—Csikszentimihalyi, Mihaly, 1996, *Creativity, Flow and the Psychology of Discovery and Invention*, HarperCollins.

13.2—"Dishing Out DSL Proves No Easy Feat," by Sal Salamone in the online publication: www.teledotcom.com (December 13, 1999).

13.3—Customer-managed relationship—Bank Administration Institute, `http://www.bai.org/retaildelivery/rd_news.html#adopt`.

13.4—Cremeans, John E. (editor), 1998, *U.S. NAICS Manual*, North American Industry Classification System: United States, Bernan Associates.

13.5—The U. S. Department Of Commerce, Economics, *Statistical Abstract of the United States, 1998: The National Data Book*, Bernan Associates.

13.6—The U.S. Industry and Trade Outlook 2000, McGraw-Hill Companies and the U.S. Department of Commerce/International Trade Administration.

13.7—2000 National Trade and Professional Associations of the United States (National Trade and Professional Associations of the United States, 2000 ed.) by Buck Downs (editor), Emily C. Bausch (editor), Sarah E. White (editor) Columbia Books, Inc.

13.8—Gaquin, Deirdre A. (editor), *2000 County and City Extra: Annual Metro, City, and County Data Book (County and City Extra, 2000)* Bernan Associates.

13.9—*Transportation and Public Utilities USA, 1999, Finance, Insurance, and Real Estate USA, 1998, Manufacturing USA, 1998, Service Industries USA, 1998,* and *Wholesale & Retail Trade U S A : Industry Analyses, Statistics, and Leading Companies (Wholesale and Retail Trade USA, 2nd Ed.),* 1998, GALE Group.

14.1—Inmon, W. H., 1996, *Building the Operational Data Store,* John Wiley and Sons.

16.1—Gamma, Erich… et al., 1995 *Design Patterns,* Addison Wesley.

Resources for Applied Integration Modeling

Appendix B includes resources for applying integration modeling to projects of any size, including

- Web Sites Offering Resources for EAI, Integration Modeling, Patterns, and Enterprise Resource Planning
- Sample Preliminary Project Introduction
- Sample Contributor Introduction
- Sample Open-Ended Interview Questions
- Sample Cover Letter for Interview Questions
- Sample Project Plan: Integration
- Checklist: Factors That Indicate an Increased Need For Integration

Web Sites Offering Resources for EAI, Integration Modeling, Patterns, and Enterprise Resource Planning

`http://www.eaijournal.com/`

A resource for e-business and application integration. It is published monthly as a magazine and as a Web site that is continually updated. The journal's mission is to provide news, expert insight, and analysis into how to deploy integrated e-business systems that span an enterprise and its partners.

`http://www.advisor.com/whome.nsf/w/ZEAI`

Covers innovations, strategies, and practices for e-business. Lists publications, events, products, services, and resources.

`http://www.cs.wustl.edu/~schmidt/patterns.html`

This site gives information on patterns, pattern languages, and frameworks.

`http://hillside.net/patterns/patterns.html`

A source for information about all aspects of software patterns and pattern languages.

`http://www.erpassist.com/nav/t.asp?t=402&p=402&h1=402`

A comprehensive source of information on ERP software, vendors, and issues.

`http://eai.ittoolbox.com/`

EAI information portal providing news, forums, mail lists, technical documents, and more.

Sample Preliminary Project Introduction

The following is an example of the kind of information that must be conveyed to project contributors by the office of the senior executive sponsoring or championing the project. Deliver this information by phone, memo, or email approximately one week before the requested meeting date.

MEMORANDUM

To: Identified contributor

From the office of: *(fill in executive's name)*

By: Administrative assistant of senior executive (CIO, CTO, VP of Technology, for example)

Re: Forthcoming Integration Project

(Fill in specific project name)

The purpose of this communication (email, memo, or phone call) is to introduce the integration consultant(s) who will be visiting your business area next week to discuss your requirements and concerns regarding the upcoming project: *(fill in project name)*.

(Integrator's name) has been selected by my office to represent the information technology organization to all business and technical area contributors. His/her purpose is to understand the point of view of your particular business area as it relates to the project and to solicit your feedback on the project's goals and requirements.

The goal of the requested meeting is to understand the integrated business process sufficiently to support and enable it through the integration and technology improvements under consideration.

Your cooperation in this matter is critical to the success of the project, and will be greatly appreciated. Please indicate your availability for the dates requested below:

Date option 1, time

Date option 2, time

Sample Contributor Introduction

The following are examples of introductory information that can be provided to the contributor at the start of the interview. Figure B.1 lists the goal, method, and approach of the project. Such an introduction helps set the expectations of the contributor and is useful because the goal, method, and approach of an integration project are likely to be different from those your contributor has previously experienced with typical software development projects.

BUSINESS INTEGRATION
Process Model

Goal:

  Understand the Integrated Business Process
  in order to Support and Enable it through Technology

Method:

  Interviewing
  to build:
  Business Requirements Model
    • Map of Current Business Functions
    • Business Usage of Current Application System
    • Business Process Components and Major Interfaces
    • Integration Views

Approach:

  Iterative and Improvisational for Early Returns
  Mix of Formal and Informal As Needed
  Pragmatic With Mid-Course Corrections
  Planning uses "Management By Objectives" Model

Figure B.1 The Business Integration Process Model sets the expectations of the business area contributor who will be interviewed.

Figure B.2 depicts the steps of the process that will be followed to complete the business integration project. It should also be reviewed at the start of the interview so that the contributor has a clear understanding of the process in which he is being asked to participate. Not only does this put the contributor at ease, but it also makes it easier for him to find opportunities to contribute to that process.

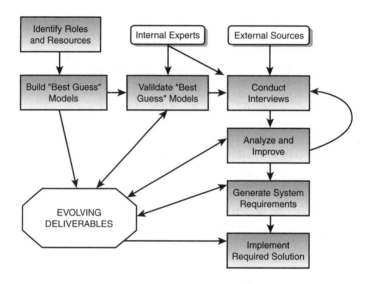

BUSINESS INTEGRATION
Process Model

Figure B.2   The Business Integration Process Model shows the steps that will be taken in the course of the integration project.

The specifics of these two figures might need to be adjusted, depending on the particular goals and structures of the individual integration project. These samples are presented to give you a starting point to produce a workable version of your own.

Sample Open-Ended Interview Questions

The following is a sample meeting agenda with some open-ended interview questions for the development of scenarios and viewpoint analysis models. You can tailor the questions to be somewhat more specific to the goals of a specific integration project. However, I do not advise you to make the questions so specific that they close down discussion and the volunteering of information you wouldn't know enough to request. You actually want the contributor to take the discussion "off track" because this often leads to important information.

The agenda is provided in advance of the actual interview to give the contributor time to review the questions and gather any materials that he feels might be relevant. A brief cover letter explaining the expectations is delivered with the agenda.

One-Hour Interview

Specific Business Area

(Name of Interviewee)

AGENDA

(The following questions are intended to initiate a dialogue about what in your view constitutes success for the current Integration Project. Feel free to start with the topics of most interest in your viewpoint and disregard the ones that hold less interest.)

1. Briefly describe the responsibilities of your position.
2. Where does your role fit in with the organization, goals, and objectives of the company?
3. What are the main issues and concerns you see for your area of responsibility?
4. Do you have any written materials documenting processes in your area that you would be willing to share with us? (Please indicate your confidentiality requirements for any materials provided.)
5. What information do you need to get your job done?
6. What information do you wish you had?
7. What are the processes that use the previous information, and how does the information flow from one to the next?
8. What information do you create? How? On what is it based?
9. What are the most immediate business problems facing your organization?
10. What are the solutions to the most immediate business problems facing your organization?
11. Where is the "low-hanging fruit" for the project?
12. What "quick-hits" would you like to see delivered?
13. What else?

Sample Cover Letter for Interview Questions

To: Business area contributor (fill in name)

From: Integrator name(s)

Re: Interview—Integration Project

(Fill in specific project name)

Attached is a set of interview questions. Please review these questions and gather any relevant materials that you feel would be of interest prior to the scheduled interview.

Your participation in the integration project is critical to its success. The interview itself is not expected to exceed one hour, although you are welcome to extend the time if you feel it is necessary.

Thank you for your participation, and we look forward to meeting with you on February 15 at 1:00 p.m.

Regards,

Integrator name

Cc: project champion or sponsor

Sample Project Plan: Integration

The sample project plan for an integration project is shown first in a high-level model, which illustrates the main phases of the plan and how they are scheduled. Figure B.3 shows phase number and task names versus their scheduling on the timeline. Note that phases one through three are run concurrently for company A, B, and so forth. They converge on the milestone target date where the companies' tasks are performed in partnership and must be synchronized. Subsequent phases are executed together by partnering companies, running sequentially. Note also that although the model shows no overlapping between subsequent phases, it has been simplified for the sake of clarity. In real-world projects, there will be overlap between phases of integration projects, which is acceptable. The integration project plan is not designed for a lock-step implementation where each phase must be thoroughly complete before the next can begin.

Integration Project Plan

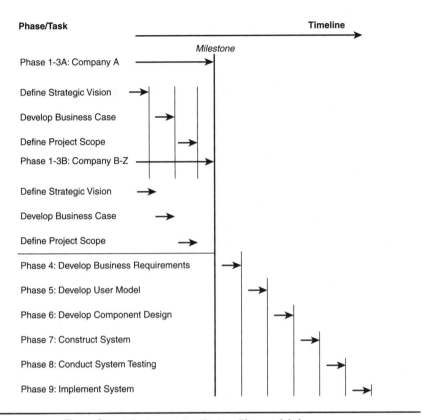

Figure B.3   The Integration Project Plan model shows a
high-level illustration of the phases of the project.

The following is a sample generic project plan for an integration project. It emphasizes the initial stages, giving detailed activities for stepping through the partnership
negotiations required by integration projects. Final stages are shown in less detail
because they are more straightforward and should follow standard software development procedures.

Phase 1A: Company A—Define Strategic Vision

- Determine goals and parameters for integration project
- Develop scenarios and viewpoint analysis models
  - Conduct interviews with project owners and stakeholders
  - Conduct interviews with project partners

- Compile and consolidate interview results
- Update scenarios and viewpoint analysis models
- Conduct review of project goals and parameters
- Define target customer or audience
    - Identify target customer or audience
    - Conduct interviews and focus groups with target customer or audience
    - Define user scenarios based on customer or audience interviews
    - Conduct review of user scenarios
    - Compile user scenario results
- Initiate marketing strategy
    - Identify technology components of marketing strategy (research, data extracts, and so forth)
    - Implement technology components of marketing strategy
- Delineate expected budget range
    - Identify expected project costs
    - Identify expected project benefits
    - Develop cost versus benefit analysis

Phase 2A: Develop Business Case

- Build economic models
    - Identify expected project costs
    - Identify expected project benefits
    - Develop cost versus benefit analysis
- Validate product or service strategy
    - Generate usage statistics on current products
    - Generate usage statistics on current services
    - Acquire usage statistics on competitor's products and services
    - Review and validate product and/or service strategy
- Compile business case with economic models and statistically supported product/service strategy

Phase 3A: Define Project Scope

- Interview project owners to clarify the project vision
- Review current automated or manual system information

- Identify and extract relevant system information for project file
- Identify the absolute limits (time, cost, and so forth)
- Prepare project scope document

Phase 1-3B: Company B-Z—(These three steps run concurrently with Company A's performance of the same three previous steps.)

- Perform Define Strategic Vision
- Perform Develop Business Case
- Perform Define Project Scope

The remaining steps are conducted jointly between integration project parties.

Phase 4: Develop Business Requirements

- Develop details of specific project vision
  - Analyze and define data needs
  - Develop data definitions
  - Define business process specifications
  - Develop object and event models
- Develop narrative list of project requirements
  - Review specific project vision and extract required functionality
  - Identify impacted areas
  - Define critical success factors (required functions)
  - Define mechanisms to support critical success factors
  - Identify performance and access requirements
  - Identify technical restrictions
  - Review regulatory requirements
  - Review corporate standards and procedures
  - Assemble requirements list
- Establish initial project approach plan
  - Review criteria for project approach selection
  - Assess organizational factors
  - Assess technology factors
- Define technology solution
  - Develop comparative document
  - Define process improvements
  - Explore technical alternatives

- Acquire vendor participation through RFI, RFP, and so forth
- Conduct research to synthesize solutions
    - Create alternative solutions comparison matrix
    - Develop recommended approach
- Analyze comparative documents against the business requirements
- Develop recommendation
- Conduct internal review of recommendation
- Assemble project approach plan
- Develop project plan
- Assess customer's perception of proposed product or service value
    - Develop customer value models
    - Review value models with customer
    - Update value models based on customer feedback

Phase 5: Develop User Model

- Walk through business process models
- Identify the portions of the business process to be automated
- Develop use-case models of selected functions from the business process
- Develop scenarios, based on use cases, to illustrate how the user interacts with the proposed or changed system
- Evaluate evolving logical data model
- Review available vendor documentation and synthesized solutions from research
- Define user interface
    - Develop site design or graphical user interface
    - Define screens, queries, reports, and other outputs
    - Define entries, selection options, and other inputs
    - Define edits, business rules, and metadata
    - Design navigation plan for site or system GUI
- Assemble level 1 prototype
- Identify user access profile
- Assemble user view model

Phase 6: Develop Component Design

- Define the technical architecture requirements
    - Identify required development language
    - Determine required application, database, and Web servers
- Confirm logical data model
- Define sources of required information
- Determine features the project will implement
    - Develop list of features
    - Review feasibility and cost information
    - Prioritize list
    - Develop release schedule for top priority features
- Identify required technology and tools for implementing selected features
    - Select tools and techniques for development
    - Acquire tools and techniques for development
- Define human resource requirements
- Locate and select appropriately skilled service providers
- Identify needed vendors for the project (data providers, ISP, hosting, and so forth)
- Develop release strategy
- Design application, solution, system
    - Assess existing automation
    - Design physical database structures
    - Develop application architecture
    - Develop programmer work package

Phase 7: Construct System

- Establish construction and test environment
- Code and test required components
- Develop job execution plans
- Develop user guide

Phase 8: Conduct System Testing

- Establish testing environment
- Conduct functional requirement testing
- Conduct user interface testing
- Conduct integration testing
- Conduct stress testing (traffic volume, database, and application server performance)
- Conduct regression testing
- Conduct acceptance testing
- Monitor and tune production performance

Phase 9: Implement System

- Develop implementation plan
- Conduct review with technical support providers
- Perform system installation
- Conduct ongoing monitoring and tuning

Checklist: Factors That Indicate an Increased Need for Integration

Experiencing one or more of these factors means greater need for integration:

Company

- System development without architectural planning
- Previous data integration failures have created negative perceptions to be overcome
- Dramatic changes in the role of marketing
- Dramatic changes in the role of IT

Industry

- Rapid industry consolidation
- Convergence is blurring the lines between industries
- Decreasing technology life cycles
- Reduced product development cycles

Index

D

F